Doing Research with Children

3rd edition

Doing Research with Children

A practical guide

Anne Greig, Jayne Taylor
and **Tommy MacKay**

Los Angeles | London | New Delhi
Singapore | Washington DC

Los Angeles | London | New Delhi
Singapore | Washington DC

SAGE Publications Ltd
1 Oliver's Yard
55 City Road
London EC1Y 1SP

SAGE Publications Inc.
2455 Teller Road
Thousand Oaks, California 91320

SAGE Publications India Pvt Ltd
B 1/I 1 Mohan Cooperative Industrial Area
Mathura Road
New Delhi 110 044

SAGE Publications Asia-Pacific Pte Ltd
3 Church Street
#10-04 Samsung Hub
Singapore 049483

Editor: Katie Metzler
Assistant editor: Anna Horvai
Production editor: Ian Antcliff
Copyeditor: Sonia Cutler
Proofreader: Jeremy Tonynbee
Indexer: Henson Editorial Services
Marketing manager: Ben Griffin-Sherwood
Cover design: Jennifer Crisp
Typeset by: C&M Digitals (P) Ltd, Chennai, India
Printed by MPG Books Group, Bodmin, Cornwall

First edition published 1999; reprinted 1999, 2001, 2002, 2004, 2006, 2008

Second edition published 2007

Library of Congress Control Number: 2011945821

British Library Cataloguing in Publication data

A catalogue record for this book is available from the British Library

ISBN 978-0-85702-885-3
ISBN 978-0-85702-886-0 (pbk)

Contents

Boxes

Figures

Tables

About the authors

Anne Greig is an educational psychologist and a Practice Tutor on the MSc in Educational Psychology at Strathclyde University. Her PhD was on preschool relationships at the Attachment Research Unit at Cambridge University. Her post-doctoral work was on the impact of maternal depression on the development of preschool children at the UEA. As an applied, chartered psychologist and psychotherapist, Anne has developed interest in the areas of autism, attachment, CBT and mental health.

Jayne Taylor is Chief Operating Officer for the Hertsmere Commissioning Locality and leads various projects for the clinical commissioning group. She also works part-time as Associate Head of Leadership at West Hertfordshire Hospitals NHS Trust where she leads two postgraduate courses in Leadership and Management. Her PhD was on coping with chronic illness in childhood and over a long career she has written a number of books about children, health and research.

Tommy MacKay is a child psychologist who has been engaged for many years in teaching research methods to postgraduate students and professionals in many disciplines, as well as doing his own research with children and young people. His ten-year research study on children's literacy in West Dunbartonshire has won many national awards. UK Prime Minister Gordon Brown wrote of him, 'Tommy MacKay is a visionary and an inspiration' with 'an absolute refusal to accept that anything was impossible'.

PART I

The special nature of children and young people in research – theories and approaches

summary of some of the major research themes will be discussed later in this chapter. While it is important that we are grateful for the knowledge we have, we must, however, ensure that we are always moving forward, always searching and always pursuing greater understanding.

There are many, many ways of achieving new knowledge, but the key to this achievement, regardless of the field we work in, is training. We acknowledge that few of our readers will go on to make pure research their living, but we also recognize that professional people, both during initial training and after qualifying, need a sound knowledge of how to apply research and how to undertake research. This book is about applying research practically and undertaking research practically. It is essentially a practical book, which is specifically designed for professionals who work, or intend to work, with children and who have to undertake research as part of their education or who need to undertake research, even on a very small scale, as part of their professional lives.

This book is also practical in that it recognizes the reality of studying children in the further pursuit of knowledge. Children do not exist in vacuums and their lives are naturally complex; they have to be if children are to enter adulthood with the repertoire of skills and behaviours that are essential for modern living. We have therefore taken a holistic perspective of the child and the child's environment, recognizing that research training must be cognizant of the many variables that influence development and behaviour. We have drawn from the fields of biology, education, health, psychology and sociology in our discussions about research and in our considerations of child participants. We are explicit in our acknowledgement that children are special and that research, and research training, involving children must also be special.

Not only are children special, but they also hold a very special place in society. While some of the research undertaken in pursuit of gaining understanding of children has been appalling in terms of what children have been expected to do and suffer, the majority of work has been undertaken sensitively and has followed correct ethical principles. We will focus on this theme in Chapter 10 but should give recognition in this opening section to the distinctive position children hold in contemporary society. This has not always been the case, however, or at least that is the impression one is left with when studying historical perspectives of child care. As we will discuss later in the chapter, the child of today has rights which are universally held, widely adhered to and, in most Western societies, monitored by legislation.

Children are special

As we have briefly mentioned above, children are very special people. Defining what we mean by special is, however, a complex and difficult task. Perhaps what we mean is that children are different from the adults who control and describe the world as we know it. Perhaps it is because children are necessary for the survival of our species. Perhaps it is because children are an enigma – we do not understand so many things about them and they therefore puzzle us. Perhaps it is none or all of these things. What is evident is that children have, from biblical times to the present day, been singled out to varying extents as being exceptional beings who have been afforded special consideration. Children are seen as an outward celebration of life, as the next generation and as the future of mankind. They also eventually grow and develop into adults, which perhaps gives us further insight into why they are considered special. The famous and infamous names from our history lessons at school were all once children themselves, which leads us to wonder why they developed in the way they did. We can sometimes look back at the childhood experiences of some adults (including ourselves) and pinpoint events or experiences that we think might account for why an adult turned out as they did, but often there are no such clues and we are left wondering.

Special and very special

It is not the intention of this book to give a detailed history of the place of children in society – there are many texts that adequately fulfil that aim. However, because we wish to focus on doing research with children, we must spend a few moments looking at the child within our society so that we can explore the wider contexts of this research.

People have children for a number of reasons. They are seen, by some, as desirable assets (Agiobu-Kemmer, 1992), as insurance to provide for adults in their old age or as a sign of one's fertility. Some religions dictate that the purpose of marriage is for the procreation of children, and indeed in 17th-century England childlessness was even considered to be a judgement against sin (Fraser, 1985). On a macro level, any society must ensure that it reproduces itself if it is to survive. On an individual level, many cultures hold the expectation that adults will eventually marry and produce children. There are also those who have children because they do not believe in the use of, or do not have access to, reliable contraception.

Whether people have children by accident or by design, once born children have certain rights, which are upheld by law. Children have the fundamental right to life, and child murderers can expect and receive the severest of punishment. Children also have the right to protection from harm and from neglect, they have the right to go to school and receive an education, among other things. In the UK, the Children Acts 1989 and 2004 in England and Wales and the parallel legislation in Scotland and Northern Ireland, together with several charters, including the *Convention on the Rights of the Child* (United Nations Children's Fund, 1989), detail explicitly the rights of children, as we will discuss in following chapters. Rights, however, only lay down the minimum expectations society holds for its children. For the majority of parents and people within society, children are their future and they strive to ensure that the mistakes of one generation do not extend to the next. People generally want for children those things they did not have themselves: they want children to have more opportunities, less hardship, more success and so on.

To ensure that children attain what society wishes for them, each generation must be analysed and evaluated, and steps taken to rectify past mistakes. We must have an understanding of children and how they develop, what factors adversely affect their progress and what factors will best promote their optimum development. Gaining this understanding is the driving force behind past, present and future research with children and crosses all professional boundaries. Biologists, educationists, geneticists, psychologists and sociologists have all striven for this greater understanding of children, albeit with differing philosophies, research traditions and methodologies.

If we accept the special status of all children within society we must also recognize that there are many children who, for a variety of reasons, must be considered to be very special. These children differ from their peers because, for example, they are exceptionally gifted or because of a physical or psychological dysfunction or because they are particularly vulnerable. These children have been, and are, the focus of a great deal of research activity that aims to discover why they are different, and the effects of their difference in terms of their present and future development. What we should emphasize here is that their rights and our responsibilities as researchers and professionals remain at least the same as for all children. In many cases, undertaking research with these very special children requires even greater training, as we will discuss in the following section. A particular challenge for the researcher is that of balancing the need for children's participation and inclusion in research activity with the need to protect very vulnerable children. We discuss this more fully in Chapters 9 and 10.

Special but not new

It is very easy for a new generation to fall into the trap of making assumptions about the past. Professionals generally, as part of their training, study aspects of the history of their profession and will gasp in horror at how children were treated. Take, for example, the past practice of separating sick children from their parents during hospitalization because it was felt that parents upset children, or the punishment meted out to children in schools for the good of their 'moral' development. The important point to recognize here is that these things happened not because those professionals did not view children as special, but because they did. It is only when common practices are questioned that change occurs, otherwise the status quo will persist endlessly. We should not think ourselves superior in any way, for without doubt our own professional practices will be questioned in years to come. We can only ensure that we do our best to question all our practices and strive, as far as possible, to base our practice on sound research and evidence. This involves two different, but related notions. First, all professionals have a responsibility to ensure that they are aware of current research, can intelligently interpret it and incorporate sound research into practice. This will be discussed fully in Chapter 4. Second, we should all constantly ask questions, and where there is a lack of research we should encourage investigation (see Chapter 2 for further discussion). This may mean undertaking research ourselves or enabling and facilitating others to do so. However, such activity requires training, particularly when the research involves children (as we shall discover during the rest of this book), because, as we have already said many times, children are special. We are fortunate to be living in an age where great value is placed on meeting the needs of children and young people. A recent publication by the Department of Health (2010: 4) makes this clear – 'nothing can be more important than getting it right for children and young people.'

Training for research

As all the professions move towards *all graduate* status, in the future all professionals should have undertaken some research training by the time they qualify. This is seen by many as a positive benefit of raising the academic expectations of initial training programmes.

A significant proportion of child-care professions, the notable exceptions being teaching and nursing, require that those who enter the profession undergo generic training before specializing with children. Generic training aims to ensure a broad base of knowledge and in many instances gives the professional a 'taster' of work with a variety of groups, including different age groups. Research training has also tended to be generic, with little consideration given to the differences between undertaking research with children or adults. There are, however, very important differences. Children are not miniature adults nor, as we have already stated, do they exist in isolation. The social and emotional relationships of the child are more fluid than at any other time of the human lifespan and cannot be ignored. For example, studying the child in a laboratory situation without also studying the child in the naturalistic setting will limit the understanding gained (Dunn, 1996; Greene and Hill, 2005). We will explore this throughout the rest of the book.

It is also important to differentiate between the study of children in general and the study of those children whom we have defined as very special. All children, for all sorts of reasons, are vulnerable, and this vulnerability is heightened in some children. These children are already in many ways often singled out because they are different, which is frequently what makes them attractive and interesting research participants. Researchers who study these children do, however, require special skills so as not to accentuate differences overtly and to the detriment of the particular child. The avoidance of harm necessitates particular skills in terms of understanding the nature of childhood, possessing knowledge about issues such as informed consent and, not least, being sensitive to differences. Schaffer (1998) discusses this point and questions past practices of focusing on the negative aspects of differences. The current trend of moving away from investigating the negative effects of difference exhibited by some children and towards a focus on the resilience of similar children is a welcome development (see also Lewis and Kellett, 2004).

Research awareness versus research skills

Research training is a far broader concept than undertaking a small survey or experiment. We mentioned in our introduction that research training also involves applying research to our practice, and this is probably the more important skill. There is little point in belonging to a profession that has a sound research base if current research is not integrated into our practice. If the research is ignored and not acted on, not only will a great deal of research time and money be wasted, but children and their families will continue to receive care that is less than they deserve.

In many instances, a profession's research base relies on experienced researchers, often located within university departments, undertaking research that produces recommendations that should then be put into place by practitioners. This is explored further in Chapter 4. The point is that both research skills and research awareness are needed, but for most practitioners it is the skill of being able to incorporate research into their practice that becomes paramount. Practice should be evidence based, but the evidence does not need to be derived from personal research but from a wider knowledge of research being undertaken within, and outwith, a profession and how it can inform practice.

Small-scale research – how valuable?

As part of initial training some students have the opportunity to undertake a small piece of research, although this is not as commonplace as it once was. The purpose of undertaking small-scale research as part of training is to give an opportunity to experience first hand what the process of doing research is about while being supervised by a more experienced researcher. It is less focused on outcomes and more about learning the 'doing'.

Getting hands-on experience of doing research does help to increase understanding of the rigour and organizing abilities that are required by the good researcher. It is an opportunity to see the end-to-end process and to try out different approaches, data collection tools, sampling techniques, analysis, report writing and so on.

Although small-scale research cannot replace studies conducted on a larger scale, which lead to generalization of knowledge, learning the discipline of doing research thoroughly can help professionals throughout their careers when faced with problems or questions that do not have easily identified solutions. Applying the systematic process learned through doing research to investigate a problem thoroughly to come up with an evidence-based solution is a competency that will be of enduring value. Actually doing research – no matter how small scale – does provide great opportunity to learn a range of skills, which will be useful throughout professional life.

Inter-professional research skills

We have mentioned that training for research with children should be different from training for research with adults. A further complication is that the care of children is rarely a uni-professional activity and yet there is a wide diversity of what professionals are taught and consequently a diversity of opinion about research. Research traditions tend to exist in most professions, ranging from the positivistic, deductive approaches favoured, for example, by doctors and pharmacologists, to the more qualitative, inductive approaches favoured by social scientists, many nurses and some teachers (see Chapter 3). If we are to take a truly holistic approach to caring for children and consequently researching with children, it is important that a more inter-professional approach is adopted. Not only do professionals in contemporary practice need to be aware of their own research traditions, they should also be skilled in recognizing and valuing the research traditions of colleagues outside their profession (Repko et al., 2012).

One of the greatest hurdles to overcome here is the rigid and hierarchical perspective that some professions hold in relation to methodologies. Yin (2008) discusses this issue and suggests that a more appropriate view of research methodologies is a pluralistic one. Different research strategies can be employed in different ways and rigidity only serves to hamper innovation. For example, case studies, according to Yin, can use exploratory, descriptive and explanatory strategies, just as experiments (traditionally seen as the only way of finding causal relationships) can have an exploratory motive. The important issue here is that where problems arise in practice relating to a child or a group of children, and research is undertaken, the process is, of course, important but so too is the outcome. At a 'grass-roots' level it does not matter very much if one method or during which he discovered the 'law of effect' and Skinner's (1938) work with pigeons and rats, which defined the learning process referred to as operant conditioning. The application of these theories to human learning, and to learning in children in particular, was notable, and the work of these early researchers formed the basis of further research into human learning and human personality. Albert Bandura (1977), for example, used Skinner's theories about behavioural consequences and blended them with his own ideas producing the theory (along with others) of social learning (a detailed account of this and other cognitive theories can be found in Chapter 2).

The work undertaken on the psychology of learning has had much wider application and has led to the advancement of practice in other professions concerned with the care of children. Sociologists have borrowed these theories: for example, Eppel and Eppel (1966) looked at the influence of early learning on later moral behaviour. Educationists have also used learning theories (as one would expect) to inform classroom activities (Bruce, 2004; Child, 1997; Greenhow et al., 2009; Panton, 1945; Raban et al., 2003), and health care professionals, particularly those involved with health promotion activities with children (Davis et al., 2011; Klebanoff and Muramatsu, 2002; Taylor and Thurtle, 2005), have borrowed such theories to underpin their work.

Clearly, then, the impact of one profession's work has had a major impact on the practice of others. What is also interesting is to note that the impetus for much of this work came before, between and just after the two world wars. It is also interesting to speculate as to why learning became, and remains, so high on the research agenda. The lack of evidence in this area leads us to speculation and we do not pretend to have any or all of the answers. Perhaps the pioneering work in Germany by Froebel (see Woods, 2005) led to some action by educationists, perhaps academic comparisons with other developed countries prompted the need to ensure that children did not fall behind, or perhaps concern about the moral behaviour of adolescents was the prompt. The list of possibilities is endless.

Adolescent deviance, delinquency and morality

The moral values and standards of adolescents has long been a subject that has fascinated researchers, and it is the second major theme on which we focus. Concern was evident for a very long time before the 1950s and 1960s, but it was during these two decades that it became an explosive subject and the focus of a great deal of research. There was much speculation as to whether deviance and delinquency were attributable to genetic or environmental influences, or a combination of both, and particular emphasis was placed on increasing the understanding of the effect of early environmental variables on later delinquent behaviour. This is a fine example of what Schaffer (1998) described as focusing on those who showed abnormal behaviour rather than focusing on those who showed normal behaviour.

Again, because of a lack of evidence, we are left to speculate as to why there was such a burst of activity in this field during these decades. The origins of activity probably lay in the interest in a group of young people who had been born during, or just after, the Second World War and who lived their adolescence during the 'flower power' era with its perceived association with sexual freedom, illicit drug taking and a greater questioning by young people of traditional and cultural practices. What we saw here was perhaps a society trying and needing to find a cause for adolescent behaviour in the 1960s because the behaviour was so alien to them. Or perhaps society needed to find some answers because it wished to be absolved of any guilt on its own part in what was seen as declining adolescent morals. How much more comfortable it feels to be able to blame the birth control pill, television, drugs or alcohol, or the 'pop' music scene, than to attribute blame to oneself.

Whatever the reasons, as we have already stated, research into this area acquired an incredible impetus that influenced educationists, psychologists and sociologists, and that had a major influence on professional practice at the time. The publication of many studies in paperback form and adaption for a general readership, also influenced the media and public opinion. Notable studies included a study of the moral values and dilemmas of adolescents (Eppel and Eppel, 1966); a study by Morse (1965) titled *The Unattached*, involving three social workers working for three years with young people who had experienced varying degrees of family breakdown; Eysenck's (1964) study of *Crime and Personality*; and Storr's (1964) exploration of the effects of childhood on later perverse or deviant sexual behaviour. There are many, many more.

The interest in adolescent deviance, delinquency and morality is still one that fascinates us today although the focus of this work has tended to move away from issues such as family breakdown, which is now a part of everyday life for millions of children. The focus over the last decade has been much more interested in cultural differences, the influence of religion on young people's morality and the impact of widespread migration (Duriez and Soenens, 2006; Rutland et al., 2010; Svensson et al., 2010; Wikström and Svensson, 2010; Woods and Jagers, 2003).

Children's relationships

The third major research theme that deserves our attention relates to the relationships children have with their parents, in particular, and the effects of 'unusual' relationships on child development. This theme had been apparent in literature earlier in the 20th century but became high on the agenda after Bowlby (1951) made bold claims about how important early caring relationships are to the ability only been confined to doctors undertaking medical research but has widened its focus to include researchers from education, psychology and sociology who have added further to the body of knowledge within their own professions, and to the professions of others, by studying the effects of HIV and AIDS from a wide variety of perspectives (Bauman et al., 2002; Goodwin et al., 2004; Richter et al., 2009; Scanlan, 2010).

Child health is our last brief example of an area of research activity and, as we stated at the beginning of this section, it is impossible to do justice to all areas of research with children, nor do we attempt to do so. The intention of these examples is to look at how research is steered and to highlight how research is, and should be, reactive to society's problems. In our examples we have looked particularly at how issues such as culture and migration have influenced the research agenda. We have also set out to give examples of how research in one area will impact on other areas, leading to a cascade of research focusing on a similar topic but which has its own peculiar approach and perspective.

Conclusion

Research is vital to the health of a profession and likewise reflects the health of a profession. Professions can stagnate and fail to increase or build on existing knowledge bases, as we have seen throughout the past few decades. At other times, however, a particular research theme has emerged from society and has captured its imagination. At these times researchers from many professions will, individually or in collaboration, focus on different aspects of the same topic. When this happens real progress is made.

Research is not only vital for the health of a profession but is also essential for the client group the profession serves – in this case, children and their families. The rest of this book is about the importance of research for the good of our chosen client group, who are special people and who deserve special consideration.

References

Agiobu-Kemmer, I.S. (1992) *Child Survival and Child Development in Africa. Bernard van Leer Studies and Evaluation Paper 6.* The Hague: Bernard van Leer Foundation.

Ainsworth, M.D.S., Blehar, M.C., Waters, C.C.E. and Wall, S. (1978) *Patterns of Attachment: a Psychological Study of the Strange Situation.* Hillsdale, NJ: Erlbaum.

Bandura, A. (1977) *Social Learning Theory.* Englewood Cliffs, NJ: Prentice Hall.

Bauman, L.J., Camacho S., Silver, E.J., Hudis, J. and Draimin, B. (2002) 'Behavioral problems in school-aged children of mothers with HIV/AIDS', *Clinical Child Psychology and Psychiatry*, 7 (1): 39–54.

Bowlby, J. (1951) *Maternal Care and Mental Health.* Geneva: World Health Organization.
Bruce, T. (2004) *Developing Learning in Early Childhood.* London: Paul Chapman Publishing.
Carlson, N.R., Miller, H.L., Heth, D.S., Donahoe, J.W., and Martin, N.G. (2010) *Psychology: The Science of Behaviour*, 7th edn. Boston: Pearson.
Child, D. (1997) *Psychology and the Teacher.* London: Continuum International Publishing Group Ltd.
Crawford, S.E. and Alaggia, R. (2008) 'The best of both worlds? Family influences on mixed race youth identity development', *Qualitative Social Work*, 7 (1): 81–98.
Davis, D.S., Goldmon, M.V. and Coker-Appiah, D.S. (2011) 'Using a community-based participatory research approach to develop a faith-based obesity intervention for African American children', *Health Promotion Practice*, 12 (6): 811–22.
Department of Health (2010) *Achieving Equity and Excellence for Children: How Liberating the NHS Will Help Us Meet the Needs Of Children and Young People.* London: Department of Health.
Douglas, J.W. (1975) 'Early hospital admission and later disturbances of behaviour and learning', *Developmental Medicine and Child Neurology*, 17 (4): 456–80.
Dunn, J. (1996) 'The Emanuel Miller Memorial Lecture 1995. Children's relationships: bridging the divide between cognitive and social development', *Journal of Child Psychology and Psychiatry*, 37 (5): 507–18.
Dunn, J. (2004) 'Annotation: children's relationships with their non-resident fathers', *Journal of Child Psychology and Psychiatry, and Allied Disciplines*, 45 (4): 659–71.
Dunn, J. and Deater-Deckard, K. (2001) *Children's Views of their Changing Families.* York: Joseph Rowntree Foundation.
Duriez, B. and Soenens, B. (2006) 'Religiosity, moral attitudes and moral competence: a critical investigation of the religiosity-morality relation', *International Journal of Behavioral Development*, 30 (1): 76–83.
Eppel, E.M. and Eppel, M. (1966) *Adolescents and Morality: a Study of Some Moral Values and Dilemmas of Working with Adolescents in the Context of a Changing Climate of Opinion.* London: Routledge and Kegan Paul.
Eysenck, H.J. (1964) *Crime and Personality.* London: Paladin.
Foundation for the Study of Infant Deaths. Available at: www.fsid.org.uk (accessed 15 February 2012).
Fraser, A. (1985) *The Weaker Vessel: Woman's Lot in Seventeenth-Century England.* London: Methuen.
Goodwin, R., Kozlova, A., Nizharadze, G. and Polyakova, G. (2004) 'HIV/AIDS among adolescents in Eastern Europe: knowledge of HIV/AIDS, social representations of risk and sexual activity among school children and homeless adolescents in Russia, Georgia and the Ukraine', *Journal of Health Psychology*, 9 (3): 381–96.
Greene, S. and Hill, M. (2005) 'Researching children's experience: methods and methodological issues', in S. Greene and D. Hogan (eds), *Researching Children's Experiences: Approaches and Methods.* London: Sage Publications Ltd. pp. 1–21.
Greenhow, C., Robelia, B. and Hughes, J.E. (2009) 'Learning, teaching and scholarship in a digital age. Web 2.0 and classroom research: What path should we take now?', *Educational Researcher*, 38 (4): 246–59.
Guidubaldi, J., Cleminshaw, H.K., Perry, J.D., Nastasi, B.K. and Lightel, J. (1986) 'The role of selected family environment factors in children's post divorce adjustment', *Family Relations*, 35 (1): 141–51.
Hawthorn, P. (1974) *Nurse, I Want My Mummy!* London: Royal College of Nursing.
Hetherington, E.M. and Stanley-Hagan, M. (1999) 'The adjustment of children with divorced parents: a risk and resiliency perspective', *Journal of Child Psychology and Psychiatry, and Allied Disciplines*, 40 (1): 129–40.

Hetherington, E.M., Cox, M. and Cox, R. (1979) 'Play and social interaction in children following divorce', *Journal of Social Issues*, 35 (4): 26–49.

Hetherington, E.M., Cox, M. and Cox, R. (1985) 'Long-term effects of divorce and remarriage on the adjustment of children', *Journal of the American Academy of Child Psychiatry*, 24 (5): 518–30.

Husson, R.N., Comeau, A.M. and Hoff, R. (1990) 'Diagnosis of human immunodeficiency virus infection in infants and children', *Pediatrics*, 86 (1): 1–10.

Kennedy, I. (2010) *Getting it Right for Children and Young People: Overcoming Cultural Barriers in the NHS so as to Meet Their Needs*. London: Department of Health. Available at: www.dh.gov.uk/en/Publicationsandstatistics/Publications/PublicationsPolicyAndGuidance/DH_119445 (accessed 16 February 2012).

Klebanoff, R. and Muramatsu, N. (2002) 'A community-based physical education and activity intervention for African American preadolescent girls: a strategy to reduce racial disparities in health', *Health Promotion Practice*, 3 (2): 276–85.

Kulka, R.A. and Weingarten, H. (1979) 'The long-term effects of parental divorce in childhood on adult adjustment', *Journal of Social Issues*, 35 (4): 50–78.

Lewis, V. and Kellett, M. (2004) 'Disability', in S. Fraser , V. Lewis, S. Ding, M. Kellett and C. Robinson (eds), *Doing Research with Children and Young People*. London: Sage Publications Ltd. pp. 191–205.

Madianou, M. and Miller, D. (2011) 'Mobile phone parenting: reconfiguring relationships between Filipina migrant mothers and their left-behind children', *New Media and Society*, 13 (3): 457–70.

Miller, M.F., ZVITAMSO Study Group, Humphrey, J.H., Iliff, P.J., Malaba, L.C., Mbuya, N.V., Stoltzfus, R.J. (2006) 'Neonatal erythropoiesis and subsequent anemia in HIV-positive and HIV-negative Zimbabwean babies during the first year of life: a longitudinal study', *BMC Infectious Diseases*, 6: 1.

Morse, M. (1965) *The Unattached*. Harmondsworth: Penguin.

Newson, J. and Newson, E. (1963) *Patterns of Infant Care in an Urban Community*. Harmondsworth: Penguin.

Office for National Statistics (2003) Gateway to UK National Statistics. Available at: www.statistics.gov.uk/hub/index.html (accessed 16 February 2012).

Panton, J.H. (1945) *Modern Teaching Practice and Technique*. London: Longmans, Green and Co.

Pavlov, I.P. (1927) *Conditioned Reflexes*. Oxford: Oxford University Press.

Prose, N.S. (1990) 'HIV infection in children', *Journal of the American Academy of Dermatology*, 22 (6 Pt 2): 1223–31.

Raban, B., Ure, C. and Waniganayake, M. (2003) 'Multiple perspectives: acknowledging the virtue of complexity in measuring quality', *Early Years: Journal of International Research & Development*, 23 (1): 67–77.

Repko, A.F., Newell, W.H. and Szostak, R. (2012) *Case Studies in Interdisciplinary Research*. Thousand Oaks, CA: Sage Publications, Inc.

Richter, L., Chandan, U. and Rochat, T. (2009) 'Improving hospital care for young children in the context of HIV/AIDS and poverty', *Journal of Child Health Care*, 13 (3): 198–211.

Robertson, J. and Robertson, J. (1989) *Separation and the Very Young*. London: Free Association Books.

Rutland, A., Abrams, D. and Killen, M. (2010) 'A new social-cognitive developmental perspective on prejudice: the interplay between morality and group identity', *Perspectives on Psychological Science*, 5 (3): 279–91.

Scanlan, S.J. (2010) 'Gender, development, and HIV/AIDS: implications for child mortality in less industrialized countries', *International Journal of Comparative Sociology*, 51 (3): 211–32.

Schaffer, H.R. (1998) *Making Decisions about Children: Psychological Questions and Answers*, 2nd edn. Oxford: Wiley-Blackwell.
Skinner, B.F. (1938) *The Behavior of Organisms*. New York: Appleton–Century–Crofts.
Song, M. (2010) 'Is there 'a' mixed race group in Britain? The diversity of multiracial identification and experience', *Critical Social Policy*, 30 (3): 337–58.
Stern, D.N. (1977) *The First Relationship: Infant and Mother*. Cambridge, MA: Harvard University Press.
Stine, G.J. (1997) *AIDS Update 1997: An Annual Overview of Acquired Immune Deficiency Syndrome*. Upper Saddle River, NJ: Prentice Hall.
Storr, A. (1964) *Sexual Deviation*. Baltimore: Penguin Books.
Svensson, R., Pauwels, L. and Weerman, F.M. (2010) 'Does the effects of self-control on adolescent offending vary by level of morality? A test in three countries', *Criminal Justice and Behavior*, 37 (6): 732–43.
Taylor, J. and Thurtle, V. (2005) 'Child health', in J. Taylor J. and M. Woods (eds), *Early Childhood Studies: an Holistic Introduction*, 2nd edn. London: Hodder Arnold. pp. 244–56.
Taylor, J. and Woods, M. (eds) (2005) *Early Childhood Studies: An Holistic Introduction*, 2nd edn. London: Hodder Arnold.
United Nations Children's Fund (1989) Convention on the Rights of the Child. Available at: www. unicef.org/crc/ (accessed 16 February 2012).
Wikström, P-O.H. and Svensson, R. (2010) 'When does self-control matter? The interaction between morality and self-control in crime causation', *European Journal of Criminology*, 7 (5): 395–410.
Wong, D.F., Chang, Y., He, X. and Wu, Q. (2010) 'The protective functions of relationships, social support and self-esteem in the life satisfaction of children of migrant workers in Shanghai, China', *International Journal of Social Psychiatry*, 56 (2): 143–57.
Woods, M. (2005) 'Early childhood studies: first principles', in J. Taylor and M. Woods (eds), *Early Childhood Studies: an Holistic Introduction*, 2nd edn. London: Hodder Arnold. pp. 1–22.
Woods, L. and Jagers, R. (2003) 'Are cultural values predictors of moral reasoning in African American adolescents?', *Journal of Black Psychology*, 29 (1): 102–18.
World Health Organization Expert Committee (1951) *Expert Committee on Mental Health: Report on the Second Session, Geneva, 11–16 September 1950. Technical Report Series (World Health Oragnization) No. 31*. Geneva: World Health Organization.
Wright, R., Houston, S., Ellis, M., Holloway, S. and Hudson, M. (2003) 'Crossing racial lines: geographies of mixed race partnering and multiraciality in the United States', *Progress in Human Geography*, 27 (4): 457–74.
Yin, R.K. (2008) *Case Study Research: Design and Methods*, 4th edn. London: Sage.

Recommended reading for further study

Lewis, V., Kellett, M., Robinson, C., Fraser, S. and Ding, S. (2004) *The Reality of Research with Children and Young People*. London: Sage in association with the Open University.
Taylor, J. and Woods, M. (eds) (2005) *Early Childhood Studies: An Holistic Introduction*, 2nd edn. London: Hodder Arnold.
Tisdall, K., Davis, J.M. and Gallagher, M (2009) *Researching with Children and Young People: Research Design, Methods, and Analysis*. Los Angeles, CA: Sage.

TWO

Theory for research and practice with children and young people

The aims of this chapter are:

- to show why theory is important when doing research with children and young people;
- to provide an overview of the relevant main psychological and sociological theories and their implications for doing research with children and young people;
- to highlight the importance of *context* as well as *content* in research with children and young people.

Situation 1 A mother, having watched a controversial chat show, asks a nursery teacher if she should withdraw her child from day care and give up work because she now believes that children of working mothers suffer and that a group care setting is not as good as being at home with mother. What should the nursery teacher do and say to this mother?

Situation 2 A nurse is concerned about the possible effects and potential damage to families in which there is a child with a long-term illness requiring frequent and intensive separations between the child and the family. Is there anything the nurse can do to better understand the process and at the same time provide support for the families?

Situation 3 Following the publication of a story in a popular women's magazine, the helpline of a fostering and adoption support group is besieged with callers seeking advice on the value of cultivating a relationship between an adopted child and the biological mother. What can these callers be reasonably told?

Situation 4 A paediatrician notices that anxious children of very anxious parents do not respond well to standard forms of advice and intervention. What steps should the paediatrician take to help the parents understand the impact they are having on their children and to enhance their outcomes?

Situation 5 The manager of a youth club located in a deprived inner-city tower block observes that youngsters of all ages are struggling to play constructively together and to form friendships in a lasting and appropriate manner. How should the manager take forward these concerns and make changes?

Situation 6 A family counsellor needs to work with the bitterly separating parents of three children aged 4, 8 and 13 who are causing great concern at school. What approach should the counsellor take with the parents to improve the outcomes for the children and what challenges are there to bringing about change?

The practitioner or researcher is not alone in the quest for answers on important and complex issues like these that affect children and young people. For each practice situation described in situations 1–6, there is an established knowledge base of related theory and research. This knowledge is there to inform and guide those who work or research in the field of child care and development. For instance, there is a great deal known about child–carer attachments, separation and loss. There is a lot known about the relative contributions of home and day care, or parent and teacher to child education. Some of these questions are not, however, so well represented in theory and research as others. Relatively little is known about fathers compared with the extensive research on mothers, or about the effects of factors, such as age and gender, on resilience to trauma. Not much is known about the costs and benefits of maintaining relationships between an adopted child and their biological mother. This does not mean that there is no role for theory in these cases. On the contrary, existing theories in related areas can be adapted or new theories created and this will guide and generate much needed research in important but neglected areas.

Nevertheless, the mere mention of the word 'theory' can drive terror into the hearts of research students and practitioners alike – the former because of the overwhelming range of possible and often complex theories that they are only beginning to touch on in lectures, and the latter because they have come to rely on their practice, experience or intuition and may feel threatened that the knowledge they have is no longer valued. For those of us who teach about the role of theory in research and practice, it is apparent that, in the undergraduate population and even beyond into the classrooms, wards, homes and communities, 'theory' can be regarded as a dirty word.

In this chapter we hope to show that the nature of theory is, in fact, rather like that of a valuable, important and useful friend. The undergraduate needs to realize that a sound grasp of theory – like all good friendships – needs to be worked on and developed over time. The intuitive practitioner need not feel insecure, because experience creates an advantage in being able to recognize and use theory effectively. We all need to appreciate that theory is not a mystical thing visited upon us by superior beings, but is instead an ordinary part of everyday thinking and of being human.

The fact is that theorizing is a natural, human compulsion that helps us to organize our perceptions of the world and therefore make it easier to predict and control. For instance, a mother who notices withdrawn behaviour and school refusal in her eight-year-old child is confronted by an unpredictable situation that disrupts routine and poses a threat to longer-term adjustment and security. Finding the reason for the behaviour, describing it, explaining it, predicting it and controlling it is a matter of survival. Theories have been described as nets cast to catch what we call 'the world', to rationalize, to explain and to master it. In the world of child development, you may have a theory that the eight-year-old has a behavioural disorder because of an underlying problem in the child's relationship with the mother. You will then investigate the nature of this relationship to describe what is wrong and to implement changes. Or you may have the theory that the child's behaviour is simply a consequence of an ineffective parental regime of rewards and punishments. You will then describe that regime, explain the problems, predict patterns and bring about changes that will control or alter the behaviour. As both these examples suggest, theory can be viewed as a stage on which observations and experiments can be conducted and serve an important practical function by guiding research and practice.

Why do people who work with children need theory?

Every individual who deals with children and young people has this very human need to make sense of them. If little Ben is creating mayhem in his reception class, foster placement or medical ward, the requirement to observe his behaviour, describe what he is doing and find both explanations and solutions is essential. The explanations generated can help predict not only Ben's behaviour but may also be generalized to other similar children and situations. Ultimately, it should be possible to understand or predict and to devise a means of controlling, preventing or curing such behaviour. These processes of describing, explaining, predicting and controlling are the very essence of theory, and professionals in education, health and welfare need to do all of these things on a daily basis. In many cases, far-reaching decisions about a child or young person's future will have to be made on the basis of such theorizing. A sound understanding of theory is, therefore, of the utmost importance.

There are, however, many different theoretical perspectives in human development, many different ways of 'seeing' the world and, consequently, many different explanations and solutions for any one given situation. For example, a mother seeking advice on the disruptive behaviour of her child could, potentially, receive diverse and incompatible explanations and solutions depending on which professional is consulted. An educational psychologist may theorize that a learning disability is underlying the disruptive behaviour and recommend additional support for learning. A health visitor may theorize that food intolerance often underlies child behaviour disorders and refer the child to a dietician. A social worker may theorize that social hardship and inadequate parenting are the source of the behaviour problem and implement a programme of parenting skills and social support. In more extreme situations, theoretical perspectives may influence the approach of professionals at the threshold of important decisions, such as the need to be educated in a special school or to be looked after in a residential setting. Theory, therefore, could potentially have a massive impact leading to a range of possible futures for a given child or young person, and seeking to improve the ways in which different professional groups can understand the theories and practices of one another and work together in the interests of children and young people is an important goal.

Finally, another reason why people who work with children and young people need theory is because much of the policy and legislation that dictate the roles, practices and rights of both practitioner and child/young person are formulated on the basis of various established bodies of theoretical knowledge. According to the guidance on the Children Act (Department of Health, 1990), the implicit child-care principles have been developed over a long period of time and have many roots, including knowledge from child development, psychology, psychiatry and sociology. The importance of understanding the nature of these underlying theories is obvious. It will lead to a better understanding of the nature of the job to be done as well as the nature of children and young people.

Theories for guiding and interpreting research and practice with children and young people

Nature versus nurture

The question about the extent to which children and young people's minds and behaviour are a product of their biological make-up or of the environment exerting an influence on them has been around in philosophy since the ancient time of Plato, through to the 17th and 18th century, and philosophers such as René Descartes (1596–1650), John Locke (1632–1704) and Jean-Jacques Rousseau (1712–1778). This is widely known as the nature–nurture debate: Plato and Descartes proposed that at least some ideas (thinking) are innate. Locke, however, took the view that the infant is born with a mind that is a blank slate or *tabula rasa*, and consequently that all knowledge is a product of experience writing itself on the blank slate. Rousseau, on the other hand, thought that infants were born with an inherent sense of right and wrong. He went further to propose some enduring theories of development, such as the process of maturation and the concept of developmental stages.

Nowadays, those of us with a professional obligation to study and understand children and young people accept the position that while there is often an interplay between nature and nurture, it is not usually as clear cut as it appeared in the articulation of the great debate. For example, we know that puberty appears in all young people at roughly the same age regardless of culture and country of origin. However, diet and other maturational factors such as parenting, developmental delay, hormonal disorders, and individual differences such as temperament do exert an influence on the precise age at which the young person finally begins and ends puberty.

All of the theories for doing research with children and young people that follow do accept that there is an interplay between the nature and the nurture of the child or young person. Where they differ is in their views about which of the two is the dominant factor in determining the developmental outcomes for the growing individual.

Nature over nurture

Biological theories, discussed in more detail later on in the chapter, in essence propose that the way human physical and psychological development unfolds over time is partially or wholly genetically programmed and that human development and behaviour are also influenced by biological processes and mechanisms such as hormones and neurochemistry. This position is not one that considers the social and other environments to be uninfluential, but it is a position that acknowledges the robust framework of developmental taxonomies that have an extraordinary evidence base, well backed up with scientific observation and research.

The cognitive developmental theorists Jean Piaget (1896–1980) and Lev Vygotsky (1896–1934), also discussed later on in the chapter, believed that infants are predisposed to construct their own psychological reality, but Vygotsky gives greater weight to how that constructed reality is influenced by the external, social experiences rather than biological maturation.

Nurture over nature

Behaviourists such as Ivan Pavlov (1849–1936) and B.F. Skinner (1904–1990), also discussed in this chapter, believed that it is possible to use inherent reflexes, which drive individuals to seek rewards and avoid punishment (pleasure versus pain), to entirely shape behaviour from the outside using classical conditioning and operant conditioning using schedules of negative or positive reinforcement, and that behaviour can be weakened by using punishment. In social learning theory, Albert Bandura introduced the notion that a direct reinforcer is not always necessary for learning to occur in social situations. Merely observing or modelling the actions of others motivates learning too.

Theories that focus on the interplay of nature and nurture

Freud's (1901/1976) theory of psychosocial development, Bowlby's (1979) work on attachment theory, Erikson's (1950/1963) views of psychosocial development, Bronfenbrenner's (1979, 1986, 1992) ecological model of development, and theories about risks and resilience from the field of developmental psychopathology are those that give equal measure to the impact of what is evolving within the child in terms of determined unfolding patterns and the impact of the wider environment, from the broadest cultural sense to the localized setting of within close relationships. Sociological theories also require that researchers use methods that enable us to delve deeper into the subjective reality of the child or young person's world (Rutter, 2006).

There are a number of other theories and research evidence bases that are relevant for supporting a programme of research on children and young people. These include theories on: parenting; social networking theory; life stressors and coping with adversity; prosocial development; gender development; the impact of trauma and loss; sibling relationships; peer relationships; morality and conscience; memory development; the impact of school (language and literacy); and self-esteem are just a few that spring to mind. A detailed examination of all of these areas is beyond the scope of this book, but they are easily accessed via a library and other electronic sources.

Psychological theories

In doing research with children and young people we have a range of theories to choose from. The main theories informing human development and research are drawn from the discipline of psychology. Until shortly after the Second World War psychology was characterized by competing 'schools'. Thereafter the discipline grew and diversified enormously, and the old schools that psychologists adhered to tended to be replaced with a variety of fields of study, each using various theoretical perspectives. These perspectives might offer different explanations of the phenomena being studied, and each can be seen as providing possible insights without having to be mutually exclusive. The five different perspectives reviewed here have been chosen to represent the main approaches in contemporary psychology as reflected in key foundational texts for the discipline, such as Davey et al.'s (2004) *Complete Psychology*. These are physiological, psychodynamic, behaviourist, humanistic and cognitive. The popularity of these theories owes much to their ability to inform us about the child or young person in interaction with the environment either as originally formulated or as they have been revised by subsequent theorists. The classic example of explaining a handshake, as shown in Box 2.1, illustrates the differing emphases of these theories.

BOX 2.1

Theoretical perspectives

A group of teenagers arrive at a party and are introduced to some friends. They all shake hands. Why do people engage in this particular behaviour? The handshake can be approached by each of the selected theories in a different way:

PHYSIOLOGICAL	The handshake might be the result of particular sets of neural and muscular processes, or it might be due to a gene for sociability.
PSYCHODYNAMIC	The handshake could be the result of a desire for physical contact.
BEHAVIOURIST	The handshake could be the result of previous conditioning, having been associated with some reward.
HUMANISTIC	The handshake might be the result of a need for acceptance.
COGNITIVE	The handshake could be the result of purposive mental processes – for example, consciously deciding to show friendship.

Although individual theorists will have a preferred approach to finding explanatory frameworks, all of these perspectives may make a contribution to our understanding of child behaviour and development.

Source: Davey, G.C.L., Albery, I.P., Chandler, C., Field, A.P., Jones, D., Messer, D., Moore, S., Stirling, C. (eds) (2004) *Complete Psychology*. London: Hodder & Stoughton. Reproduced by permission of Edward Arnold (Publishers) Ltd.

Physiological approaches

The physiological approach focuses on the biological basis of behaviour and of psychological functioning. The underlying assumptions are that behaviour is determined by biological factors, and that whatever the contribution of other influences the best explanation of behaviour will be framed in biological terms. The roots of this approach go back to the beginnings of psychology as a discipline in its own right, when there was a preoccupation with the sensory and motor correlates of mental events. In 1860, Gustav Fechner published his *Elemente der Psychophysik*, translated from German as *Principles of Psychophysics* and in 1874 Wilhelm Wundt wrote his *Grundzüge der physiologischen Psychologie*, translated from German as *Principles of Physiological Psychology*.

In many respects the rise of psychoanalysis and other psychodynamic theories changed the focus of psychology from biological explanations to an interest in inner mental life as shaped by early childhood experience. Currently, with the decline of the influence of psychodynamic theories (see later in the chapter) on mainstream psychology and with the developments that have revolutionized technology, the place of biological explanations for behaviour has become much more prominent. Three main fields of interest inform the physiological approach: brain function, biochemistry and heredity.

It is in the field of brain function that the advances in technology have had the most far-reaching impact. The study of brain–behaviour relationships has been revolutionized by these advances. Diagnostic procedures such as functional magnetic resonance imaging (fMRI), positron emission tomography (PET), computed tomography (CT) and computerized axial tomography (CAT) scanning and regional cerebral blood flow (rCBF) (Gazzaniga et al., 2002 describe these and other procedures) have transformed our knowledge of how the brain works. Some of these methods allow us to study the brain at work in live situations, and to watch the effects of the performance of different tasks both at the level of gross brain structures and in much finer detail. It is also possible to study brain impairments and the impact they have on behaviour. Biochemical studies also inform the investigation of the workings of the brain through the study of *neurotransmitters*, chemicals in the brain that affect behaviour and mood. For example, low levels of serotonin are associated with depression.

The study of heredity capitalizes on the vast increase in genetic research in recent years, both in animal and human studies (Plomin et al., 2002), but studies of genetically pre-programmed behaviour are long established in psychology. They include not only the investigation of individual differences in intelligence and personality but also of universal commonalities, such as nurturing routines and protective responses towards infants. For example, a sudden piercing cry from a babbling child will trigger a parental 'pattern of caring'. Consider how adults readily respond to any child in distress, adopt the young of others, respond to baby features of the young of any species and the way that babies smile, reeling adults in and eliciting positive responses such as baby talk or 'motherese'. One of the consequences of these biologically determined, interdependent chains of stimuli and responses is that the child forms a specific attachment to a particular carer, usually the mother.

John Bowlby (1907–1990) was a psychiatrist who applied psychoanalytical theory to his early writings on the mother–child relationship, particularly the view that the earliest relationships were crucially important for longer-term development and adjustment. However, he later concluded that biological principles better explain the nature of the tie between mother and child – i.e. the complex, interdependent repertoire of instinctive behaviours in both infant and parent that function to create proximity between the child and carer and lead to the creation of a bond. However, as the child has to learn who their mother is and what kind of mother she is, and the mother needs to adapt to her infant, conditions exist in which an infant and mother can fail to bond or bond in a maladaptive way. An attachment is an emotional bond in which the person feels secure and the other person is a safe base from which to explore the world around. There are far-reaching implications for this theory and the ideas and methods are further explored later in this chapter.

Implications of physiological approaches

Physiological approaches have been criticized as being too reductionist, by reducing behaviour to its basic biological components; and too determinist, in focusing on biological heredity to explain human personality and activity. However, they have provided an explanatory framework for a great deal of psychological functioning. Through systematic investigation of brain–behaviour relationships they have opened the way to a clearer knowledge of how children develop and to understanding the ways in which development sometimes goes wrong. They have provided many procedures for conducting research into human behaviour and development, and have been instrumental in establishing new approaches to addressing a wide range of difficulties both through pharmacological treatments and through specialized therapeutic techniques.

Psychodynamic approaches

The starting point for psychodynamic theories was Freud's (1901/1976, 1905/1977, 1923/1984) psychoanalysis, but other well-known psychodynamic approaches are those of Adler (1916), Jung (1921) and Erikson (1950/1963). These theories focus on dynamic, unconscious drives that govern behaviour. Freud trained as a physician, specializing in the study of the nervous system. In treating his patients, he noticed that some had illnesses for which no biological cause could be found, such as the 'mental illnesses' of hysteria, anxiety and phobia. He was inclined to cure these patients by listening to them talking freely and without interruption about their current thoughts, feelings and desires. Freud's aim was to understand the underlying processes of the patient's mind and personality and also to provide a 'talking cure'. As a result, he formulated a theory on the origins and development of the personality and its disorders. Freud believed that adult mental illness originated in childhood and that analysing what went wrong would lead to better understanding of the process of normal personality development.

According to psychoanalytical theory, the psychological system and its development is best described in three ways: it is *dynamic, structural* and *sequential*. It is *dynamic* in that the human psychological system is driven by *psychic energy*, which is biologically based. The most powerful drive is the sexual instinct, maintained by the energy of the *libido*. It is *structural* in that personality is made up of three parts, the *id*, the *ego* and the *superego*, which are in constant conflict. The *id* seeks instant gratification and has free rein until the child is about two-years-old. The *ego* develops as a rational mechanism and plays an important role in the resolution of the conflicts that arise between the drive for instant gratification and the reality imposed by carers. By the school years, the *superego* has developed, representing parental standards, which the child has internalized. It is *sequential* in that development is said to go through five fixed psychosexual stages, each representing the focus of the *libido* on a different part of the body. These are shown in Box 2.2.

BOX 2.2

Freud's five psychosexual stages

ORAL (age 0–1½)	At birth the child's neurological pleasure centre is focused on the mouth. Oral behaviours such as sucking and biting are the child's pleasure source.
ANAL (age 1½–3)	As the child's body develops, neurological awareness of the anus is in place. Elimination and retention of faeces are a source of pleasure at the same time when the child is being toilet-trained.

PHALLIC (age 3–5)	At this time there is increased sensitivity in the genital area, and both sexes are likely to find pleasure in the exploration of this area. Freud claimed that children become unconsciously sexually attracted to the parent of the opposite sex. This is called the Oedipus complex in boys and the Electra complex in girls. These complexes are characterized by the rivalry with the same-sex parent for the sexual attention of the opposite-sex parent, a fear of the same-sex parent and an attempt to deal with the resulting anxiety through the defence mechanism of identification with their rival.
LATENT (age 5 to puberty)	At this time, sexual impulses are not an issue. It is a period of resolution following the anxiety of the preschool years. Identification with same-sex peers is a feature at this stage, and sexual impulses, in whichever form they have been resolved, will remain latent, hidden until the challenges of puberty.
GENITAL (puberty onwards)	Sexual impulses resurface with the onslaught of hormonal activity and genital regrowth that accompanies puberty. During adolescence, the child should reach a mature form of heterosexual love.

Implications of psychodynamic approaches

The psychodynamic approach has almost certainly been more absorbed into everyday life than any other theory. Its basic concepts and vocabulary have become familiar and are often viewed in the public mind as representing the essence of psychology. At the same time, it must be recognized that its claims are largely untestable and they occupy an uneasy position in relation to modern scientific psychology. Nevertheless, psychodynamic theories have served to highlight the importance of early childhood experiences and relationships, and the sequential nature of the developmental tasks facing children at different ages. They have contributed to many therapeutic situations, such as play therapy with emotionally disturbed children. They emphasize how carers need to provide a sensitive and responsive type of provision which takes full account of the individual's needs for experience and stimulation. Environments and relationships should be secure and provide opportunities for the young child to play and explore. When dealing with parents, it may be necessary to explore the nature of their own early childhood and teenage experiences.

Behaviourist approaches

Behaviourism 'changed the subject of psychology from mind to behaviour' (Davey, 2004: 16). Its basic premise is that behaviour is *learned*, and it turned the focus from inner mental life to the role of the environment in shaping behaviour. It offered a strict scientific method and for many years it was the dominant force in psychology. Behaviourism continues to play an important role in theory, research and practice, and in relation to children and young people it has many applications in teaching and learning, in behaviour management and in therapeutic approaches. The roots of behaviourism are to be found in the work of the Russian physiologist Ivan Pavlov, who was interested in the way certain biological events become systematically related to changes in the environment.

Conditioning

In his famous experiments, Pavlov noticed that a hungry dog will automatically salivate when given food. Furthermore, if the dog hears a bell every time the food is presented it will learn to salivate when hearing the bell alone and in the absence of food. This process of learning to respond to a previously neutral event is called *classical conditioning*. Salivation is an unconditioned response, i.e. it is natural and reflexive; food is an unconditioned stimulus, i.e. it is naturally associated with salivation. The bell becomes a conditioned stimulus, and the salivation on hearing the bell in the absence of food is a conditioned response. A child may have a recurring nightmare at night that will eventually become a fear of darkness. These behaviourist principles were formalized into a general theory by J.B. Watson (1913) in a landmark paper entitled 'Psychology as the behaviourist views it', and then in his classic text *Behaviourism* (1930).

Operant conditioning

A further landmark was B.F. Skinner's (1938) *The Behaviour of Organisms* book. Skinner's doctoral studies at Harvard in the early 1930s, in which he trained rats to press levers in exchange for food, led him to propose that behaviour is a function of its consequences, and to add to classical conditioning another main theory of learning, operant conditioning. When individuals act spontaneously on their environment, responses that are rewarding increase the frequency of the behaviour in question while responses that are punishing decrease its frequency. Thus, children learn to repeat behaviours that are rewarded and not to repeat behaviours that are punished. The pleasant or rewarding consequences of behaviour, such as attention, smiling, praise, are known as *positive reinforcement*.

A child may be behaving badly to receive attention, and to stop the behaviour, the parent, carer or teacher may speak to, distract and otherwise give attention to the child. In effect, the child's behaviour is being reinforced through finding a successful way of getting the attention that is craved. Punishment serves to weaken undesirable behaviour either by withdrawing pleasant things or by the enforcement of unpleasant things. Many professionals will be familiar with these behaviour modification procedures, such as 'shaping', which provide a way of changing behaviour by using schedules of reinforcement.

Social learning

Albert Bandura (1977) developed behaviourist principles further with his social learning theory. He pointed out that there were other ways of learning apart from direct reinforcement. Children learn a whole range of behaviours through observation, such as how to care for a baby, make tea or hit others. Parents and others serve as models of behaviour, and Bandura called this *observational learning* or *modelling*. Furthermore, children learn not only from positive reinforcements and punishments that they themselves receive but also from those given to their models for their behaviour. In this way, children do not model all behaviour they observe, such as stealing. Gradually, Bandura took more interest in the role that thinking or cognition plays in the mediation of social learning. There are several ways in which the child's own thinking intervenes between the observation of the behaviour and its imitation. The child needs to attend to the modelled behaviour, to retain it, to retrieve it and to reproduce it. In addition, the child must want to, or be motivated to reproduce the observed behaviour. In effect, cognitive processing of attention, memory and information processing all play a role in observational learning and modelling. Thus, Bandura (1986) redefined his theory as social cognitive theory.

Implications of behaviourist approaches

Modern critiques of behaviourist theories highlight a number of limitations. They are too mechanistic, they ignore mental processes, they see behaviour as being environmentally determined with insufficient regard to biological factors and they are poor at accounting for complex behaviours such as language. Nevertheless, they have established an extremely important principle: behaviour can be learned and modified through the principles of operant conditioning, based on positive reinforcement and punishment, and children learn through observing, modelling and cognitively processing the behaviour of others. The wider theoretical developments that have focused on the importance of social and cognitive factors have provided a broad range of applications of behaviourist principles to theory and practice.

Humanistic approaches

Humanistic psychology emerged in the 1950s as a reaction to both behaviourism and psychoanalysis. It is concerned with the human dimension in psychology, with the study of the whole person and with a focus on positive strengths and psychological health in contrast to the common emphasis on mental illness and disorder. James Bugental (1964) defined humanistic psychology in terms of five postulates:

- Human beings cannot be reduced to components.
- Human beings have in them a uniquely human context.
- Human consciousness includes an awareness of oneself in the context of other people.
- Human beings have choices and responsibilities.
- Human beings are intentional and they purposively seek meaning, value and creativity.

The main names associated with humanistic psychology are Carl Rogers and Abraham Maslow. Both were concerned with the concept of *actualization*. Rogers (1951) proposed that people are born with an actualizing tendency. This drives them towards psychological health, which is achieved when the perceived self (how we see ourselves) is aligned with the ideal self (how we would like to be). It was Maslow, however, who was most closely associated with the establishment of humanistic psychology as a formal development. The new movement was known as the 'third force' in psychology, following Maslow's designation of psychoanalysis as the 'first force', the 'second force' being behaviourism. Maslow (1954) is best known for his 'hierarchy of needs', shown in Figure 2.1. To achieve psychological growth and health we must first satisfy lower needs, ultimately reaching self-actualization.

The most recent development in psychology within humanistic theory is the rise of 'positive psychology', a term coined by Maslow and adopted by Martin Seligman (Seligman, 2003; Seligman and Csikszentmihalyi, 2000). This movement has taken up the humanistic theme of emphasizing what is right with people rather than what is wrong with them. Its aim is to enable people to live lives of fulfilment, marked by health, happiness and well-being. Peterson and Seligman (2004) have reacted against the preoccupation of psychology with negative features, such as classifications of psychological disorders like anxiety and depression, by producing their own manual of the strengths and virtues that are

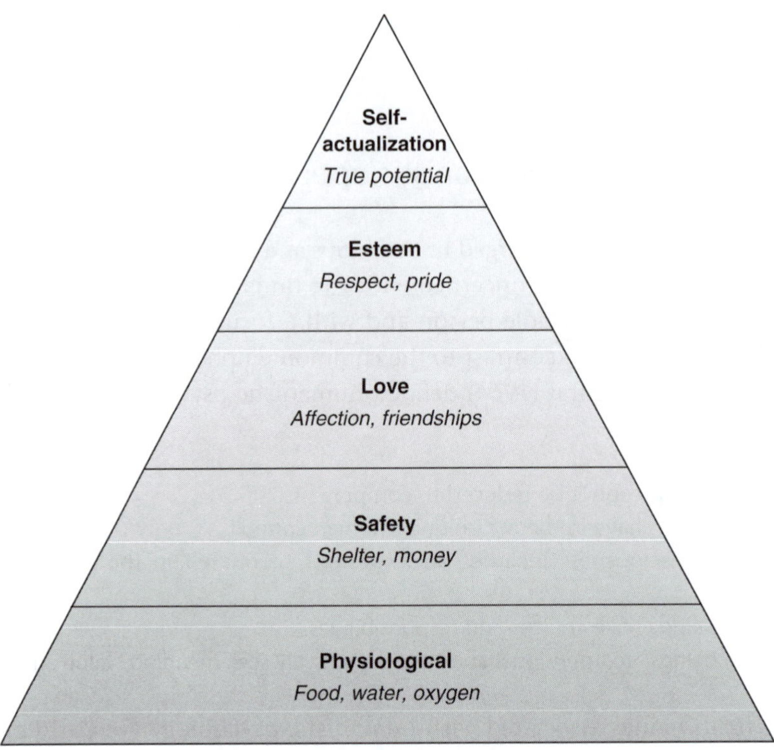

Figure 2.1 Maslow's (1954) hierarchy of needs, simplified version

found in people who are happy and fulfilled. Their approach to areas such as the assessment of children, providing them with support or conducting research with them, would be to focus on their strengths, skills and potential rather than on their difficulties and weaknesses.

Researchers in positive psychology have developed a theoretical model with three overlapping areas of happiness in life. The *pleasant life* or 'life of enjoyment' focuses on how people experience the positive emotions associated with normal and healthy living. The *good life* or 'life of engagement' examines the beneficial effects that are experienced when people are immersed at optimal level in their primary activities. The *meaningful life* or 'life of affiliation' investigates how people obtain a sense of meaning and purpose from belonging to and contributing to something greater than themselves, such as social groups, organizations or belief systems.

Implications of humanistic approaches

Humanistic psychology has been criticized for lacking a coherent, clearly defined and integrated theory. It has been seen as weak with regard to the scientific method, and its overall impact on academic psychology has been limited. Nevertheless, in many ways it has made a significant and increasing contribution, and many of its research efforts and practical applications have been invested in worthwhile areas such as the promotion of international peace and cooperation and the enhancement of social welfare. It has also been responsible for the development of various widely used strategies for providing support and counselling for children and young people, including client-centred therapy, one of the principal therapeutic approaches in psychology.

Humanistic psychology favours qualitative research methods over quantitative ones (see Chapters 3, 6, 7 and 8), viewing the qualitative approach as being most suitable to understanding the whole person and investigating the meaning and purpose of behaviour. It clearly has important implications for research and practice with children and young people. By focusing on children and young people's strengths rather than their weaknesses and by taking an interest in the whole individual and in the healthy and fulfilling aspects of everyday life, it provides a positive approach to doing research with children and young people. In addition, it promotes an approach that is likely to be appealing to all who are concerned with the welfare of the child or young person and in taking forward a positive agenda.

Cognitive approaches

Cognition means thinking, and cognitive theories are about the ways in which children and young people come to think about, know about and understand the world around them. The two main cognitive theorists are Piaget (1929/1952, 1937/1954, 1945/1962) and Vygotsky (1978). As with the other theories mentioned so far, they each regard the child as an active participant in constructing knowledge. They agree that both biology and environment are important, but vary on the emphasis they place on each one.

Jean Piaget (1896–1980) was an influential Swiss psychologist, who was also part philosopher and part biologist. As a philosopher he was interested in questions on the acquisition of knowledge, such as: What is learning? Are things always the way they appear? As a biologist he was interested in describing and recording systematically the various stages of thought children go through as they develop. In relation to human development he helped to bridge the gap that often exists between philosophy and science, by applying scientific methods to philosophical questions. From studies which began with his own children, he concluded that there are important qualitative differences between a child's understanding of the world and that of adults.

Piagetian structures and processes

Piaget believed that infants are born with mental blueprints called schemata (singular: schema) through which they adapt to the environment. Some of the earliest schemata include the sucking and grasping reflexes, which become more complex through the adaptive processes of assimilation and accommodation. In assimilation, the infant imposes existing schemata on the environment, for example, in spontaneously sucking anything that might be a nipple. In accommodation, the schema is gradually reorganized to meet the challenges of the environment, for example, the adaptation of sucking to drinking from a cup. Piaget identified four major stages of development:

- *Sensorimotor stage (0–2 years).* Reflexes gradually become more complex as various schemata coordinate. For example, grasping and looking can combine into a new schema for 'picking up'. Children gradually learn about object permanence, i.e. the continued existence of an object that goes out of sight.
- *Pre-operational stage (2–7 years).* Thinking is marked by *egocentrism* (seeing the world from one's own point of view) and *centration* (focusing on one aspect of a task and ignoring others). Piaget's classic test for this stage is that of *conservation* (of number – see Figure 2.2 – volume, mass, and so on). Children presented with two glasses of water with equal amounts think one has more if it is poured into a taller, thinner glass.
- *Concrete operational (7–11 years).* Children who pass conservation tests can now think in relative terms – that things can hurt a little or a lot – and they can grasp concepts such as 'more' and 'less', but they still think in concrete rather than abstract terms.
- *Formal operational (11 years plus).* The stage of formal logic and abstract thinking. Adolescents gain the capacity for higher-order reasoning.

As a theoretician, Piaget was more interested in the cognitive processes underlying task performance. He devised a series of tasks that enabled him to describe the development of cognitive processes such as object permanence, perspective taking, conservation and many others. His investigations enabled him to describe the sequence in which children became accomplished in various cognitive tasks. In tasks to assess children's ability to understand conservation, the understanding that some property of objects such as number or quantity is not changed by the experimenter's adjustments, is tested. Figure 2.2 illustrates the *conservation of number*, where two rows of coins are arranged so that the two rows are evenly matched in the number of coins and spacing between them. The

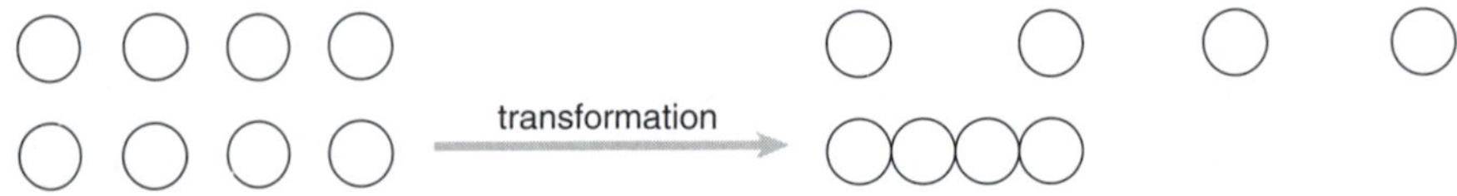

Figure 2.2 Piaget's conservation of number task

experimenter then transforms them by pushing the bottom row together and the top row coins apart.

Piaget found that, while preschool children could correctly answer the pre-transformation question 'Which row has the most coins?', they consistently failed the post-transformation question 'Now which row has the most coins?', believing that, in this example, there were suddenly more coins in the top row. Piaget also wished to test his theory of egocentrism – the proposal that preschool children are unable to appreciate that other people may view things differently. He devised *the three mountain task*, in which children had to guess whether or not another person looking at the same three mountains as themselves but from a different angle, would see the same thing as them, or different. Although Piaget found evidence to support his view that young children have a problem with perspective taking, subsequent methodological revisions demonstrated greater abilities than Piaget's initial design allowed.

These tasks are interesting to researchers for a number of reasons. They illustrate the elegant simplicity of designing tasks for children of all ages, tasks that reveal information about the inner minds of children. Many other researchers have demonstrated how simpler versions of such tasks can be devised, versions more accessible to even the youngest children, and providing evidence that certain abilities are evident in much younger children than Piaget supposed. Flavell (1978, 1985, 1988) developed simple tasks which illustrate the perspective-taking abilities in three-year-olds. These variations in turn resulted in the emergence of a new socio-cognitive theory, *the theory of mind*, the ability to appreciate the world of mental states such as ideas, beliefs, desires and feelings in self and others and how they may differ (see further in this chapter). Piaget's tasks have therefore been subject to critical evaluation and methodological revision (e.g. Donaldson, 1978; Samuel and Bryant, 1984) in elegant demonstrations of how he underestimated the impact of the social and research context and language used on children's perspective-taking abilities.

The rediscovery of Vygotsky

The work of the influential Russian psychologist Lev Vygotsky was rediscovered after years of communist censorship. Vygotsky gave much greater importance to the social and cultural origins of thought and the role played by language in its structuring. In *Mind in Society: the Development of Higher Psychological Processes,* he (1978) describes how cognitive functioning has its origins in the child's social interactions. A child may reach for an object arbitrarily, an adult intervenes and 'interprets' the child's action and thereby bestows meaning upon the event. In effect, then, every cognitive process appears first on the social plane as part of joint activity and later appears on the psychological plane after it has been 'internalized' by the child. Language is the cultural tool that enables the child to internalize thought originating with others.

An important Vygotskian concept is the *zone of proximal development* (ZPD). Vygotsky believed conversations between children and adults to be crucial for cognitive development. He found that a child's performance of a task when working with adults or more able peers gave a better indication of cognitive development than independent performance. Thus ZPD is the learning zone in which a child can accomplish a task with the assistance of others. The aim of adults is to gradually remove the support they provide and pass over responsibility for the task to the child. Of course, not all parents, carers or educators are equally skilled in identifying and working within the child's ZPD. For example, depressed parents can be less sensitive to the ZPD (Goldsmith and Rogoff, 1995). According to Vygotsky (1978), when children are playing with adults or even older children they are learning how to think. The quality of the interaction taking place should, then, tell us something about the quality of the *scaffolding* children receive from their elders. Nevertheless, the learning process is not entirely in the hands of adults. Children can or should be able to make their own creative contributions to joint activity.

The Puzzle Task (Wertsch and Hickman, 1987) is a nice example of a task that creates a situation which enables the observation of interaction in the ZPD. Preschool children and their mothers are given two complete identical puzzles. One puzzle is taken apart and the pair asked to reassemble it. Mothers are asked to help their child whenever they feel the child needs help. The quality of the interaction can then be assessed in terms of helping the child to understand the task, directly and indirectly, referring to the completed puzzle for guidance, the child's contribution to solving the puzzle, for example, asking questions, and the mother's ability to encourage the child to 'think' for themselves. Two-year-olds should be able to engage in simple puzzle tasks with a parent, teacher or carer. However, as it is possible to increase the complexity of puzzles, there is potential for similar research on children of all ages. Reasonably recent research continues to find new ways of describing and testing the ZPD (see Meins and Russell, 1997, for a classic example).

Implications of cognitive approaches

Current work in the cognitive and social cognitive areas is not driven by any integrating theoretical framework and is very diverse. However, the approach has made a very major contribution to our knowledge of child development and to theory, research and practice with children and young people. It has highlighted that:

- Children think differently from adults and there are qualitative differences in the way children of different ages understand the world around them. Whether you are a nurse explaining treatment or pain, a social worker assessing risks, a teacher planning a curriculum or a researcher working with children and young people, attempts must be made to appreciate and respond to these differences.
- The child's learning, understanding and thinking is influenced by environmental conditions, social relationships and cultural conventions. It is important to find out where the child or young person is at in terms of experience. Is the child or young person from an ethnic minority? Is there a depressed carer? How effectively are the challenges of the world brought to the child or young person?
- The focus should be on supporting children's and young people's potential at the point of development rather than on task performance. There are implications for people who work with children and young people to recognize and locate the ZPD and to help others involved with them to do so, too. This is important for nurses, teachers, social workers, parents and researchers alike.

Recent theories

The latter part of the 20th century saw an explosion in new or emergent theories that began to address the fact that the human mind cannot be reduced to any one of the five main approaches previously described. This is achieved by looking at the internal and external processes and mechanisms that mediate among them. Such theories specifically address the links between the child or young person's outer social world and inner psychological world and are therefore difficult to classify strictly in the five main approaches previously outlined. Three important theories of this type are the *theory of mind, attachment theory* and the social ecology model of the *child/young person in context* theory.

Theory of mind

A child possessing a 'theory of mind' has an ability to appreciate the world of mental states, the world of ideas, beliefs, feelings and desires. Bartsch and Wellman (1989) developed a task that demonstrates that three-year-olds have difficulty in understanding the mental states of others. In an everyday situation, if a child is shown a box of chocolates that does not have chocolates inside but instead has marbles in it, they will understand that the box does not contain what they believe it should contain. If the child then sees the box shown to another child who has just arrived, they will believe that the other child, like them, thinks that the box contains marbles. In other words, the

Figure 2.3 A 'theory-of-mind' task: Where will Sally look for her marble?

three-year-old is unable to attribute a false belief to others. The classic test for children is known as the Sally–Anne test in which Anne secretly removes an object from Sally's basket when she is gone and the child is asked to predict where Sally will look for the object when she returns (see Figure 2.3 for an illustration of this task).

The task described by Bartsch and Wellman (1989) entails enacting four scenarios with two dolls, depicting situations similar to the marbles in the chocolate box example. Practical 2.1 describes in detail how to conduct a false-belief or theory-of-mind task on preschoolers. The basic task design has been replicated and adapted in many research studies. Variations of this type of task have been particularly productive as a tool for researching with autistic children and for correlating with task performances in other areas of psychosocial functioning, such as attachment, and with emotion understanding (Baron-Cohen et al. 1985; Dunn, 1995; Fonagy et al., 1997; Greig and Howe, 2001; Meins et al., 1998). Theory-of-mind research has seen staggering levels of growth in the past decade, and as was the case with Piagetian tasks, the method is constantly evolving to include higher levels of task demand such as second-order theory of mind tasks, those that are for older participants and those that use drawings and cartoons rather than concrete props.

Denham and Auerbach (1995) devised a task for assessing the ability of preschool children to understand the emotional states of others. These tasks are similar to the false-belief tasks in that they use puppets and other props from the world of children in an effort to evaluate their ability to assess, in this case, feelings from the perspective of the dolls involved, and, in the case of the false-belief task, the intentions and thoughts of others. These authors incorporate a well-known simple method of asking young children to express their own feelings or, in a more complex task, those of others from three faces, made of fabric, wood or paper on which there are three faces drawn, each expressing a different emotion. Even very young children can use these simple prompts to express their own likes or dislikes and the feelings of others. Researchers ask children to point to faces in response to questions on feelings or post them into boxes or attach them to photographs. In this form, especially in expressing likes or dislikes, the task is a form of self-report. Denham and Auerbach (1995) have successfully employed this task in a more complicated design which involves scenarios evoking the emotions of happiness, sadness, anger and fear and which has been widely used in other studies.

PUTTING THEORY INTO RESEARCH AND PRACTICE 2.1 – CONDUCTING A FALSE-BELIEF TASK WITH CHILDREN

To conduct this practical you will need:

- approved access to a preschool child of 3–5 years of age (see Chapter 10 for guidance on ethics);
- three rag dolls – male or female – that are easily held;
- two boxes of raisins, two boxes of fish food, two boxes of plasters and two boxes of crayons. For each pair of boxes, make sure one has a picture of the presumed contents and paint out the picture on the other box.
- Remove the contents from the boxes with pictures on them.

Procedure:

1 Sit comfortably with the child at a table.
2 Introduce the child to the dolls, e.g. Sally, Anne and Bill/Ben.
3 Put the dolls aside/under the table to give the impression that they are 'away'.

4 Put the first pair of boxes on the table in front of the child and say: 'Point to the box you think has got raisins/fish food/plasters/crayons in it.'
5 Let the child have a look to establish that the pictured box is empty and the blank box contains the expected contents.

Stage 1: Prediction (getting the child to predict where the doll will look)

Say: 'Look, here comes Sally. Shall we see if she can find the ____?' Place the doll, looking from one box to the other as if 'looking', and say: 'Where will Sally look for the ____?' Note the child's response. Put Sally away.

Stage 2: Explanation (getting the child to explain the doll's intentions)

Say: 'Look, here comes Anne now.' This time show the doll going straight to the labelled box and try to open it. Say: 'Look, what's Anne doing? What does she think?' You may need to prompt the child a bit by saying things like: 'She thinks something, doesn't she ... ?' Note the child's response. Put the doll away.

Stage 3: Prediction

Bring out the third doll. Place it in front of the boxes as if looking. Say: 'Here comes Bill/Ben. Point to the box you think he will look in.' Note the child's answer. Put the doll away.

Now repeat this procedure for the other three pairs of boxes. The child scores 1 point for each correct answer and 0 points for incorrect answers.

Questions to explore after the practical:

1 How did your child's performance compare with that of others?
2 What did you learn about controlling the environment and about the sorts of strategies you need to manage the child's spontaneous contributions?
3 How did you feel doing this task?
4 Why do you think the explanation phase is important?
5 What does the literature say about the link between theory of mind (thoughts and intentions) and the understanding of feelings of self and others? How has this been addressed methodologically?

Attachment theory

The most famous accounts of *attachment theory* are found in the comprehensive works of John Bowlby (1953/1965, 1979). Since the publication of his classic work *Child Care and the Growth of Love* (1953/1965), there has been an almost unparalleled development in attachment theory and research. The central ethological premise of attachment theory is that the infant is genetically and biologically predisposed to form attachments to carers as part of an instinctive mechanism that ensures proximity to adults, safety and, through this, increased likelihood of survival of the species. However, when applied to human infants, the theory also draws on constructs from psychodynamic and cognitive information processing approaches. In their classic study, Ainsworth et al. (1978) identified two major patterns of attachment behaviour that are displayed in strange or fearful situations: a secure pattern and an insecure pattern. Insecure patterns can be further classified into avoidant or ambivalent. In practical terms, a secure child is better able to use the parents as a secure zone when exploring new and unfamiliar tasks, while the insecure child will behave in an avoidant/detached manner or in a coercive and threatening manner towards the mother. In later research that included a sample of children who had traumatic experiences of parental care (Crittenden, 1992), insecure classifications became 'defended', 'coercive' or 'defended/coercive or disorganized'. Only the disorganized pattern is viewed as dysfunctional or maladaptive and tends to be characteristic of the most severely traumatized children.

The Attachment Story Completion Task (Bretherton and Ridgeway, 1990) is a way of assessing preschoolers' quality of attachment to their carers. It involves presenting the child with five scenarios, enacted with handheld, bendy, realistic family dolls and supporting props. The first scene, in which the family celebrate a birthday, is a training session and is not assessed. In this scene the tester establishes the nature of 'the game', which is for the tester to start the story and for the child to finish it off. The child is allowed to explore and handle the toys, and the tester can establish an understanding of how to pitch the game and the most effective prompts to use, such as 'and then what happens?' or 'is this story finished now?'. The five scenes include: spilled juice, monster in the bedroom, hurt knee, departure and reunion. Each story is selected as a trigger that is likely to lead the child to represent moments in which they will be challenged and resort to attachment behaviour patterns. The issues addressed at the beginning of each story are:

- the attachment figure in an authority role;
- pain as the elicitor of attachment and protective behaviour;
- fear as an elicitor of attachment and protective behaviour;
- separation anxiety and coping;
- responses to parental return.

The child's performance is assessed for security of attachment on all five stories and given an overall classification. Both verbal and non-verbal behaviour is taken into account in terms of appropriateness of content, emotional expression and coherence of story resolution. Box 2.3 describes the procedure and how to classify the responses. Figure 2.4 illustrates doll use in the attachment story completion tasks for 'departure' and 'spilled juice'.

Figure 2.4 Attachment story completion scenes for 'Departure' and 'Spilled juice'

BOX 2.3

Attachment story completion task

General props

Two sets of family dolls, each comprising mother, father, boy child, girl child. From these sets you need to use one whole family plus the adult female from the other set as grandmother. Alternate child dolls to suit the sex of the child, i.e. an only boy – use the two male dolls; a girl who has a brother, use one male and one female. For each story begin by saying 'I'll start the story and you finish it.' Enact your part then say to the child: 'Now you show me with the dolls what happens next.'

Warm-up (a birthday cake to scale of dolls)

Enact a scene in which the mother produces a birthday cake. There may be some exploration of the toys and it may take a while to make sure the child understands the routine.

Spilled juice (table, tablecloth, bottle of juice, cakes)

Enact a scene in which the child leans over the table and spills the juice. Finish by saying: 'Then Mummy says "You've spilled the juice" … show me what happens next.'

Monster in the bedroom (no additional props)

Enact a scene where Mummy says: 'It's getting late. It's time for your bed.' Show the child going to their bedroom, seeing a monster and shouting 'Mummy! There's a monster in the bedroom!' from the bedroom.

Hurt knee (piece of green felt [grass] and grey sponge [rock])

Enact a scene where the family go for a walk to the park where there is also a high rock. The child sees the rock and says: 'Wow! Look, a high, high rock. I'm going to climb that rock.' The child climbs the rock, falls off and cries, sobbing 'I've hurt my knee'.

Departure (Granny joins the family, a box painted as a car)

Enact a scene in which Granny arrives. Then say: 'You know what I think is going to happen? I think Mummy and Daddy are going on a trip.' The parents say good-bye and 'See you tomorrow' and leave in the car, which drives away out of sight.

Reunion (same props as Departure)

Enact a scene in which it is the next day. Granny is at the window and says: 'Look children, look who's coming back'; the car, with parents in, returns.

Criteria for security/insecurity

- *Very secure*: story issues are resolved fluently, without many prompts, and appropriately.
- *Fairly secure*: slightly avoidant or odd responses on one or two stories.
- *Avoidant insecure*: don't know or complete avoidance of the issues over three stories or more, even showing some disorganized responses.
- *Insecure disorganized*: odd or disorganized responses over three or more stories even if displaying some avoidant responses.

Source: Adapted from Bretherton, I. and Ridgeway, D. (1990) 'Story completion tasks to assess young children's internal working models of child and parent in the attachment relationship', in M.T. Greenberg, D. Cicchetti and E.M. Cummings (eds), *Attachment in the Pre-school Years: Theory, Research and Intervention*. Chicago, IL: University of Chicago Press. pp. 273–308. Reproduced with permission.

Most recently, Minnis et al. (2006) reviewed some of the latest innovations in research and therapy for assessing attachment relationships with the use of computer software (West et al., 2003) and go on to describe their own research study using a specially designed computerized story completion assessment: the Computerised McArthur Story Stem Battery (CMSSB). This form of assessment is viewed as advantageous because:

- children enjoy interacting with computers and are becoming increasingly familiar with their use at work and at play;
- it can be used to access larger groups of children in community settings;
- it is less time consuming and can be used consistently.

To test the CMSSB, it was administered to two groups for comparison: a group of school children in foster care and a group of school children as a control. As anticipated, the vulnerable foster care group showed significantly poorer coherence of story narratives, less intentionality (perspective taking) and greater avoidance than the control group of school children.

The child and young person in context

When considering the various approaches to understanding children and young people, it is important to recognize that the child or young person in society is part of a social system. A system, whether biological, economic or psychological, has two basic properties: *wholeness* and *order*. All parts within are related to all other parts, and there must be an adaptive ability to incorporate change. An example might be the birth of a new baby into the family. This event will affect routine, require new routines and have an impact on relationships. In other words, any change in one part of the system brings about changes in other parts of the system.

Bronfenbrenner (1979, 1986, 1992) proposed a *social ecology* model to describe the progressive, mutual accommodation throughout the lifespan between a growing human organism and the changing immediate environment. Let us briefly imagine two children. One child has two parents, both working and happy in their jobs. The family lives in an affluent neighbourhood which is well serviced by excellent schools and other community provisions. The parents have a wide network of professionals, family and friends and the child is popular and clever at school, has close friends and attends a number of extracurricular activities and out-of-school clubs. The family has two cars and takes frequent holidays. The other child has only ever had one parent, their mother. There have been male friends but no real father figure for the child.

This mother is unemployed and receiving social security benefits. They struggle financially and do not have a telephone. They live in a rough neighbourhood and never go on holiday. The mother is clinically depressed and finds it difficult to make friends and manage her child's increasingly difficult behaviour. The child is unpopular at school, frequently gets into trouble and is prone to accidents and ill health.

As these examples suggest, the child is part of a system or network of social and environmental relationships. There are many players (family, teachers, friends) and many settings (home, play park, school, neighbourhood). Bronfenbrenner proposed four contextual structures within which individuals and places are located: microsystems, mesosystems, exosystems and macrosystems.

The *microsystem* is the immediate setting, which contains the child: the garden, the house, the play park. These are examples of physical space/activity. Microsystems also contain people, such as parents, teachers, peers and the interactions with these people. The *mesosystem* is the relationship between different settings and at different times of development: links between the home and school or hospital. The *exosystem* does not directly contain the child but does have an influence; it includes parental employment and social networks. The *macrosystem* refers to the broader cultural and subcultural settings within which micro-, meso- and exosystems are set, such as poverty, neighbourhood, ethnicity and so on.

Let us consider the model by way of the example of divorce. There are immediate concerns about the individual child. We might wonder how a particular child copes with stress associated with divorce, or if it matters what the age of the child is at the time of the divorce. A specific research question might be: what qualitative differences exist in children at different developmental levels as far as the perceptions and interpretation of the divorce process is concerned? At the micro level we may wish to examine the quality of the pre-divorce relationship between parents and child as a predictor of post-divorce adjustment. At the meso level we could examine the impact of divorce on the child's achievements and relationships at school. At the exo level, we may wonder about the availability of the non-resident parent, perhaps by asking: does physical distance from the non-resident parent affect post-divorce adjustment? At the macro level there are marriage settlement issues – for example, were discussions on child support and other concerns settled fairly and via mediation? It is also possible to consider how these various levels work in combination. In asking how post-divorce economic instability affects family relationships, specifically changes in family patterns, we are examining both macro and micro levels. Asking whether kinship and the availability of family members assist the child in post-divorce adjustment combines issues at both the macro and exo levels.

Implications of emerging theories

The human mind and behaviour are wonderfully complex. However, if we are working with or caring for an emotionally distressed child or young person who is struggling with an understanding of self and others and experiencing problematic relationships, perhaps because of a biological impairment or a traumatic early relationship or as a response to social stressors, or, most likely in the world of real-life research, a complex mixture of these, we are duty-bound to develop our understanding of them and to increase our knowledge of the ways in which we can best support them to cope. In embracing the complexity of the everyday lives of children and young people, the concept of vulnerability and resilience becomes especially important for areas of research that seek to improve the outcomes for children and young people through a better understanding of the risks they face and the social adversities that impact upon them. Resilience is defined as 'normal development under difficult conditions'.

Research and theory has found resilient characteristics in children and young people to include: being female; having secure attachments; having an outgoing temperament; being sociable and having the ability to solve social problems. Vulnerability can be defined as those characteristics of the child or young person, their family and community that might hinder healthy development. Research and theory has identified these characteristics as including: disability; racism; lack of secure attachment; difficult temperament and a lack of family, social or community support. Adversity in the environment refers to the life events and difficulties that pose a threat to the healthy development and adjustment of the child or young person and these include experiences of loss, abuse and neglect. Protection in the environment has been shown in research to include: positive experiences at school; at least one supportive adult; help with behavioural problems and a wider supportive network for vulnerable parents in the community. The principal aim for researchers who wish to improve outcomes for children and young people is to be able to more accurately assess their vulnerabilities and the adversities they face and to then improve the level of protection in their environment and increase their personal resilience.

For further readings that explore these important complex links between the child's inner and outer worlds see the work of Michael Rutter and others on risks and resilience in children (Fonagy et al., 1994; Gilligan, 1999; Rutter et al., 2004) and Robert Hinde (1997) on exploring the complexities of interpersonal dynamics. For theory and research summaries on the impact of parental mental health problems on children and young people see Dunn (1995), Fonagy et al. (1997), Greig (2004, 2005a, 2005b) and West et al. (2003) for recent reviews on childhood depression, personal, social and emotional development, and the interaction between play, language and learning. For theories of parenting see the work of Baumrind (1972), Bornstein (1995), Golombok (2000) and Quinton and Rutter (1988); for prosocial development see the work of Schaffer, (1996); for self-concept and esteem see the work of Coopersmith (1967), Dusek and Flaherty (1981); for sibling and peer relationships see the work of Dunn (1993, 2004), Dunn and Kendrick (1982) and Steinberg (1993); for the impact of loss, divorce and separation on children and young people see the work of Dunn et al. (2001), Fahlberg (1994) and Jewett (1984); and for the development of language and literacy see the work of Hulme and Snowling (2009) and Snowling and Hulme (2005). These are only some of the many theories that exist within established bodies of research that are potentially of use to anyone doing research with children and young people. A full appraisal of all of these theories is beyond the immediate scope of this book. However, this brief overview is a useful starter for those of you who wish to do real-world research in very specific domains of the lives of children and young people.

Context versus content variables in research

When we are doing research with children and young people it is important to take into account not only the whole context of the child or young person but also the whole context of the research itself. Many people conduct research projects and use their findings to develop theoretical approaches without recognizing the impact on research of the wider context within which it is carried out. MacKay (2006) has highlighted this by distinguishing between *content variables* and *context variables*. Content variables represent the actual substance or content of the research programme – the factors that have been deliberately built in as the basis of the research. For example, suppose a support teacher wants to find a better method of teaching young children who are having difficulty grasping early reading skills. They decide to introduce the newer 'synthetic phonics' approach instead of the traditional 'analytic phonics' approach that most children have grown up with. They may be using quantitative methods (Chapters 6 and 7) and setting up an experimental and a control group, or they may be using qualitative methods (Chapter 8) and investigating the in-depth experience of the children who are using the new method. Either way, the content variable in question is the phonics approach that has been adopted. This is what has been planned as the substance of the research, and if children do better with the new method presumably it is because it is better than the old method. But is it? Or might there be other factors that have brought about the change that have nothing to do with the programme at all?

This is where context variables are important. The children who are doing the old, traditional method just go on doing what they have always done. The children who have the new synthetic method, however, find that it is 'all-singing, all-dancing'. There is excitement in the air. The teacher has a new interest and enthusiasm, and a belief that their ideas will make a difference. The new method has a lot of interesting, colourful materials, and it involves doing things in a quite different way – everybody doing the actions and shouting out the letters together as they learn them. Clearly there has been a significant change in the teaching *context* and not just in its *content*. So which is the more important factor? Is it the new phonics or is it the unplanned changes that came along with it? The best known example of a context variable is the *Hawthorne effect*. In the late 1920s and early 1930s a series of experiments was carried out at the Hawthorne Works of the Western Electric Company in Chicago, Illinois, USA with a view to increasing productivity. After varying factors, such as level of illumination and timing of rest breaks, the researchers found that productivity increased *whatever* the change – including returning to the conditions operating at the outset (Mayo, 1946; Roethlisberger and Dickson, 1939). The conclusion was that the effect was simply the result of being the focus of interest and attention, resulting in changed levels of expectancy and heightened motivation.

Researchers have two choices when faced with context variables such as the Hawthorne effect. The traditional approach is to view it as a pitfall and take steps to avoid it by finding ways of giving groups the same experiences as much as possible. However, many people reading this book are likely to be practitioners who want an answer to the question: 'How can I carry out research with children and young people that will really make a difference to their lives?' MacKay (2006) sought to answer this question by taking a quite different approach to context variables. If a factor like the Hawthorne effect can have a positive impact, then instead of avoiding it why not celebrate it and build it in deliberately to research interventions? In applying this approach to raising the educational achievement of a whole population, he set out to maximize the impact of the context variables and focused on five key factors: vision, profile, ownership, commitment and declaration. These factors were formally articulated and embraced as part of the research strategy and they became the vehicle for conveying the content of a changed curriculum. The research was presented as being 'visionary' and was given a very high profile. The message to all who participated was that they were involved in something very important. This in turn promoted commitment and ownership. The project belonged to everyone and all were motivated to play their part in making it succeed. 'Declaration' was also introduced. There were great expectations and they were declared boldly. In one of the studies, children in six of the schools received exactly the same intervention as all others – with one difference. They and their teachers made a bold declaration three times a day that their results were going to improve. The children in these six schools achieved higher levels of improvement than the children in the comparison schools.

These observations should highlight the many factors that influence research outcomes. They represent both a caveat and an opportunity. The caveat is that if you want to carry out some pure research to investigate, for example, whether a new methodology is a better one, then you should be aware of the context variables that may 'contaminate' what you are doing and find ways of controlling these. The opportunity is that if you are charged with 'making things better' and you want to maximize the effects of your innovation, then overall impact will be enhanced if you bring to your project a clear vision and inspire excitement and commitment in those who are participating.

Sociological theory

In our efforts to better understand and make sense of children and adolescents either in an everyday sense or in a research exercise, sociological theory requires us to look at and test the realities of our attitudes towards them. The sociological theory approach is one that goes beyond a psychological–ecological perception of the child and young person in society. It argues that all our attitudes, perceptions and beliefs about children and adolescents are – like all of our attitudes – socially constructed. That is, those realities we accept as established knowledge about children and young people, how they think, feel and behave, are not actually objective realities; rather they are a construction of the machinery of human meaning making.

What we commonly describe as childhood and adolescence do not in reality have a natural distinction that marks a child or young person off as being in a certain category of childhood or adolescence. For example, one universal and internationally agreed definition of childhood is to be found in the United Nations Convention on the Rights of the Child (www.unicef.org/crc/): the period from birth to 18 years of age. Despite this, across the world and within different places and subcultures even in our own localities, there is considerable variation in how children and adolescents are seen and treated by the more senior members in society and in policies and practices. Categories of childhood and adolescence, therefore, have actually been socially constructed by human society to better understand and manage the category members.

A consequence of this is that there is no universal reality or definition of the child or adolescent. Certain cultures have their own social construction on the younger members of its society and how one culture categorizes children and young people will not necessarily be the same as that of any other culture. For example, in modern western societies, children and adolescents are legally constructed and defined as having rights, they are required to go to school and to have protection; they have access to tailored television, media and other consumer products. We speak of the 'early years', 'teens' and 'preteens'. Nevertheless, historically, this has been very different. In the Victorian era, children and young people were not socially constructed in the same way. Similarly, in other cultures today, children and young people have a very different life experience because of the way their societies have socially constructed them. They may be married by arrangement at an age that is unthinkable in Western society, carry significant responsibilities of work and have no rights of protection. With our socially constructed view of children and young people, based on our own beliefs and attitudes, there is no objective truth that declares what children and adolescents actually are. While we may all feel very grown up at 18 years of age when we are given the key to the door, are able to buy alcohol, get married, vote, and so on, our parents may well still regard us as a child for many years beyond that.

Postmodernism and discourse theory

Postmodernism is a theoretical approach that accepts the principles of social constructionism as previously outlined. This theoretical paradigm dates back over 50 years and dictates that what one may view as childhood or adolescence is actually socially constructed and determined by time, space and culture (Aries, 1962). This approach challenges the view that there is a natural or universal conceptualization of childhood and adolescence, and instead, it proposes that these states are social inventions. The approach is not meant to be a mutually exclusive one with respect to biological determinism. Readers with a biological and psychological scientific background will recognize their own within-field arguments of the nature–nurture debate here. The aim of postmodern social constructionism is to switch the focus well away from those aspects of childhood/adolescence that are both naturally given within the child and altered within the child by virtue of a nature–nurture interaction. Instead, the focus is on the totally extraneous social forces that shape their world and how their world is viewed and managed by others. For those of us wishing to do real-world social, educational and health research with children and adolescents it is therefore a useful theory, but it is not universally accepted and its practical relevance has often been questioned (Howe, 1994). Another useful feature of the postmodern, social constructionist paradigm is that it offers us the concept of 'discourse'. A discourse refers to a whole set of interconnected ideas that work together and are held together by a particular ideology or world view such as a discourse of 'parenthood', a discourse of 'community' and a discourse of 'feminism'. In this way, there can be said to be a discourse of 'childhood' and of 'adolescence', each of which has its own knowledge base, beliefs, values and ethics about how the worlds of childhood and adolescence work.

There can also be different 'discourses' within the social construction of childhood and adolescence depending on different 'takes' on it. For example, one take is that the inherent goodness and vulnerability of children and young people means they require protection. This is a 'need-to-provide welfare discourse'. Another take is that children and young people are inherently bad and require discipline and civilization. This is a 'need-to-control discourse'. Clearly these two polarized views of children and young people motivate different ways of relating to and acting on behalf of them and the need for social structures and procedures to support them. For the most part, society manages to juggle these two separate discourses of childhood and adolescence as both address different aspects of meeting all the needs of the child or young person in society. Social science has recognized for some time the need to accept the complexities of the lives and worlds of children and adolescents and the anxieties that adults have in attempting to reconcile their complexities.

Implications of sociological theory

One of the criticisms of social constructionism is that while it does offer us some understanding of the confusion we encounter when we are motivated to act on behalf of children and young people, it is far less clear what it has to offer in helping people decide what is to be done on behalf of children and young people. According to Howe (1994), the postmodern theory of social constructionism does have practical relevance for children and young people if the following approaches are taken: pluralism; participation; power and performance.

Pluralism

Children are complex and multidimensional. No one discourse will ever sufficiently give all explanations and meet all the needs of the child. This means there is the necessity of recognizing that there are different positions and finding ways of constructively managing conflicting views, respecting and tolerating diversity and uncertainty.

Participation

In the constructionist context there is no absolute truth, nor one single remedial course of action, and it is crucial that all those who are entitled to a view do have their views respectively taken into account if a creative solution that is agreed by all is to happen.

Power

In constructionism, there is a need to be consciously aware that all those involved in the world of the child or young person has their own brand of power (professionals, carers, parents, and children and young people themselves), each capable of protecting their self-interests.

Performance

This is about bureaucratic, institutional and academic power and social constructionism requires that this is looked at critically in terms of how self-serving these powers are in terms of what they profess and what they do and they are to be judged regarding the consequences of their power for children and young people.

Theory, research and practice: the rise of critical studies

During recent years, all aspects of theory, research and practice both in psychology and in other disciplines have been challenged by the rise of the *critical movement*. This has seen the development of critical psychology (Fox and Prilleltensky, 1997), critical social work (Fook, 2002), critical teaching (Wink, 2004) and critical sociology, with its own international *Journal of Critical Sociology*. The central argument is that science is not and cannot be apolitical and value-free. The debate about values in science is one that challenges the entire research agenda by asking questions about the priorities, aims and methods of research. All of the assumptions on which traditional paradigms for theory, research and intervention are based are called into question, and wider questions are raised about the impact of research and practice in the arena of social justice and human welfare.

The attempt to provide an agreed-values framework to underpin the priorities of research is not without significant challenges. In promoting the belief that 'fundamental human needs, values and rights must be met and upheld for a better and more just society to emerge', Prilleltensky and Nelson (1997) propose five core values that may be found generally agreeable among researchers and practitioners working with children and young people. These are: health, caring and compassion, self-determination and participation, human diversity and social justice.

Clearly the agenda of the critical movement could have many implications for how we apply theory and how we conduct research with children and young people. At the very least, it should cause us as researchers to pause and think about our aims and methods, and the impact these will have on our young participants. (See also Chapter 10 on the ethics of doing research with children and young people.)

Conclusion

Children and young people are complex beings in a complex world. How, then, do we begin to do research with them? Do we focus on their individual characteristics? Their playful interactions with peers? Their relationships with friends, siblings and carers? How can we capture the ways in which children and young people are embraced, supported, punished or isolated by the society and culture in which they live? The remainder of this book is devoted to helping to address questions of this kind.

PUTTING THEORY INTO RESEARCH AND PRACTICE 2.2 – WHICH THEORY?

Return to the six situations described at the beginning of this chapter. In groups, either discuss each situation or do so selectively, according to the group interests, and address the following questions:

1 Which theory or theories best describe and explain the issues involved?
2 Why is a particular theory suited and why are others unsuited?
3 To what extent is the chosen theory/theories limited in dealing with each situation?
4 Discuss the potential risks/vulnerabilities/adversity/resiliences that can be taken into account, if any, in each scenario.

References

Adler, A. (1916) *The Neurotic Constitution: Outline of a Comparative Individualistic Psychology and Psychotherapy*. New York: Moffat, Yard.

Ainsworth M.D.S., Blehar, M.C., Waters, E. and Wall, S. (1978) *Patters of Attachment: a Psychological Study of the Strange Situation*. Hillsdale, NJ: Erhbaum.

Aries, P. (1962) *Centuries of Childhood: a Social History of Family life*. New York: Vintage Books.

Bandura, A. (1977) *Social Learning Theory*. Englewood Cliffs, NJ: Prentice Hall.

Bandura, A. (1986) *Social Foundations of Thought and Action: A Social Cognitive Theory*. Englewood Cliffs, NJ: Prentice Hall.

Baron-Cohen, S., Leslie, A.M. and Frith, U. (1985) 'Does the autistic child have a "theory of mind"?', *Cognition*, 21 (1): 37–46.

Bartsch, K. and Wellman, H. (1989) 'Young children's attribution of action to beliefs and desires', *Child Development*, 60 (4): 946–64.

Baumrind, D. (1972) 'Socialization and instrumental competence in young children', in W.W. Hartup (ed.), *The Young Child. Reviews of Research*, Vol. 2. Washington, DC: National Association for the Education of Young Children.

Bornstein, M.H. (1995) *Handbook of Parenting*. Mahwah, NJ: Lawrence Erlbaum Associates.

Bowlby, J. (1953/1965) *Child Care and the Growth of Love*. Harmondsworth: Penguin.

Bowlby, J. (1979) *The Making and Breaking of Affectional Bonds*. London: Tavistock Publications.

Bretherton, I. and Ridgeway, D. (1990) 'Story completion tasks to assess young children's internal working models of child and parent in the attachment relationship', in M.T. Greenberg, D. Cicchetti and E.M. Cummings (eds), *Attachment in the Preschool Years: Theory, Research and Intervention.* Chicago, IL: University of Chicago Press. pp. 273–308.

Bronfenbrenner, U. (1979) *The Ecology of Human Development: Experiments by Nature and Design*. Cambridge, MA: Harvard University Press.

Bronfenbrenner, U. (1986) 'Ecology of the family as a context for human development: research perspectives', *Developmental Psychology*, 22 (6): 723–42.

Bronfenbrenner, U. (1992) 'Ecological systems theory', in R. Vasta (ed.), *Six Theories of Child Development: Revised Formulations and Current Issues.* London: Jessica Kingsley. pp 187–249.

Bugental, J.F.T. (1964) 'The third force in psychology', *Journal of Humanistic Psychology,* 4 (1): 19–26.

Coopersmith, S. (1967) *The Antecedents of Self-Esteem.* San Francisco CA: W.H. Freeman.

Crittenden, P.M. (1992) 'Quality of attachment in the preschool years', *Development and Psychopathology*, 4 (2): 209–41.

Davey, G.C.L., Albery, I.P., Chandler, C., Field, A.P., Jones, D., Messer, D., Moore, S., and Stirling, C. (eds) (2004) *Complete Psychology*. London: Hodder & Stoughton.

Denham, S.A. and Auerbach, S. (1995) 'Mother–child dialogue about emotions and preschoolers' emotional competence', *Genetic, Social, and General Psychology Monographs,* 121 (3): 311–37.

Department of Health (1990) *The Care of Children: Principles and Practice in Regulations and Guidance*. London: HMSO.

Donaldson, M.C. (1978) *Children's Minds*. New York: Norton.

Dunn, J. (1993) *Young Children's Close Relationships: Beyond Attachment*. London: Sage.

Dunn, J. (1995) 'Children as psychologists: the later correlates of individual differences in understanding of emotions and other minds', *Cognition & Emotion*, 9 (2–3): 187–201.

Dunn, J. (2004) *Children's Friendships: the Beginnings of Intimacy*. Malden, MA: Blackwell.

Dunn, J. and Kendrick, C. (1982) *Siblings: Love, Envy, & Understanding*. Cambridge, MA: Harvard University Press.

Dunn, J., Deater-Deckard, K. D. and Joseph Rowntree Foundation (2001) *Children's Views of Their Changing Families*. Layerthorpe,York: YPS for the Joseph Rowntree Foundation.

Dusek, J.B. and Flaherty, J.F. (1981) *The Development of the Self-Concept During the Adolescent Years*. Chicago, IL: University of Chicago Press for the Society for Research in Child Development.

Erikson, E.H. (1950/1963) *Childhood and Society*, 2nd edn. New York: Norton.

Fahlberg, V. (1994) *A Child's Journey Through Placement.* Indianapolis, IN: Perspectives Press.

Fechner, G.T. (1860) *Elemente der Psychophysik*. Leipzig: Breitkopf und Härtel.

Flavell, J.H. (1978) 'The development of knowledge about visual perception', in C.B. Keasey (ed.), *Nebraska Symposium on Motivation*, Vol. 25. Lincoln, NB: University of Nebraska Press.

Flavell, J.H. (1985) *Cognitive Development*, 2nd edn. Englewood Cliffs, NJ: Prentice Hall.

Flavell, J.H. (1988) 'The development of children's knowledge about the mind: from cognitive connections to mental representation', in J.W. Astington, P.L. Harris and D.R. Olson (eds), *Developing Theories of Mind.* New York: Cambridge University Press. pp. 244–67.

Fonagy, P., Redfern, S. and Charman, T. (1997) 'The relationship between belief–desire reasoning and a projective measure of attachment security (SAT)', *British Journal of Developmental Psychology*, 15 (1): 51–61.

Fonagy, P., Steele, M., Steele, H., Higgit, A. and Target, M. (1994) 'The Emanuel Miller Memorial Lecture 1992. The theory and practice of resilience', *Journal of Child Psychology and Psychiatry, and Allied Disciplines*, 35 (2): 231–57.

Fook, J. (2002) *Social Work: Critical Theory and Practice*. London: Sage.

Fox, D. and Prilleltensky, I. (1997) *Critical Psychology: an Introduction*. London: Sage.

Freud, S., Strachey, J. and Richards, A. (1901/1976) *The Psychopathology of Everyday Life*. Pelican Freud Library (4). Harmondsworth: Penguin.

Freud, S., Strachey, J. and Richards, A. (1905/1977) *Three Essays on the Theory of Sexuality*. Pelican Freud Library (7). Harmondsworth: Penguin.

Freud, S., Strachey, J. and Richards, A. (1923/1984) *The Ego and the Id*. Pelican Freud Library (11). Harmondsworth: Penguin.

Gazzaniga, M.S., Ivry, R.B. and Mangun, G.R. (2002) *Cognitive Neuroscience: the Biology of the Mind*, 2nd edn. New York: Norton.

Gilligan, C. (1999) 'Children's own social networks and network members: key resources in helping children at risk', in M. Hill (ed.), *Effective Ways of Working with Children and their Families*. Philadelphia, PA: Jessica Kingsley.

Goldsmith, D.F. and Rogoff, B. (1995) 'Sensitivity and teaching by dysphoric and nondysphoric women in structured versus unstructured situations', *Developmental Psychology*, 31 (3): 388–94.

Golombok, S. (2000) *Parenting: What Really Counts*? London: Routledge.

Greig, A. (2004) 'Childhood depression – part 1: Does it need to be dealt with only by health professionals?', *Educational and Child Psychology*, 21 (4): 43–54.

Greig, A. (2005a) 'Personal, social and emotional development', in J. Taylor and M. Woods (eds), *Early Childhood Studies: An Holistic Introduction*, 2nd edn. London: Hodder Arnold. pp. 57–77.

Greig, A. (2005b) 'Play, language and learning', in J. Taylor and M. Woods (eds), *Early Childhood Studies: An Holistic Introduction*, 2nd edn. London: Arnold.pp. 99–116.

Greig, A. and Howe, D. (2001) 'Social understanding, attachment security of preschool children and maternal mental health', *British Journal of Developmental Psychology*, 19 (3): 381–93.

Hinde, R.A. (1997) *Relationships: A Dialectical Perspective*. Hove: Psychology Press.

Howe, D. (1994) 'Modernity, post modernity and social work', *British Journal of Social Work*, 24 (5): 513–32.

Hulme, C. and Snowling, M.J. (2009) *Developmental Disorders of Language Learning and Cognition*. Chichester: John Wiley.

Jewett, C.L. (1984) *Helping Children Cope with Separation and Loss*. London: BAAF.

Jung, C. (1921) *Psychological Types, or the Psychology of Individuation*. New York: Harcourt and Brace.

MacKay, T. (2006) *The West Dunbartonshire Literacy Initiative: the Design, Implementation and Evaluation of an Intervention Strategy to Raise Achievement and Eradicate Illiteracy: Phase 1 Research Report*. Dumbarton: West Dunbartonshire Council.

Maslow, A.H. (1954) *Motivation and Personality*. New York: Harper.

Mayo, E. (1946) *The Human Problems of an Industrial Civilization*. Boston, MA: division of Research, Graduate School of Business Administration, Harvard University.

Meins, E. and Russell, J. (1997) 'Security and symbolic play: the relation between security of attachment and executive capacity', *British Journal of Developmental Psychology*, 15 (1): 63–76.

Meins, E., Fernyhough. C., Russell, J. and Clark Carter, D. (1998) 'Security of attachment as a predictor of symbolic mentalising abilities: a longitudinal study', *Social Development*, 7 (1): 1–24.

Minnis, H., Millward, R., Sinclair, C., et al. (2006) 'The Computerized MacArthur Story Stem Battery – a pilot study of a novel medium for assessing children's representations of relationships, *International Journal of Methods in Psychiatric Research*, 15 (4): 207–14.
Peterson, C. and Seligman, M.E.P. (2004) *Character Strengths and Virtues: A Handbook and Classification*. Washington, DC: American Psychological Association.
Piaget, J., Tomlinson, J. and Tomlinson, A. (1929/1952) *The Child's Conception of the World*. New York: Harcourt, Brace and Co.
Piaget, J. (1937/1954) *The Construction of Reality in the Child*. New York: Basic Books.
Piaget, J. (1945/1962) *Play, Dreams and Imitation in Childhood*. New York: Norton.
Plomin, R., DeFries, J.C., Craig, I.W., et al. (eds) (2002) *Behavioral Genetics in the Postgenomic Era*. Washington, DC: American Psychological Association Books.
Prilleltensky, I. and Nelson, G. (1997) 'Community psychology: reclaiming social justice', in D. Fox and I. Prilleltensky (eds), *Critical Psychology: An Introduction*. London: Sage. pp. 166–84.
Quinton, D. and Rutter, M. (1988) *Parenting Breakdown: The Making and Breaking of Inter-Generational Links*. Aldershot: Avebury.
Roethlisberger, F., Dickson, W., Wright, H.A., Pforzheimer, C.H. and Western Electric Company (1939) *Management and the Worker: an Account of a Research Program Conducted by the Western Electric Company, Hawthorne Works, Chicago*. Cambridge, MA: Harvard University Press.
Rogers, C.R. (1951) *Client-Centred Therapy, Its Current Practice, Implications, and Theory*. Boston, MA: Houghton Mifflin.
Rutter, M. (2006) *Genes and Behaviour: Nature-Nurture Interplay Explained*. Oxford: Blackwell.
Rutter, M., O'Connor, T.G. and the English and Romanian Adoptees (ERA) Study Team (2004) 'Are there biological programming effects for psychological development? Findings from a study of Romanian adoptees', *Developmental Psychology*, 40 (1): 81–94.
Samuel, J. and Bryant, P. (1984) 'Asking only one question in the conversation experiment', *Journal of Child Psychology and Psychiatry, and Allied Disciplines*, 25 (2): 315–18.
Schaffer, R.H. (1996) *Social Development*. Oxford: Blackwell Publishers.
Seligman, M.E.P. (2003) *Authentic Happiness: Using the New Positive Psychology to Realise your Potential for Lasting Fulfilment*. New York: The Free Press.
Seligman, M.E. and Csikszentmihalyi, M. (2000) 'Positive psychology. An introduction', *American Psychologist*, 55 (1): 5–14.
Skinner, B.F. (1938) *The Behavior of Organisms*. New York: D. Appleton-Century.
Snowling, M.J. and Hulme, C. (2005) *The Science of Reading: a Handbook*. Malden, MA: Blackwell.
Steinberg, L.D. (1993) *Adolescence*. New York: McGraw-Hill.
Vygotsky, L.S. (1978) *Mind in Society: Development of Higher Psychological Processes*. Cambridge, MA: Harvard University Press.
United Nations Children's Fund (2012) Convention on the Rights of the Child. Available at: www.unicef.org/crc/ (accessed 26 March 2012).
Watson, J.B. (1913) 'Psychology as the behaviourist views it', *Psychological Review*, 20: 158–77.
Watson, J.B. (1930) *Behaviourism*. New York: Norton.
Wertsch, J.V. and Hickman, M. (1987) 'Problem solving in social interaction: a microgenetic analysis', in M. Hickman (ed.), *Social and Functional Approaches to Language and Thought*. Orlando, FL: Academic Press. pp. 251–66.

West, P., Sweeting, H., Der, G., Barton, J., and Lucas, C. (2003) 'Voice-DISC identified DSM-IV disorders among 15-year-olds in the West of Scotland', *Journal of the American Academy of Child and Adolescent Psychiatry,* 42 (8): 941–9.

Wink, J. (2004) *Critical Pedagogy: Notes from the Real World.* New York: Pearson/Allyn and Bacon.

Wundt, W.M. (1874) *Grundzüge der physiologischen Psychologie.* Leipzig: W. Engelman.

Recommended reading for further study

Layard, P.R.G., Dunn, J. and Good Childhood Inquiry (2009) *A Good Childhood: Searching for Values in a Competitive Age.* London: Penguin.

Roberts Boyd, D. and Bee, H.L.(2009) *Lifespan Development*, 5th edn. Boston, MA: Pearson/Allyn and Bacon.

Bjorklund, D.F. and Hernández Blasi, C. (2012) *Child & Adolescent Development: An Integrated Approach.* Belmont, CA: Wadsworth.

THREE

Theoretical frameworks

The aims of this chapter are:

- to introduce the major conceptual approaches to thinking about and conducting research with children and young people;
- to explore the differences and potential overlaps between qualitative and quantitative research designs;
- to provide a practical guide for choosing an appropriate conceptual approach.

Reflect briefly on the many occasions you say 'I have a theory ...' followed by something like 'there is a man whose job it is to coordinate all your bills so that they all arrive on the same day' or 'the middle child develops relationship difficulties in adulthood'. Whether your theories are comic, absurd or revolutionary, they are based on observation. It may be the tenth time this year that you have noticed the sickening thud of all your bills coming through the letter box at once. It may be the fourth generation in your family where the middle child has never had a successful long-term partnership. Some observations and theories are worth testing and some are not. If we do indeed prove that there is a 'bill coordinator', there is not a lot we can do about it. However, establishing a link between adult relationship difficulties and birth order is informative, useful and sets up an intriguing trail of research questions, answers and interventions.

The overwhelming importance of children and young people in our lives makes them, arguably, theorized about more than anything else. When it comes to understanding and helping them, lay theories and casual observations simply will not do. A more cautious, reliable, valid and insightful approach, indeed a 'scientific' approach, is needed when it comes to entering, understanding or predicting the world of children and young people.

Epistemological frameworks or ways of knowing children and young people

The philosophical basis to a research framework largely relates to the researcher's position regarding the nature of science and knowledge. The scientific revolution that first emerged in the 16th century, grew to a full 'enlightenment' by the 18th century. The Enlightenment of 18th-century Europe promoted empirical and scientific knowledge, and intellectual interchange, while opposing superstition and intolerance. Our knowledge and understanding of the whole of creation is 'enlightened' by a rational, evidence-based and truly scientific approach that leads to progress and modernization. The industrial revolution then brought in great advances in science and technology that grew out of observable, quantifiable, general or universal truths and that changed the way we see the world and the way in which we live.

In more recent times, however, a movement that calls itself *postmodernism* has been exerting considerable influence on social research and other disciplines such as architecture, art and literature. This approach challenges everything that is upheld by *modernism* and, in its most extreme form, its central tenet is that 'there is no objective truth or reality' (Alvesson, 2002; Blaikie, 2007). In less extreme forms, postmodernists do not want to imply that truth and reality do not exist, but wish to emphasize that our own understanding of what is real and true is a complex and relative processes. That is, one's truth or reality is relative rather than universal.

Social science and social research have been affected by the 'relativistic' position that has arisen out of the postmodernist movement. The search for a methodology that addresses the justifiable need for the understanding of these specific, local, personal and community forms of truth that are not quantifiable, has presented a considerable challenge to the traditional scientific, modernist research approach. As we discuss later in the chapter, simply because social science research is about people who are not only physical objects, but who also possess interpretative minds and social processes, a new type of research method, the qualitative method, is required that goes beyond simple description and quantification. The rise in qualitative methods has been slow to find a truly 'scientific' format, but its progress is both definite and necessary in any research that seeks to fully address the human condition. The approach is now, arguably, sitting side by side with quantitative methodology in a scientific paradigm of social science research that takes account of all aspects of humanity whether biologically determined or relatively defined. The debate is maintained between the extremists of both positions, but for those of us who work in the field of human social research, in the real world, a pragmatic approach is recommended and this is discussed later on in the chapter.

We go on now to apply these two fundamental approaches, quantitative and qualitative, to the real-world example of research involving children and young people. We discover what is meant by positivism and constructivism, explore what is similar and what is different about these approaches and learn how to take an evidence-based and pragmatic approach in choosing an appropriate method for a real-world research project with children and young people.

A scientific approach to researching children and young people

As we have discussed in the previous section, there is a pseudo-debate between researchers in the physical sciences (biologists, geologists, chemists and so on) and the social sciences (psychologists, sociologists, educationists and so on). This debate rests on the belief that the theories, methods and explanations one might use in investigating a digestive system, rock, fossil or chemical compound are, of necessity, different from those used when investigating human action, thought and development. Simply and correctly put, a fossil is not a human being. The matter is, however, not that simple at all when we consider how humans are also physical, biological and chemical: for instance, the way in which body chemicals control human characteristics and even how humans both adapt to and alter their physical, geographical and social environments. For researchers interested in the complex problems and the holistic nature of human subjects, the consensus is that one needs to use an eclectic or heuristic approach to the theories, methods and findings in research questions about human subjects.

Research that involves children and young people and the social worlds in which they live needs to be seen from as many angles as possible. It needs to draw on a wide range of theories and methods from the sciences, social sciences, humanities and arts. As noted by William James, 'Psychology is a science and teaching is an art and sciences never generate directly – out of themselves. An intermediary inventive mind must make the application by using its originality' (1899: 3).

Novice researchers, therefore, will do well in taking Robson's (2011) advice to seek out the value of conducting a 'scientific' study, to keep prejudices in check and to clear away some of the common misconceptions about the scientific approach. At the same time, it is important when researching children and young people in the real world to have a broad interpretation of 'science' to include a whole range of qualitative and interpretative methods that are nevertheless done with rigour, transparency and open to evaluation by self and others. This is a matter of good research and professional practice. Developmental researchers across disciplines have recognized the limitations of a strict form of 'scientism' and have been actively developing theories (see Chapter 2) and methods (see Chapters 6, 7, 8 and 9) to deal with it.

The revision of what is meant by 'science' here is a result of two recent challenges: a social science paradigm shift and new legislation on children and young people. The need for a paradigm shift has been recognized within the social sciences for some time now and calls for the inclusion of a broader range of qualitative and interpretative methods. This is to better address the fact that children and young people are in a dialectical relationship with other people and also with cultural and historical contexts. The Children Act 2004 (National Archives, 2012) contents enforce a range of regulations relating to the rights of children and young people to be consulted about matters that affect them. Consequently, creative researchers have been inventing new methods to ensure reliable and valid consultation with children and young people. We now have to think carefully about our research in terms of being 'on', 'with', 'about' and even 'alongside' children and young people, where the latter refers to children and young people as researchers themselves!

In the next section, we will address the traditionally distinct approaches to theory and research and go on to address their similarities, differences and overlaps.

The science of positivism and constructivism

The radical progress in scientific discoveries and new technologies characteristic of the Industrial Revolution resulted from an approach to theory and research known as *positivism*. The positivist assumption about the nature of children and young people is that they are accessible through the same scientific procedures one would use on a rock, fossil or chemical. Young humans are natural, physical beings and are subject to the same laws and principles that govern the structure of the universe. They are determined, knowable, objective and measurable. As a research method, positivism is a process whereby the researcher seeks to establish the truth or falsity of a theoretical statement, such as 'little girls who wear red shoes run faster than little girls who wear black shoes'. Such statements are also known as hypotheses, the truth value of which is tested through methods of observation or experiment. This method also requires systematic, controlled procedures to aid verification processes, the aim of which is to discover universal order, to create generalizations together with theories and laws that allow predictions across settings and individuals. The collection and analysis of numerical data is favoured, and the method is also known as quantitative. An often cited example of a good positivistic theory is the *law of gravity*. This theory explains falling apples, the behaviour of roller coasters and the position and movement of planets in the solar system. With very few statements about the mutual attraction of bodies, this theory explains a large number of events that can be observed or experimentally tested.

Historically, the advent of schools to prepare young people for a technologically literate society coincides with the need to better understand how their minds work

Figure 3.1 Subjective conceptualization affecting positivist investigation

and develop. Developmental researchers with a positivist approach assume that law-like relationships can be drawn among constructs they identify, operationalize and measure. Hence, children and young people are studied in controlled settings, variables are isolated, measured and correlated with other variables, and predictions are made to populations represented by the samples being studied. For instance, a study on one preschool may be generalized to all preschools in that area.

Theories of human development derive from psychology, a social science in favour of positivist methodology. Hence, theories on the nature of attachment relationships between a mother and her child, based on observations of bonding instincts and behaviour in geese, can be used to explain much of, if not all of human social behaviour and development. This could be construed as research 'on' children and young people. It is an approach that seeks explanation.

The trouble with doing research with human subjects – as opposed to forces, fossils and feathered animals – is that both the researcher and research participant have a conceptualization of the research situation and what is expected to happen. The cartoon in Figure 3.1 makes the methodological point that the control of a positivist investigation is seriously undermined by the possibility of a human, subjective conceptualization of the research situation on the part of both researcher and participant. Not only does the researcher need to contend with how the participant perceives and responds to the research situation, they are also dealing with a personality who could, unintentionally or otherwise, sabotage the entire exercise.

It is the human capacity for language, thought and action that poses a challenge for positivist methodology. Buchanan (1994) discusses how the natural processes of the physical sciences are independent of the language used to describe them, but human practices are not. For instance, a single human gesture can have several different meanings depending on the person and the context. Consider the meaning of a raised hand in the following contexts: a child in class when the teacher asks a question; a teenager playing in the park at football; a child waving to his mother as she leaves them behind; in a group of children who have been asked to vote on indoor or outdoor activities. Furthermore, should we wish to define the construct of 'well-being' for a child or young person, which definition is right – diet and exercise, normal growth and development of physical and psychological functions, or courage, wisdom and modest living? Consider how a teenager may be disturbed and angry by their father's absences yet, once a parent themselves, becomes appreciative of their father's sacrifice. These examples illustrate how complex the business of interpreting and defining human behaviour is and how it is bound to the context, time and what it actually means to the people involved. Dealing with very young children or those with intellectual or communication difficulties adds further complications for positivist research. The child's capacity for language, action and self-reflection is not only qualitatively different from that of adults but these capacities are also qualitatively different for different age groups and for different levels of ability of children and young people.

There is, however, an alternative conceptualization of the nature of children and young people and of the theory and research methods that should be applied to them. This alternative approach is called *constructivism*. Constructivist researchers perceive the child or young person as a subjective, contextual, self-determining and dynamic being. Children, young people and their carers are social, relational beings who are engaged in joint action. As they interact they construct joint meanings within a given context. In this way, meaning is constructed symbolically in interaction with others. Children, young people and their carers are inextricably part of the worlds they study. They are both the observed and the observer. Children and young people, and their relationships, are dynamic across individuals, context and time. Furthermore, the meanings constructed and the actions taking place in everyday situations are also located within specific cultural and historical practices and time. This could be construed as research 'with', 'about' and 'alongside' children and young people. It is an approach that seeks understanding.

Constructivists argue that, in a subjective world, where understanding and knowledge are symbolically constructed and held in convention and social unity with others, it is inappropriate to seek samples, control and isolate variables, quantify behaviour and generalize to a larger population of people. Instead, the constructivist researcher makes an effort to understand how the worlds of children and young people operate, by somehow entering those worlds, describing and analysing the contextualized social phenomena found there. The constructivist view that actions, thoughts, intentions and meanings cannot be conveyed

Table 3.1 Theoretical frameworks for scientific research with children and young people

Positivism (explanatory research on)	*Constructivism (understanding research with)*
The nature of the child/young person is objective, knowable and determined. The child/young person can be observed, controlled, measured and quantified. However, there is only a similarity between the child/young person and natural/ physical processes, and theories are inexact, cannot be proven, and are only probable.	The nature of the child/young person is subjective, not objectively knowable or measurable. The child/young person have their own perspective, but are also socially determined and theories are inextricable from context and culture

in an analogous way with numbers, but need a more qualitative handling of data, has lead to the approach being described as *qualitative*.

Instead of control, constructivists want naturally occurring social behaviour, in place of isolated variables, they seek a contextualized holistic examination of participants' perspectives. Instead of measuring, correlating and predicting, constructivists describe and interpret (Hatch 1995: 122). Table 3.1 summarizes the two principal theoretical frameworks for doing research with children and young people.

Theoretical frameworks for scientific research with children and young people

Doing research with children and young people could be described as a systematic and scientific search for information that aims to improve our knowledge of them. This definition begs two further questions: what is meant by knowledge and what is meant by scientific? The answers to these questions rest on which framework – quantitative and/or qualitative – the researcher has chosen to work with. In the next section we address the differing conception of knowledge and science in each framework. As a starting point, let us consider some of the sources of knowledge about children and young people as more or less scientific, where scientific is taken to mean impartial, reliable, valid and controlled. The ways in which we come to 'know' about children and young people include *authority*. We are told what the nature of children and young people is by parents, so-called experts and politicians. Thus, knowing that 'children should be seen and not heard' because this is what some higher authority has told us, is not 'scientific'. Another way of knowing about them is through personal belief or conviction. So, for instance, you may be convinced that they are incapable of knowing and expressing what their needs are despite evidence that contradicts it. This kind of 'tenacity' is not scientific and can be tantamount to prejudice. Knowledge that passes itself off as a logical inevitability or a priori knowledge that 'goes without saying' is not scientific. For example, if you define intelligence as 'an innate, permanent ability to adapt to the environment and solve problems' then it is a matter of logical necessity that measures of intelligence should be correlated across infancy, childhood, adolescence and adulthood. A scientific test of this type of knowledge about children and young people is likely to be disconfirmed because it fails to take into account 'other factors', which potentially affect the phenomenon in question.

Deduction and induction

There are two principal methods of scientific activity: deduction and induction. Deduction in science emphasizes theories (ideas and explanations) from which we can 'deduce' likely outcomes. An example that is often given for this is that you may never have seen an omelette fly into an electric fan but you could make an excellent prediction of the likely outcome. Induction in science emphasizes data (measures, numbers, observations). In gathering data together, patterns and relationships among the numbers become obvious: if the numbers are 2, 4 ... you might predict the next number as 6 or 8 or 16 but you do not have enough figures to predict which one should be next. If you obtain another figure, which is 16, you can now predict the next number as 256 because each number is multiplied by itself to obtain the next number. It is apparent from this example that the larger amount of numbers available, the easier it will be to reliably discern such patterns and relationships.

As a concrete example of deduction, you may start out with a theory that working mothers have poorer relationships with their children than non-working mothers. To test this theory, you simply challenge it by predicting the outcome in the opposite direction – that working mothers will have a better relationship with their children than non-working mothers *or* the hypothesis can be nullified to 'there will be no difference between working mothers and non-working mothers in their relationships with their children'. You then set up an experiment that will clarify the relationship between the two variables, A (the number of hours worked) and B (quality of the relationship). However, to test this hypothesized relationship, it is necessary to define concept A and B to provide a measure of each variable. These measures can then be observed in two groups of mothers: those doing little or no work (group 1) and those doing a lot of work (group 2). The type of knowledge this test reveals is considered scientific because it is empirical, impartial, reliable, valid and controlled. It is also open to verification and correction, as it can be replicated, modified and improved by other researchers. If you do indeed find the answer that supports your theory, this will be a powerful scientific finding.

As a concrete example of induction, you may not have a particular theory to deduce from but prefer instead to observe, measure and examine potential patterns among the data produced. You may simply observe some mothers and children, noting the frequencies of things indicative of a good quality relationship, such as involvement, positive affect and so on. These patterns may, in themselves, create a theory or suggest the application of an existing one. If you do come to a conclusion, it is still scientific but not as powerful as it would be if you had made an actual prediction about what you would find.

An often-cited analogy of the different ways of using deduction and induction is that of building a house. In deduction you start at the top with the roof, the overarching bit at the top and work your way down to the ground. Here you are most interested in predicting, depending on what a given roof looks like, what the house underneath should look like. In induction you start at the bottom with the ground and work your way up and stick the overarching roof on at the end in a way that explains what you happened to have built below. However, to take the analogy further, most research involving children and young people could be described as a functional combination of both, with a bit of roof or foundation to start, maybe a wall, another bit of roof, and so on.

The quantitative framework for doing research with children and young people

The quantitative research framework is based on assumptions about the objective nature of children and young people, knowledge and research methods. Such an approach is based on the scientific activity of deduction – the procedure for testing existing theory. The notion that theory pre-exists in a law-like form is consistent with the view that the child or young person is objective in nature and that their behaviour, understanding, knowledge or meanings are structured, determined and universal. Hence, the quantitative framework entails a methodology in which theory exists and is tested empirically to be proven or not proven. In the house construction analogy it is a top-down procedure (see Figure 3.2). The basic methodological tool for conducting quantitative research is experimentation.

According to McCall (1994) scientific research on children and young people entails two conceptual levels: theoretical and empirical. The theoretical level (deduction) is about general concepts, principles, laws and hypothesized relationships. The empirical level (induction) is about defining the concepts into observable, measurable variables and conducting observations that describe the hypothesized relation. In his simple model of a 'scientific study' (see Figure 3.3), McCall (1994) points out that we should be aware of the working assumptions of researchers that operate at each level. Each one of these working assumptions

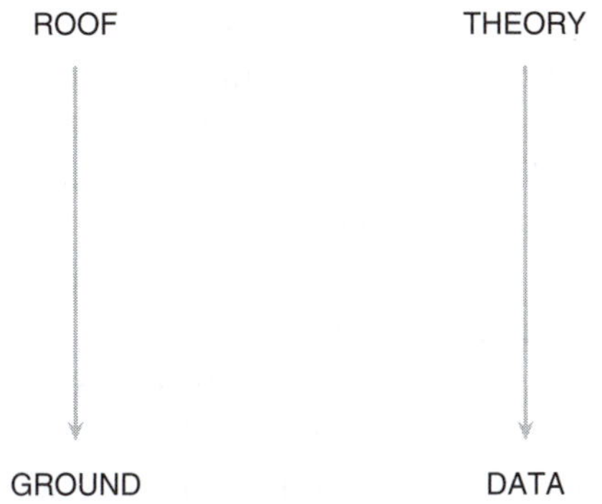

Figure 3.2 A top-down view of theory and data

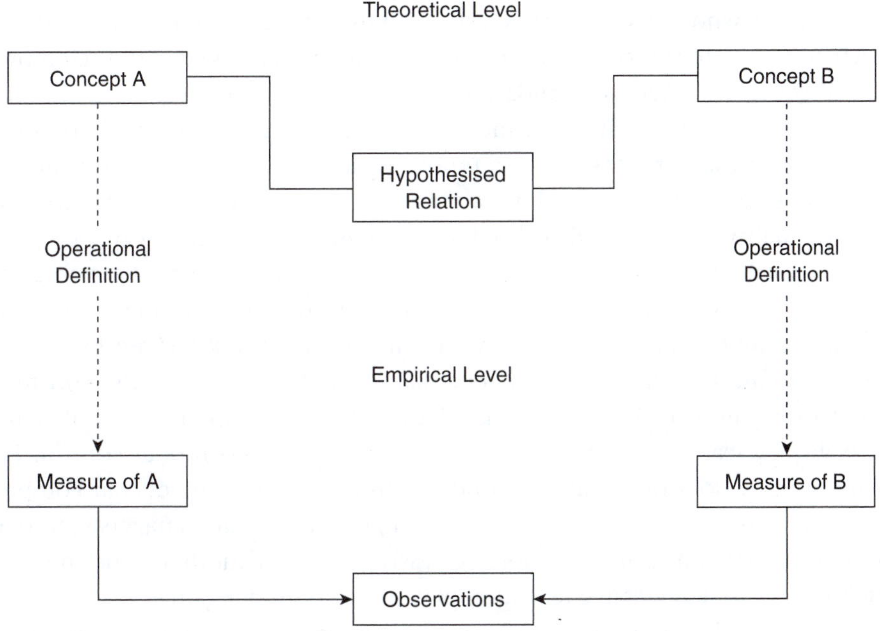

Figure 3.3 A simplification of McCall's model for behavioural research

Source: Adapted from McCall, R.B. (1994) 'Commentary', *Human Development*, 37: 293–8. Reproduced with permission of S. Karger AG, Basel.

exists because researchers and their young participants are not forces or fossils and because human science is not a perfect science.

At the theoretical level, the reality of the basic concepts can be challenged. For instance, a researcher may be working on the assumption that intelligence is an innate, permanent ability to adapt to the environment and solve problems and is therefore stable across infancy, childhood, adolescence and adulthood. In fact, when intelligence is tested over time, this does not appear to be the case. While this could be due to a problem with measures, it could also be because the researcher is working on the wrong assumption about the stability of intelligence.

Also at the theoretical level, the hypothesized relationship between variables A and B may not be a valid one. For instance, you may hypothesize that, all other things being equal, mothers who work longer hours will be more tired and therefore spend less quality time with their children than mothers who do not work long hours. An empirical test of this hypothesis is likely to fail because, in the case of research with human participants, it is not easy to hold 'all other things equal'. Things like guilt, overcompensation and fluctuations in energy levels could easily apply in this example.

Another example could be of a hypothesis that is not sufficiently specific or comprehensive. So, for instance, the rather ambiguous and ill-defined hypothesis that 'children who spend more time with their mothers get better school grades' is much better written as 'children who spend 1 hour each evening with their mothers will get better grades on standardized achievement tests (SATs) than children who spend 15 minutes with their mothers each evening'. The second hypothesis is more specific about measures and implies a particular empirical relationship.

Working assumptions also penetrate at the level of measurement, influencing the quality, validity and reliability of our measures. When a test of some hypothesized relationship between A and B fails, we could simply be measuring it wrongly but it could also be because the concept we are trying to measure is much more complex than we have assumed. The example given by McCall (1994) is that infant behaviours are remarkably unreliable even across short-term observation intervals. Where, he asks, does unreliability end and lack of stability begin? Researcher assumptions can also disrupt observational control. For instance, how does one deal with findings from separate studies that compromise each other? One study, for example, might report that teenagers who play more computer games are also more aggressive, while in another study the finding might be that aggressive teenagers play more computer games.

In deciding what to observe, it is impossible to do so with complete objectivity for, as Goethe noted, 'we see what we know'. Can we ever be certain that what we see is all there is? Or what we see or know is right?

Having described McCall's analysis of a quantitative framework for research in human behaviour and development, it is tempting to reject the model entirely in favour of something more qualitative. This would be foolish, however, as McCall goes on to argue:

> Suppose one defines a better football team to be one that has a better win–loss record and a poorer football team to be one that has a poorer win–loss record. Better teams beat poorer teams, everything else being equal. But if this were so obvious, no-one would play the game. The fact is that everything else is

> not typically equal. Poorer teams beat better teams on occasion which is why professional football fans often assert that any pro-team can beat any other pro-team 'on a given day'. The implication is that many hypotheses are not all-or-none, but are probabilistic. Even if they appear to be a priori in nature, our empiricism helps to define that probability, that degree of relationship, that extent of influence, recognising the portion not accounted for is due to other factors (which we conveniently call 'error' but which nevertheless consists of potentially identifiable causes). (1994: 297)

The fact is that scientific enquiry is rarely tidy, and researchers need to think more about the conceptualizing of variables, specifying theoretical relation or hypothesis and ensuring reliability of measures. Even when measurement problems arise, they are still informative if only because they challenge the working assumptions of the researcher.

A qualitative framework for doing research with children and young people

The qualitative research framework is based on assumptions about the subjective nature of children and young people, knowledge and research methods. The qualitative approach is based on the scientific activity of induction – the procedure for generating new theories and in which theory emerges from the data. The notion that theory is created from or emerges from data is consistent with the view that the child or young person is subjective in nature and that their understanding, knowledge and meanings are subjective, and emerge in interaction with others in a given context. Hence, the qualitative framework entails a methodology in which theory is 'grounded' in data such as observations, interviews, conversations, written reports, texts and their interpretations. In the house construction analogy, it is a bottom-up procedure (see Figure 3.4) and the basic methodological tool is interpretation.

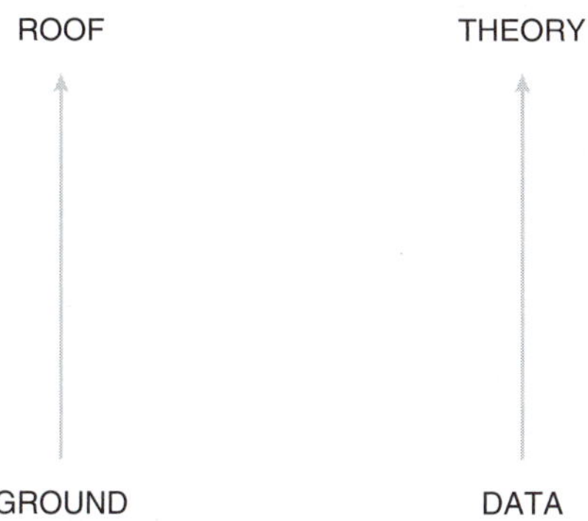

Figure 3.4 A bottom-up view of theory and data

Interpretivist scientists seek to understand the social world from the point of view of the child or young person living in it. By way of constructs and explanations, interpretivists attempt to make sense of how they understand their experiences and how this affects the way they feel towards others. Interpretivism has roots in those branches of psychology and sociology that acknowledge the need to understand and capture subjective experiences and meanings. Humanistic psychology, for instance, begins with a view of the child as their own psychologist, creating meanings for themselves out of their experiences and interactions. When a child encounters problems, the belief is that the child should be enabled to look within themselves for both the problem and the solutions. Interpretative sociology encourages entering the child's (and the young person's) world and meanings to get their perspective from the inside out. This is necessary because situations, meanings and problems are defined in interaction with others. The concept of labelling is a good example of how a child might be socially defined as a problem and ultimately become one.

Framework of working assumptions

How would McCall's simple model of quantitative research on children and young people work on qualitative research at the theoretical and empirical levels, and what are the working assumptions of qualitative researchers at each level? This is shown in Figure 3.5.

This inductive variation could also be analysed in terms of working assumptions held by qualitative researchers at each level. At the empirical level, the assumption is that it is possible to engage in methods such as observation, interview, report or text analysis in a theoretical vacuum, with no guiding definitions, concepts or constructs. So, for instance, if your aim is to explore the quality of the relationship between a working mother and her child, it is virtually impossible to do so without some guiding perspective or sensitizing concepts on what to look for, why and how.

Also at the level of interpreting the research, there is the qualitative aim of discovering or entering the subjective experience and perspective of the child or young person. Given that the researcher and participant are simultaneously both the observer and the observed, the research experience itself is mediated on several levels by the intersubjective relationship between researcher and participant. Participants have their own tacit and declared understandings; researchers have their own perspectives and interpretations. The relationship is also mediated at a cultural level by conventional meaning systems and power relations which are interpreted within social and institutional contexts.

In essence, then, the subjective nature of both researcher and participant is just as problematic for the scientific, qualitative interpretivists as it is for quantitative experimentalists.

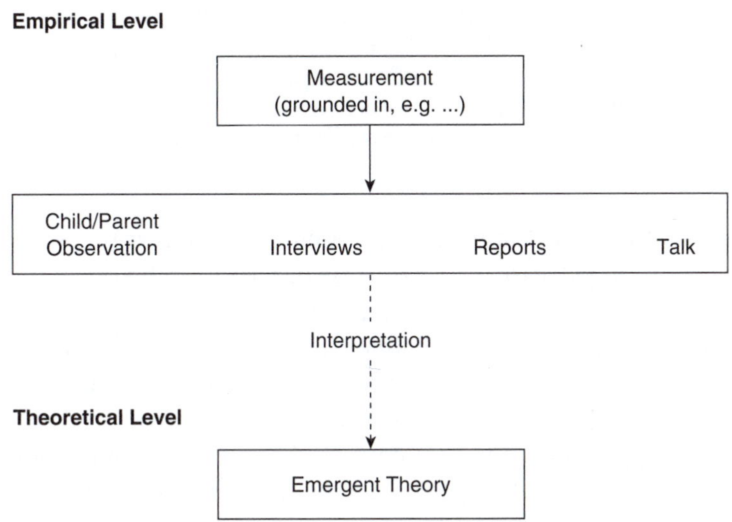

Figure 3.5 A qualitative version of McCall's two conceptual levels of research

Source: Adapted from McCall, R.B. (1994) 'Commentary', *Human Development*, 37 (5): 293–8. Reproduced with permission of S. Karger AG, Basel.

Henwood and Pidgeon (1995) propose what they call a 'constructivist version of grounded/inductive theory' for dealing with the impossibility of atheoretical research, and they express it in a procedural framework. Qualitative researchers, they argue, *must* have a perspective from which to build their analyses and recommend a functional relationship between the data and its interpretation. In this way, researchers' perspectives can guide the questions asked and provide a balance between possessing a grounding in the discipline and pushing it further.

At the empirical and interpretive level, in dealing with the problems of intersubjective understanding and meanings, Hatch (1995) proposes a theoretical framework based on *activity theory*. According to this theory, the goal of interpretive research is to understand the meaning that children and young people construct in their everyday action, situated in a cultural, historical setting and in mutually interacting intentional states of the participants. This entails a method that goes beyond simply detailing what people are doing and into an exploration of the meanings and intentions that underlie these activities. The required unit of analysis includes both the individuals and the culturally defined environment which is grounded in a set of assumptions about roles, goals and means used by the participants in the activity setting.

In applying this framework to doing research with children and young people, Graue and Walsh (cited in Hatch), advise:

> ... motivation/intention is central. Individuals are motivated to do some things and not others ... need to pay careful attention to young children's actions and ideas. ... To get a sense of motives, it is important to watch children's interactions closely, to listen to their explanations of actions and to be respectful of their voices. It requires basic methods of interpretive research, plus attention to the connections between the local context and the broader culture and history. (1995: 148)

In summary then, qualitative research attempts to capture the ways in which our young research participants make sense of the research events under investigation. In an important sense, then, qualitative research enables the voice of the participant to be heard. It is perhaps not surprising then that qualitative methods that specifically deal with the child's or young person's perspective have only recently begun to be addressed. As we have discussed elsewhere in the book, the assumption has long been held that children and young people are either unable or not entitled to have a point of view. Obviously, the younger the child, the less likely the child is to be heard in research. The dominance of the experimental method in developmental psychology has meant that the value of creating valid methods of obtaining the child's or young person's perspective in research has simply been overlooked. Attempts to address this are now proving fruitful, particularly in the field of child and family social work research, and in the new sociology of childhood. These techniques are extensively reviewed in Chapter 9.

Practitioner research

The reality is that most people who do research with children and young people are practitioners who need to study them as part of their job. This type of 'action research' takes place with people outside of laboratories, in the real world of hospitals, clinics, schools, nurseries, homes and the community. Real-world research is not only about people but also takes full account of the advantages arising from the enquirers and participants being people themselves. According to MacKay (cited in Greig):

> Research is basically 'enquiry': but enquiry which is carried out systematically and with the rigour of those who basically adopt the scientific method. I don't really go in for a 'researcher/practitioner-researcher' distinction, any more than I go in for an 'academic/applied' distinction. I simply view research as occurring at various levels and as being of various kinds. What we have in mind with 'practitioner-research' is what is done in messy, real-world situations rather than in laboratories, often (but not only) using a qualitative rather than a quantitative paradigm, often using small samples in single establishments, which don't always lend themselves to RCTs (random control trials), frequently answering questions and priorities that originate with service users rather than the researcher, and often done not for its own sake alone but as a more systematic and enhanced approach to service delivery. (2001: 77)

In consequence, the methods used in practitioner research tend to be mainly qualitative, but also quantitative and require a broad interpretation of what is meant by 'scientific'. These topics are covered in more detail in Chapters 6, 7 and 8.

Choosing an approach

As we discussed previously, quantitative research demonstrates results in terms of numbers (it quantifies or measures) and usually employs statistics, for instance, measuring the effect of unfamiliar or strange situations on the heart rate and saliva samples of four-year-old children. Qualitative research is concerned with unique situations and phenomena and would describe in detail and interpret with a view to explaining the object of study: for example, a case study of one boy's disruptive behaviour at a playgroup, with interviews of both parents and teachers about his wider social environment; or detailed, intensive long-term observations of one child referred to social services. It is generally accepted in research that, in choosing either or a mixed approach, it is best to be guided by the nature of research questions, the participants, the sort of findings you require and what you intend to do with them. This topic is covered in detail in Chapter 5. The relationship between qualitative and quantitative research can be exclusive, but the two approaches have remarkable potential for overlap in practice. Multiple overlaps can be manifested in eclectic studies: for instance, an experiment on the self-esteem among poor readers could include some in-depth case studies of one or two children. Or a child with behavioural difficulties could be studied as a case, observed intensely over a long period of time and in a variety of social contexts, all supplemented by health and education records and interviews of parents and professionals who know the child. At the same time, the child might be assessed using questionnaires or tests on the extent of the behavioural disorder and the child's mental age, both of which are standardized and 'quantitative'. Interpretative tasks could also be included, such as measuring the child's attachment to parents through projective tests or using a technique of story completion in playing with family dolls. It may also be possible to undertake an experimental regime of 'interventions' assessing the child before and after treatment.

Nevertheless, there are clear boundaries, notably in distinguishing the approaches as experimental and non-experimental. Conceptualized strictly in this way, the approaches become polarized. Qualitative becomes non-experimental research which is subjective, insider, holistic, naturalistic, valid, inductive, exploratory, ungeneralizable and discovery-oriented. Quantitative becomes experimental research that is objective, an outsider, particularistic, controlled, reliable, deductive, outcome-oriented, generalizable and verifiable. This distinction between qualitative and quantitative approaches to research is more useful for the purposes of description and argument than it is a reality, because many psychologists and sociologists engage in a principled mixture of the two. It is a fallacy to assume, for instance, that theoreticians always behave or think like positivists or 'hard' scientists. Freud is a good example. Despite his background as a biologist and clinician whose ideas about human behaviour and development were essentially reductionist – i.e. all behaviour can be explained by simple biological processes – his approach to theory, research and practice has been much criticized as 'unscientific' (Eysenck, 1952). Similarly, Piaget, also by training a biologist, intent on a taxonomy of human knowledge and acquisition and who conducted actual experiments with children, has been accused of less than vigorous scientific methods (Donaldson, 1978). It is also a mistake to assume all psychologists aspire to 'hard' science. Even early in the 20th century, Vygotsky – a contemporary of Piaget – condemned the misuse of 'positivist' approaches to child behaviour and development, such as standardized tests. These, he argued, did not address the child's individual motives, talent and potential for development or the important effects of the historical, cultural and social context on the research situation.

Researchers are now addressing the potential similarities or shared goals in conducting qualitative and quantitative research that is 'scientific'. There is a very good argument that any scientific research needs to have a standard of rigour that adheres to issues of reliability and validity. Both approaches can attempt to make the research in question replicable. This is a controversial issue regarding qualitative research, but a consensus is now emerging that, by documenting the decision trail in qualitative research, a process synonymous with specifying methodological details in quantitative reports is achieved (Yin, 2003). In this way, it becomes more a matter of making more sense, to other researchers, of the methods used and conclusions drawn, rather than replicability. In both cases, it is essential to gather appropriate evidence so that a judgement can be made about the significance of the findings. Harding (cited in Henwood and Pidgeon):

> ... makes the important distinction between 'weak' and 'strong' objectivity in science: weak objectivity occurs when the inevitable layers of subjectivity are overwritten or obscured. In moving towards strong objectivity, the researcher makes public the full range of interpretative processes involved in knowledge production. Research that seeks to reveal rather than obscure the hand of the researcher and social bases for knowledge, by this account, has some claim to providing more adequate knowledge. (1995: 118)

Figure 3.6, originally for young children but also applicable to older children, and Practical 3.1 provide a procedural framework for choosing an approach to doing research with children and young people.

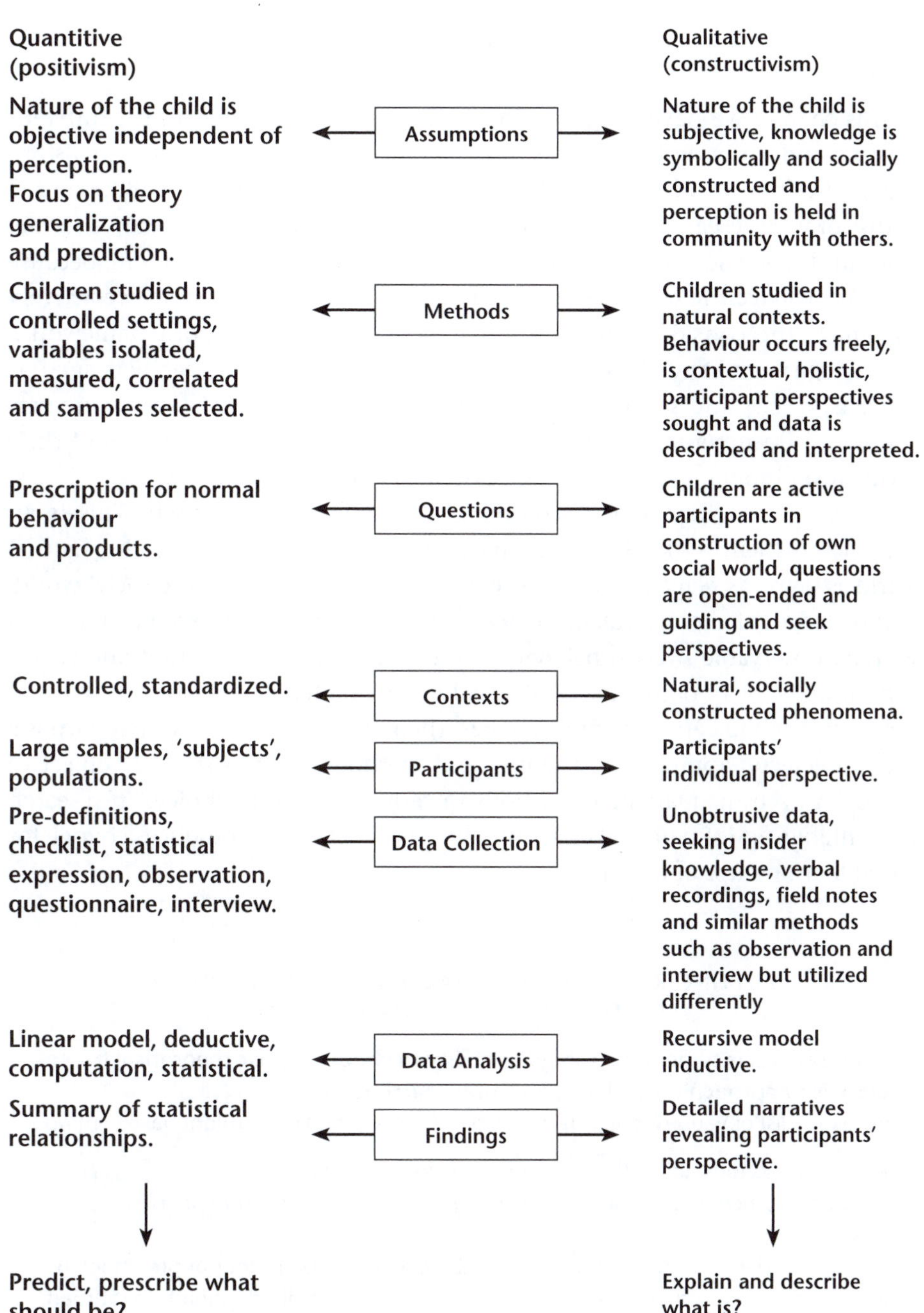

Figure 3.6 A comparison of quantitative and qualitative frameworks for research with children and young people

Source: Based on Hatch, J.A. (ed.) (1995) *Qualitative Research in Early Childhood Settings*. Westport, CT: Praeger. Adapted with permission.

Conclusion

In this chapter we have sought to introduce novice researchers to the different existing and evolving frameworks or paradigms that guide research and also to the debates that surround them. We believe that it is possible, depending on the nature of your research aims, to use either the qualitative or quantitative framework in doing research with children and young people. Furthermore, because we acknowledge the complex nature of children and young people, we actively encourage the consideration of research designs which use both frameworks. Psychologists and sociologists, ethnographers, practitioner–researchers such as teachers, nurses and social workers, those who study trends in social structures via official documentation or records, and youngsters who do research of their own, are all individuals researching in the real world.

Earlier in the chapter we recommended a pragmatic approach. This is an approach which: seeks a philosophical middle ground; accepts the natural world as being as real and valid as the psychological world and the social world; acknowledges the powerful influence of both internal and external forces in shaping observable human behaviour and understanding; sees that knowledge is both objectively observable and socially constructed and relative; has a cautious approach to certainty; finds the best theoretical fit for the research purpose; uses an eclectic approach to theories and methods; seeks a strongly objective approach even in qualitative methods in terms of making choices in research accountable; and, finally, takes action, links to practice and produces change for individuals, groups and societies.

PUTTING RESEARCH INTO PRACTICE 3.1 – DECIDING TO GO QUALITATIVE OR QUANTITATIVE

This practical is to demonstrate your ability to choose a basic theoretical framework for approaching various types of research issues.

Below is a list of various, potential research projects a researcher might have in mind.

- You are curious about the self-esteem of poor readers.
- You are concerned about the body image of children and young people receiving surgery.
- You wonder how the birth of a new baby affects the behaviour of preschoolers.
- You are interested in the effects on preschool children of adoption from abroad.
- You wonder how children and adolescents feel about their parents' divorce and subsequent contact arrangements.
- You are interested in the child-raising practices of different UK cultures.

Either alone or in groups, consider these potential projects with respect to the series of questions listed below, which help you to decide the nature of the enquiry.

- What is the underlying philosophical system – objective, intuitive/subjective, multiple?
- What is the purpose of the enquiry – describing everyday reality, finding causes or explanations?
- What is the nature of your research question(s)?
- What is the nature of the phenomenon being studied?
- What do you think of advice from colleagues who hold opposing views on this?
- What are your personal ideas?
- Is there a way to use both methods? In everyday practice, multiple methods would be needed to explore the richness of reality.

References

Alvesson, M. (2002) *Postmodernism and Social Research*. Buckingham: Open University Press.

Blaikie, N. (2007) *Approaches to Social Inquiry*, 2nd edn. Cambridge: Polity.

Buchanan, D.R. (1994) 'Reflections on the relationship between theory and practice,' *Health Education Research*, 9 (3): 273–83.

Donaldson, M.C. (1978) *Children's Minds*. New York: Norton.

Eysenck, H.J. (1952) 'The effects of psychotherapy: an evaluation', *Journal of Consulting Psychology*, 16 (5): 319–24.

Graue, M.E. and Walsh, D.J. (1995) 'Children in context: interpreting the here and now of children's lives', in J.A. Hatch (ed.), *Qualitative Research in Early Childhood Settings*. Westport, CT: Praeger.

Greig, A. (2001) 'The educational psychologist as practitioner-researcher: Reality or dream?', *Educational and Child Psychology*, 18 (4): 75–88.

Hatch, J.A. (ed.) (1995) *Qualitative Research in Early Childhood Settings*. Westport, CT: Praeger.

Henwood, K. and Pidgeon, N. (1995) 'Grounded theory and psychological research: New developments in understanding science', *The Psychologist*, 8 (3): 115–18.

James, W. (1899) *Talks to Teachers on Psychology: And to Students on Some of Life's Ideals*. London: Longmans, Green and Co.

McCall, R.B. (1994) 'Commentary', *Human Development*, 37 (5): 293–8.

National Archives (2012) Children's Act 2004. Available at: www.legislation.gov.uk/ukpga/2004/31 (accessed 26 March 2012).

Robson, C. (2011) *Real World Research*, 3rd edn. Chichester: John Wiley and Sons.

Yin, R.K. (2003) *Case Study Research: Design and Methods*, 3rd edn. Thousand Oaks, CA: Sage.

Recommended reading for further study

Robson, C. (2011) *Real World Research: a Resource for Social Scientists and Practitioner-Researchers. Chapters 1 and 2*. Oxford: Blackwell Publishers.

PART II

Doing research with children and young people – reviewing, designing and conducting research with children

FOUR

Evaluating research with children and young people

The aims of this chapter are:

- to introduce sources of evidence and how to access evidence;
- to provide a step-by-step guide to evaluating published research.

Learning to be able to critically evaluate research is an important skill for those in training and for the discerning professional after qualification. First, researchers need to be knowledgeable about what has gone on before in their particular field so that they make informed judgements about how they should proceed with their own research. As we discussed in Chapter 1, it is important that research adds to the body of knowledge of the profession, and while the replication of research can be useful, it is generally desirable that research should be cumulative and build on previous work to discover new facts or relationships. The researcher then needs the skills of critical evaluation to identify research problems that have been studied before, to explore methods and approaches that have been taken and, not least, to discover what previous researchers have found through investigation. As we discuss in Chapters 3, 5, 6, 7 and 8, important decisions have to be made when undertaking research about how to design appropriate research strategies. Thorough analysis of the work of others in the field will provide a sound foundation for further study by equipping the researcher with the knowledge to make informed, evidence-based judgements.

Second, it is recognized that excellent practice is not only about undertaking research and pushing forward the boundaries of knowledge, but it is also about being aware of what is going on in our own, and related, professional fields and applying knowledge to our own practices. We must, as professionals, ensure that we are up to date, and one of the main ways of doing this is to access and read professional journals and scholarly works. We must, however, be discerning in what we choose to apply to practice, because to apply all that we read could and probably would lead to much confusion. New and emerging theories are often reported in journals. These theories, generated through inductive processes, are largely untested, so their wholesale incorporation into practice is premature at this stage (see Chapters 3, 5 and 8 for further discussion). However, reporting these theories is important so that debate is stimulated around a particular problem and further research in that area is triggered. It is only by accumulating evidence in a field of knowledge that a consensus view of a particular issue can be formed and tentative conclusions drawn.

It therefore becomes very important that the professional practitioner is aware of the whole, emerging debate and not just part of it. A good example over the last decade or so is the debate about the effects of the measles, mumps and rubella (MMR) vaccination on children and the potential links to autism. Clearly, a professional who had only read one side of the debate without investigating the subject more fully might inappropriately change practice and be open to professional criticism. It is important that the reader can understand the status of a piece of research, be able to evaluate it critically and intelligently use the data. In the early stages of an academic debate this may mean doing nothing more than to follow the developments of the debate. Taking and using only random parts of an ongoing research debate and considering only selected bits of the debate without awareness of the whole picture is unacceptable in contemporary practice.

This chapter follows through the process of accessing and critically evaluating the literature, while stressing the necessity of always placing research within a wider theoretical or conceptual framework. Two key contrasting studies, one that broadly fits within a *qualitative* framework and the other within a *quantitative* framework, will be used as examples of this process to give a practical focus and to act as case studies for future critical analysis. These articles are available in full via Sage; websites (www.sagepub.co.uk/greig).

Accessing the literature

There is an ever-increasing and wide range of sources of information in a particular field. In some areas the amount of research and literature available can be daunting, making it important that you narrow down your field of enquiry. If you do not do this you may find yourself swamped with the volume of information. The process of refining your search can be difficult, and it may be necessary to undertake some general reading first so that you can identify what are referred to as *keywords*. This general reading can usually be achieved by accessing an academic library, such as those found in most universities and colleges, or by accessing literature on the World Wide Web (WWW).

After you have identified your keywords, there is a range of sources you can use to identify literature. Increased use of information technology has made this task very much easier. The WWW has revolutionized the process, and the arduous task of sifting through cards and bibliographies in the library has become a thing of the past. The skill now is to become familiar with the technology and most librarians will be only too happy to help. There are also some good texts that will help you with this process (Ford, 2011; Ó Dochartaigh, 2007).

After you have identified a range of references, judgments are required as to which are going to be appropriate for your requirements. Some information sources will provide you only with a title, while others will provide an abstract. Some journals are fully available on the WWW so that you have access to the whole article. Others will require you to become a subscriber. If you are enrolled as a student at an academic institution you should ask which journals the institution subscribes to as you may be able to get free access to the articles you need.

The next stage is to gather your literature in a manageable form (either in a paper-based form or electronically) so that you can begin the process of critical analysis. This may lead to further searching as, for example, in the case of key research articles that may reference other pieces of work you may also need to look at. If a key article appears in a particular journal and you believe the article will stimulate debate, you should access that particular journal on a regular basis so that you do not miss the developing discussion. In some professional fields there are specific and pertinent journals in which such debate will occur while in other professions there are literally hundreds of journals relating to a particular field. If, however, a discussion and debate article appears in a particular journal, it is normal practice for the debate to continue in the same journal.

Evaluating research

The most usual and appropriate way of evaluating research is the use of the research process as a model for evaluation. However, many students, when evaluating research, fall into the trap of using the research process as an inflexible model. Research should always be rigorous and scientific in its enquiry, but different approaches to research inevitably require that researchers place differing emphasis on the various stages of the process. An approach that is too rigid will result in confusion for readers as they attempt to 'fit square pegs into round holes'. The reader may make unfounded criticism of the research and the researcher. The following section gives a balanced view of how to approach the evaluation of research, by focusing on two studies that adopt different research approaches so that the need for flexibility and contextualization can be fully appreciated. Both studies are available at www.sagepub.co.uk/greig. The two studies which have been analysed are Kukulu et al. (2010), on the dietary habits, economic status, academic performance and body mass index in school children, and Bond (2010) on children's perception of how the mobile phone has impacted on the relationships in their everyday lives.

General considerations

The first stage of evaluation is almost an intuitive one and involves reading the whole piece of research at least once and reflecting on your first impressions. It is important to undertake this activity before you begin to engage in the finer detail of the study, when it can sometimes become difficult to interpret the whole (colloquially known as being unable to see the wood for the trees!). You become so engrossed that your objectivity can be compromised.

So what are you looking for at this stage? One useful simile is to consider research as a journey. Good research can be likened to a well-planned expedition. The purpose of the journey is well defined and you know what mode of transport you must take. Your route is planned, you have an up-to-date map and you have checked the feasibility of undertaking each part of the journey in the specified time. You have done your homework and know what potential problems lay in your way. You allow extra time for these eventualities. Once you have started you do not deviate from your chosen route, and if you unexpectedly have to take a diversion or you get lost you immediately consult your map and get back on your pathway as soon as possible. You definitely don't 'follow your nose' and head in the general direction of where you believe your original path lies. When you have completed your journey you might make recommendations to other people who wish to go in a similar direction, but your recommendations only relate to those parts of your journey that you have undertaken and that you therefore have direct experience of. You do not speculate about what you have not seen or heard.

When reading a well-written piece of research you should almost feel a sense of 'completeness' about the research. A good study should have a sense of 'flow'. The research approach should stem from the previous study in this field, the aims should be to expand the knowledge base, the methods should be justified and logical and the data should relate to the aims. You should be able to identify the sources of any conclusions and recommendations from the data. Although intuition is hardly a scientific or rigorous concept, when you become experienced at reading research you will know that when you feel uncomfortable about a piece of research, further detailed analysis will usually show you were right. If you read the piece of research by Kukulu et al., you will find that there is a logical flow to the study, although there is a lack of order within the introduction section (see later in this chapter). The piece of research by Bond flows less well, in part because concepts and issues are introduced later in the text. For example, the introduction states 'this article explores children's use of mobile phones in managing and maintaining relationships with friends' (Bond, 2010: 514) whereas the research methodology section states that the study aimed to explore 'children's perceptions of risk and mobile phones' (Bond, 2010: 516). The reader is left questioning what the study is actually about (it is actually about both relationships and risk). This type of anomaly will sometimes arise because of the strict word limits for published articles resulting in researchers having to summarize full research reports down significantly. Meaning and flow can sometimes get lost in this process.

After you have taken a global view of the piece of research it is time to start looking at the study in finer detail, and we have included in the following sections a step-by-step guide to this process using examples of real studies. Prior to doing this, there are other questions you should ask yourself before you become engrossed in detail. The first relates to the researcher or researchers: who they are, what job they do and why they are undertaking the research. On reflection this is not such a strange thing to do. You are studying the piece of research to establish a base for your own study or to potentially change practice. Both will probably cost time and ultimately money. Therefore, you should apply a similar logic as you would if you were employing someone to take up work for you and ask if they have the right qualifications for the job and what is their motivation for doing the work. This is particularly important when looking at research involving children, as we have discussed in Chapter 1. Both the Kukulu et al. (2010) and Bond (2010) studies give the names and places of work of the research team. However, we have no information in either articles about the roles of the researchers or their qualifications.

The second general point relates to the title of the work and whether it is an accurate reflection of the study itself. One of the duties of researchers is to communicate the results of their efforts (see Chapter 11), and to do so the piece of research, if published, should be accessible. In an age where technology is so important and the use of databases is commonplace, the use of keywords to access literature has become very important, as we have already discussed. You should therefore ask yourself whether the title of the work contained keywords and gave you an insight into the nature of the study. Short, snappy titles might be clever but are unimpressive when you are searching databases and wading through hundreds of titles. The study by Kukulu et al. contains the keywords *dietary habits, economic status, academic performance, body mass index, school children* and *comparative study*, so it does provide detail of what the study is actually about. In the study by Bond, the main title 'Managing mobile relationships' only reflects the study content when the subtitle 'Children's perceptions of the impact of the mobile phone on relationships in their everyday lives' is considered. The whole title allows you to know what it is you are going to be reading about. In both articles additional keywords are actually provided making the study easy to access. Both articles suggest from the title that the articles are primary research, which is important for many students who are required to analyse original research rather than secondary articles, reviews and reports. However, neither title tells you where the studies took place – the Kukulu et al. study, for example, took place in Turkey and the Bond study in the UK. This may be important if, for example, you wanted to review articles from the UK only.

Introduction and the problem being studied

Researchers, like most other writers, will usually set the scene of the research by formally introducing what they have studied and why. This may or may not be preceded by an *abstract*, which is a brief summary of the completed research. The Kukulu et al. study gives a full abstract, which includes an introduction, methods, results and conclusions drawn. The abstract still does not make clear that the study took place in Turkey.

Kukulu et al. abstract

> The changes in dietary habits and way of life of adolescents can lead to some nutrition problems. The purpose of this study was to compare dietary habits of children living in metropolitan and non-metropolitan areas regarding their physical characteristics, socio-economic milieu and educational level. A total of 737 students studying in the 6th, 7th and 8th grades of two different primary schools took part in the study. Data were collected by a questionnaire including dietary habits of participants. Furthermore, the weight and height of students were measured and their body mass index was calculated. During the study, while 4.3 percent of students living in the non-metropolitan area were found obese, this figure was 8.4 percent in the metropolitan area. A big majority of non-metropolitan students have breakfast and lunch at home. Metropolitan students not having lunch at home have their lunch at restaurants or school canteens and generally consume more snacks. The obesity risk of students participating in the study was found to be high. Intervention programs should be organized in order to inform the students about the importance of healthy nutrition and lead them to change their current consumption behavior.

The study by Bond also provides an abstract stating what the study explores and that it is 'based on the accounts of 30 young people'. The abstract does not make clear how the data were collected.

Bond abstract

> This article explores English children's use of mobile phones in managing and maintaining friendships and relationships in their everyday lives. Based on the accounts of 30 young people aged between 11 and 17, this research adopts a social constructivist perspective to offer a theoretical framework which explores how children themselves actually use mobile phone technologies and understand risk in their everyday lives. This is an interpretative account that offers a methodological rationale for hearing children's voices and viewing them as experts on their own lives.

The introduction to the problem being studied is crucial not only in terms of what follows but also in determining whether you feel it is worth reading the rest! Many busy people will only read the abstract and the first paragraph and discard pieces of work that do not come up to scratch, even though we all know that introductions are notoriously difficult to write and probably do not reflect with accuracy what follows. Abstracts and introductions are the gateway to the rest of the article and should encourage the reader to feel impelled to enter to see what else is on offer.

Kukulu et al. combine their introduction with a review of the literature, making it challenging for the reader to identify what the problem being studied is actually about and what points relate to the work of others. The opening paragraph of the introduction of the Kukulu et al. study makes clear that dietary habits are formed in childhood and then places the study within the context of the global problems of obesity and being overweight in children. The study goes on in the second paragraph to discuss the impact of school on healthy nutrition and that unhealthy nutrition will adversely affect school performance and educational attainment. However, since the single study cited is by Considine and Zappala (2002), a study undertaken in Australia, we must question the generalizability of this work to the Kululu et al. study, particularly as finally in paragraph three we are introduced to the location of the study, which is Turkey. In paragraph three the rate of obesity in Turkey is introduced – linked to the increased availability of fast food and sugary drinks. In paragraph five of the introduction the Turkish school system is introduced and the authors cite literature relating to the effects of having breakfast. They then propose that if schools did not serve fast food and introduced better quality food to menus then 'obesity will be reduced and children's diets will improve' (Kukulu et al., 2010: 356). They go on to discuss the priorities that schools have to build classrooms as opposed to investing in better school food – but there are no evidence sources cited to back up this claim. The authors also write that the problem is more pronounced in developed regions but again do not provide evidence for this. Finally, at the end of this combined introduction and literature review, the aim of the study is stated: 'to compare the dietary habits of school children living in metropolitan and non-metropolitan areas according to their physical and familial characteristics as well as their location of residence and school performance' (Kukulu et al., 2010: 357). We have to conclude, however, that the aim does not logically flow from the small sections of literature cited. The key study about educational attainment was an Australian study. Other studies cited, for example, Deveci et al. (2007) and Bakar et al. (2007) are published in Turkish and, without being able to read these articles, it is difficult to understand the nature of the work that has been undertaken or indeed if the references are primary research or not. There appear to be a number of assumptions made for which evidence is not provided.

The study by Bond also has a combined introduction and literature review. As we have mentioned previously, the study starts out by clearly stating that the article is about 'children's use of mobile phones in managing and maintaining relationships' (Bond, 2010: 514). Literature is then introduced and at first reading it seems very puzzling that the first two references are from 1999 and 1925, respectively. While mobile phone use was fairly common in 1999, this was certainly not the case in 1925! However, reading the text again, Bond is referring to theories she is basing her work on, e.g. the 'sociology of giving' (2010: 514). Bond goes on to state that her work will argue that the 'mobile phone is viewed by children as essential to supporting relationships, offering security and reassurance but simultaneously creating anxiety and insecurity' (2010: 514). She goes on to expand on the notion of the 'pure relationship' proposed by Giddens (1992) and 'sociability', discussed by Simmel and Hughes (1949). In paragraph two, Bond cites further work from the 1990s around 'modernity' and people's relationship with technologies. She then introduces additional information about her own study stating that the role of the mobile telephone will be outlined with regard to 'friendships, intimate relationships and bullying' (2010: 515). Bond goes on in the next paragraph to say that 'recently research has been undertaken to explore the concept of risk within children's experience' and that 'James et al. (1998) suggest ...' (2010: 515). What is not clear is if the evidence base, i.e. the recent research, is attributed to James et al. (1998) or not. First, a 1998 publication is not recent, and second, the reference is to a book about theorizing childhood. The remainder of this paragraph goes on to explore the boundaries between adulthood and childhood and engages into an interesting discussion about public space, which has relevance later on in the study.

Bond's last two paragraphs of the combined introduction and literature review focus specifically on mobile telephone use among young people. A range of literature is used, including primary research, although it is not clear from reading the text which citations are primary sources. The literature is also dated for a study published in 2010, with one reference from 2009 (actually published in 2008), which is a book about mobile telephone use in the Asia-Pacific region and does not relate specifically to young people. The next most recent reference is dated 2005, with other citations about mobile telephone use dating from between 1999 and 2003. The age of the references and citations is not always crucial. However, in a subject such as mobile telephone use it seems absolutely imperative that current literature is used as the technology is constantly evolving.

As we have stated previously, both studies combined their introduction with a review of the literature and we have commented about the nature of that literature in the previous paragraphs. The literature review is a vital component of a research study, and with the exception of certain approaches to research undertaken within a qualitative framework, where the related literature is studied at a later point, it is usual to include a literature review after the introduction so that the reader can grasp what has been undertaken in this field before, thus setting the background to the study. We have referred before to the importance of research adding to the body of a profession's knowledge, and this should be demonstrated so that it becomes clear as to how this research will contribute to the profession by building on what has gone before.

There are few hard and fast rules about what literature should be included, and this is largely dependent on the field of study. For example, in relation to the age of the literature used, a study looking at current pharmacological interventions for children who are human immunodeficiency virus (HIV)-positive is likely to refer to very recent literature, whereas a study looking at the long-term effects of institutionalization on adults who were in care as children is likely to use a much broader scope of literature dating back over several decades. Regardless of the topic, it is usual to refer to 'classic' literature and 'seminal works' even if they are dated. Each discipline has its own repertoire of such research: for example, in nursing there is Hawthorn's (1974) study *Nurse, I Want My Mummy!*, in psychology we have the Isle of Wight studies by Rutter et al. (1970), and so on. We did feel that the study by Bond might have used more recent literature, as it is about mobile telephone usage among young people and, just like our example of current pharmacological interventions, which is a rapidly changing environment, the same is true of mobile telephone usage.

All literature should, however, clearly relate to the topic under study, and the researcher should give a balanced view, particularly where there is debate. The strengths and weaknesses of each piece of literature should be discussed and then compared and contrasted with other literature. The literature review should also provide a link between the problem and how it is investigated (we refer back to the notion of a good study which will 'flow'). If there is only a very limited literature review, it might be that the particular journal puts word count constraints on the researcher who is preparing the work for publication or it might be that there is a very limited amount of relevant literature available because of a lack of previous research in the field. In the case of the latter, the researcher should tell you that this is so.

Research questions, aims, objectives and hypotheses

From the literature review there should logically follow clear statements about the purpose of the research, usually expressed in terms of aims, research questions, objectives or hypotheses or a combination of these depending on the type of research. In Chapter 5 we discuss the importance of research questions and in Chapter 3 we discussed the use of hypotheses within a quantitative framework. Within qualitative frameworks formal hypotheses are inappropriate because they test existing theory and, as we have previously discussed, qualitative research uses inductive processes to build theory.

Aims, questions, objectives and hypotheses are pivotal to the research process, and the study should address these through investigation. When evaluating research the reader should seek to make judgements about the relevance of aims, questions, objectives and hypotheses and should refer back to them when evaluating later parts of the study to ensure that they have not become lost in the debate. This is all part of the completeness of the study. In the study by Kukulu et al., the study aim is stated at the end of the combined introduction and literature review section but the authors do not make explicit what they are seeking to test. The reader has the task of making assumptions about hypotheses to be tested and it is only possible to make these assumptions after you have read the complete article. The study by Bond, makes reference to a study aim at the start of the 'research methodology' section 'to explore children's perceptions of risk and mobile phones' (2010: 516) but also states in the 'introduction' that the article 'explores children's use of mobile phones in managing and maintaining relationships' (2010: 514), and as previously noted there does appear to be a level of disconnection between these two statements.

The sample

In our experience, students undertaking research often become confused over the meanings of samples and populations, and yet understanding these is important if the reader is to make sound judgements about the accuracy of data analysis, reliability and validity. Samples are drawn from, and aim to be characteristic and representative of, a population. Sampling strategies are designed to achieve that aim. If sampling is poor it can be disastrous (see also Chapters 5, 6 and 7 for further discussion). Researchers should be absolutely clear about who or what provided them with their data and justify how they selected their sample.

Within a quantitative framework the ideal is to use probability sampling where each member of a population has an equal chance of being included in the sample. In practice this is rarely possible and certainly much of the research within the caring professions uses convenience sampling (selecting convenient participants) or some form of pseudo-random sample drawn from a convenience sample. Within a qualitative framework samples tend to be smaller, convenient and therefore non-probable, with each member of the population having an unequal chance of being selected. Qualitative researchers do, however, employ strategies for trying to ensure that their chosen sample has characteristics that are largely similar to the population from which it is drawn. One type of qualitative sampling is purposive or judgemental, where the researcher selects participants who could not be identified through other sampling strategies, employing judgement to ensure that the sample is selected on the basis of the information required (a sort of hand picking of people who you know will have the knowledge or experiences you require).

The sample in the study by Kukulu et al. was constituted from two schools randomly selected 'from among 39 primary schools situated in the rural regions of Antalaya, a city located in the south-western part of Turkey' (2010: 357). It is not clear from this statement as to whether one school was from a rural area and one from the city – in fact the statement is very confusing. The authors tell us that the sample included 737 students and that there were 340 girls and 397 boys but we are not told how many children were from which school or what the total population of the 39 schools was. We assume that the total sample is the combined total of the children in the sixth, seventh and eighth grades and then children were identified as living in a metropolitan area or a non-metropolitan area. We are told that the children were aged 'between 10 to 14–15' (Kukulu et al., 2010: 357), which raises questions as to why the authors were unable to identify the upper age limit of their sample. We are also told that the children who joined the study agreed to participate and that no child refused.

The study by Bond states that non-probability sampling, generated through 'snowballing through social networks' (2010: 516) was used. Bond mentions that this approach meant that she did not encounter the'disadvantages of gate-keeping' (2010: 516). She tells us that there were 30 children in the study aged between 11 and 17 years and that the sample included 16 girls and 14 boys. Bond is explicit that that the sample is not representative and was limited in terms of ethnicity and social class. She further tells us that the children came from three different schools – state, church-aided and private – but no further information is given as to whether the school type made anydifference to the results so the reader is left wondering why school type was mentioned – perhaps to demonstrate that the group was mixed in terms of schooling.

Ethical implications

In Chapter 10 we discuss fully the ethical implications of undertaking research involving children and what measures researchers should take to ensure that their research is ethical. When evaluating research it is important that the reader evaluates whether or not the researchers have followed correct ethical procedures, such as gaining permission, obtaining informed consent and so on (see Chapter 10 for a full discussion). In our two studies, Kukulu et al. tell us that they received ethical approval from the 'National Education Directory of Antalya' (2010: 358) and from the directors of the two schools in the sample. Children were asked to give their written consent to participate. There is no mention of parental consent, which would have seemed appropriate given that children were asked detailed questions about their parents. There is no mention of the ethical implications of their study or how they addressed potential ethical issues, which again would have seemed appropriate as they were measuring and weighing children and making judgements of educational attainment, which might have been distressing for some of the children.

The study by Bond, on the other hand, makes a clear statement that 'ethical considerations were of paramount importance' (2010: 516). She goes on to say that she has an enhanced Criminal Records Bureau certificate and is experienced in conducting research with children. Bond also obtained informed consent to participate from the children and their parents. Although Bond mentions the importance of ethical considerations, she does not detail how she has dealt with issues of confidentiality. The study is also looking at 'friendships, intimate relationships and bullying' (2010: 515), which makes the reader ask questions about how Bond would manage the ethical implications of disclosure of, for example, an illegal or harmful nature. This is not to say that Bond has not considered these issues but the point is that the reader simply does not know.

As you will read in Chapter 10, following correct ethical principles is a vital stage of the research process, and researchers who do not give adequate acknowledgement to this should expect to receive criticism in relation to their omission.

Data collection

In Chapters 5, 6, 7 and 8 we explore research techniques and ways of collecting data from children. When evaluating research it is important to identify precisely what the participants within the sample had to do to give the researcher the information required, what tools the researcher used to collect and/or measure the response and whether these were appropriate. Data collection tools (or instruments) include such things as interview schedules, rating scales, questionnaires and observation schedules and frequently will incorporate more than one instrument within one piece of research. Clearly, when collecting data from children the choice of an instrument will be influenced by a number of factors, including the developmental stage of the child.

Returning for a moment to our completeness theme, when evaluating research, the data collection tools should appear logical and should be directed towards meeting the aims, research questions, objectives or hypotheses. In complex studies it is a useful exercise to take each part of the study and map through how each area of data collection will work. This will also highlight any assumptions on the part of the researcher and obsolete data. It is not unusual for researchers to use an array of tools to collect data that do not apparently relate to the stated purpose of the study.

The reliability and validity of the research tools are a very important part of the research process and should be addressed by the researcher. Reliability and validity are rather like an internal quality assurance system (for further detail see Chapters 5, 6 and 7). Within a quantitative framework, issues of reliability and validity are addressed in a different way from that for research that is undertaken within a qualitative framework. In quantitative research the researcher is concerned that objectivity is achieved and bias is eliminated, that the study methods can be accurately replicated and that findings can be generalized across populations. The qualitative researcher should not ignore reliability and validity, but these are viewed differently. Replication is not generally sought, and reliability is established through verification by or with the participants.

If we look at our two studies the contrast is evident between the two research paradigms. In the study by Kukulu et al. we are told that data were collected from children using a questionnaire administered in class. Information on the questionnaire is briefly described as comprising family histories, consumption frequency patterns, age, weight, height, school performance, educational level, and the professions of the students' parents. The questionnaire also asked what the family's income level was. There is a discussion about income levels, which seemed to imply that children living in non-metropolitan areas and those living in metropolitan areas would have similar incomes – 'thus there are no significant income fluctuations in an area' (Kukulu et al., 2010: 358). This raises a number of questions about how researchers would know this and indeed how they could be assured that children would be aware of family income. After being told that the questionnaire was used to obtain information about weight, height and school performance we are then told that the study also used scales and a stadiometer to calculate body mass index. Academic performance was obtained from school records. We are not clear if self-reported measures were validated by actual measurements or if the questionnaire was not used to obtain this information. We are not provided with a copy of the questionnaire so we are left to make assumptions. There is no mention of how the researchers were assured of the reliability of the questionnaire. In terms of validity, we are told that data were collected by two trained research assistants.

In the Bond study we are told that data were collected through nine group discussions. There is no mention of a list of prompts or trigger questions so it is not clear what role the researcher took in the discussions. There is also no mention of 'member checking', which involves feeding back data to participants so that they can make judgements about whether the interpretation of data is valid.

Data analysis and results

When evaluating research it is important that the reader gains an understanding as to how data are analysed so that an accurate link can be made between the gathered data and the results. This might be as simple as a researcher describing the use of percentages or tables and graphs, or more complicated as in the use of inferential statistics. In qualitative research, data analysis may involve defining categories, employing varying levels of content analysis, coding, and so on. Quantitative and qualitative frameworks may also differ in terms of the separation of actual results from discussion arising from the results. Quantitative research will usually report results in what is defined as a 'value-free' way, which simply means presenting results without interpreting them in a wider context. There usually follows a distinct discussion that will provide interpretation within the context of the theoretical framework, previous work and the aims, questions or hypotheses.

In qualitative research the results may be structured in a similar way, but not always. For example, as we have described previously, a grounded theory approach will describe the data generated through a particular investigation and will seek to verify emerging categories through comparison with other studies. When you evaluate data analysis and results you should attempt to make informed judgements about whether the correct techniques have been used in an appropriate way. For example, if the researcher has used a particular statistical test, is the test appropriate for the type of data analysed? If a parametric test is used, are the data normally distributed, was the sample random and of sufficient size, were the measurements used at least interval, and so on? We deal with some of these issues in Chapters 5, 6, 7 and 8. Do not worry if these questions seem daunting and alien to you. The important point here is that you should be aware that there are questions you must ask, even though you might need help in identifying what those questions are.

In our two studies there is a contrast in approach to reporting results. Both studies have a separate results and discussion section although the Bond study could have reasonably combined these sections. The study by Kukulu et al. had, as would be expected, a separate results section that is followed by a separate discussion section. The study reports first descriptive findings giving percentages for parental education (mother and father separately), employment status, the number of children in the family, and reported these according to whether children were assigned to the metropolitan or non-metropolitan group. We are told that the SPSS statistical package was used for data analysis: chi-square was used to identify the relationship between the location of the school and the parents' education, their occupational status and the number of siblings, and the Fisher's exact test was used where small numbers were found (this is the correct alternative to the chi-square test in this case, although there is no evidence that they ever used this test). These are non-parametric forms of analyses and suitable for the type of data being analysed. Tables of data are provided with some explanation of the results provided in the text. There are also a number of variables introduced during the results section including the existence of 'lokanta' – restaurants that provide home-cooked food for individual children. Lokanta work through a contract usually between the child's mother and the restaurant owner who will tell the mother how many times the child eats in the lokanta, what the child eats and who the child eats with!

The study by Bond reports results in a contrasting way. Bond themes her findings under three headings: relationships, reciprocity and risk. She uses *verbatim* quotations to illustrate points that she highlights from the discussion groups.

Bond uses other published research to compare and contrast her findings to. There is a logical flow to the results and a real sense of how children use their mobile phones. There are eight pages of rich data interspersed with dialogue.

The two studies illustrate that when reporting results, the fundamental differences between qualitative and quantitative studies suddenly become very apparent. The first study analyses and describes the data using a range of descriptive and inferential statistics, whereas the study by Bond describes themes, using *verbatim* data from the interview and focus group transcripts to illustrate meaning and illustrate response.

Both studies also have separate discussion sections and at this point it is possible to see similarities that were not apparent when reporting results. Kukulu et al. provide a detailed discussion linked back to previous studies. The authors take the main findings from their results and interpret these, highlighting similarities and differences between their findings and the work of previous researchers. They use phrases such as 'this finding is in parallel with other studies conducted in Turkey on this subject' (Kukulu et al., 2010: 362). The discussion is clear and logical and is a clear strength of the study.

Bond uses the discussion section to link the findings back to the theories that underpinned her work. The discussion section reads more like a conclusion – possibly because Bond had (correctly in our view) compared and contrasted her findings to the work of others in her results section.

Conclusion, recommendations and limitations

The final aspect of the evaluation is about tying up all the loose ends and moving forwards. As with any academic piece of work, the research should be concluded, and because research is about the discovery of new facts or relationships these should be defined in terms of application to practice, future research and other recommendations. These should be made within the context of any limitations of the research: for example, a study that used a convenience sample may refer to the inappropriateness of generalization across a population and suggest that further study using a different sampling strategy be undertaken.

The conclusion is also about 'closing the loop' and emphasizing the completeness of the work. We used the simile of a well-planned journey at the beginning of the chapter, so it may be useful to view the conclusion as arriving at your destination when you sit down to relax, reflect, plan what you are going to do now that you have arrived, and look forward to your next journey.

Turning for a final time to our two studies, Kukulu et al. conclude their study by summarizing what they have found through their investigation and by referring to how their study adds to the existing body of knowledge in the field, making suggestions for further research relating to their particular findings. They also make recommendations that do not link to the study findings, such as that teachers should receive training so that they can educate children about a healthy diet. While this might make some sense, it should not have been included in the recommendations because they have no evidence to back up that this would have a positive effect.

The study by Bond had no formal conclusion although, as stated above, the discussion section highlights the major themes explored and includes a concluding statement about what the study illustrated. We felt that the lack of a conclusion meant that the study finished abruptly and without making formal recommendations.

Neither study is explicit in recognizing the limitations of their work in terms of not being able to generalize findings in their conclusions.

Conclusion

Evaluating the research of others is important for two reasons. First, to be informed about the knowledge base within your own profession you must be aware of research that has been and is being undertaken and be able to analyse that research. Second, if you wish to undertake research yourself you must be able to intelligently use previous research to guide you. The process of evaluating research is not difficult but does involve practice and a level of knowledge about the research process. In this chapter we have taken two contrasting research papers and highlighted briefly some of the areas that are important in evaluating research as an example of the considerations that should be given when reading research.

PUTTING RESEARCH INTO PRACTICE 4.1 – SEARCHING FOR INFORMATION

This exercise is designed to enable you to practise searching thoroughly in a narrow area to help you improve your skills of accessing information.

During the process of this practical keep a note of problems encountered, help received and from whom or where, solutions to problems and any other information that may be helpful in the future.

Think of an area you might like to know more about that relates to children – if you cannot think of anything look at the research ideas in Practical 3.1 for an idea. Then:

- Go to the library and find one general article or book relating to the topic and from there identify two *keywords.*
- Find out what databases are available in the library.
- Ask the librarian to show you how to use one of the databases.
- Using your keywords, search the database.
- Find out which sources of information are available in the library.

Using your keywords search the WWW to see what additional information you can find.

PUTTING RESEARCH INTO PRACTICE 4.2 – CRITICAL EVALUATION OF A KEY STUDY

This exercise aims to give you experience of critical evaluation.

- Select a study identified through your searches above.
- Follow through the process described in this chapter, keeping a note of any difficulties you experience.

References

Bakar, C., Budakoğlu, I., Erdem, Ö. and Akgün, H.S. (2007) 'Özel bir Ilköğretim Okulu Öğrencilerinin Beslenme Alışkanlıkları, XI', *Ulusal Halk Sağlığı Kongresi Kongre Kitabı*, 195.

Bond, E. (2010) 'Managing mobile relationships: children's perception of the impact of the mobile phone on relationships in their everyday lives', *Childhood*, 17 (4): 514–29.

Considine, G. and Zappala, G. (2002) 'The influence of social and economic disadvantage in the academic performance of school students in Australia', *Journal of Sociology*, 38 (2): 129–48.

Deveci, S., Baydur, H. and Kaplan, Y. (2007) 'Manisa Il Merkezinde Kentsel ve Yarıkentsel Iki Ilköğretim Okulu 6. 7. ve 8. Sınıf Öğrencilerinin Beslenme Durumları ve Kimi Antropemetrik Ölçümlerinin Değerlendirilmesi, XI', *Ulusal Halk Sağlığı Kongresi Kongre Kitabı*, 190.

Ford N. (2011) *The Essential Guide to Using the Web For Research*. London: Sage.

Giddens, A. (1992) *The Transformation of Intimacy: Sexuality, Love and Eroticism in Modern Societies*. Stanford, CA: Stanford University Press.

Hawthorn, P. (1974) *Nurse, I Want My Mummy!* London: Royal College of Nursing.

Kukulu, K., Sarvan, S., Muslu, L. and Yirmibesoglu, S.G. (2010) 'Dietary habits, economic status, academic performance and body mass index in school children: a comparative study', *Journal of Child Health Care*, 14 (4): 355–66.

Ó Dochartaigh, N. (2007) *Internet Research Skills: How to Do Your Literature Search and Find Research Information Online*. London: Sage.

Rutter, M., Graham, P.J. and Yule, W. (1970) *A Neuropsychiatric Study in Childhood*. London: Heinmann Medical.

Simmel, G. and Hughes, E.C. (1949) 'The sociology of sociabilty', *American Journal of Sociology*, 55 (3): 254–61.

Recommended reading for further study

Dane, F.C. (2011) *Evaluating Research: Methodology for People Who Need to Read Research*. Thousand Oaks, CA: Sage.

Girden, E.R. and Kabacoff, R.I. (2011) *Evaluating Research Articles from Start to Finish*, 3rd edn. Thousand Oaks, CA: Sage.

Lichtman, M. (ed.) (2011) *Understanding and Evaluating Qualitative Educational Research*. Thousand Oaks, CA: Sage.

FIVE

Designing and doing research with children and young people: the importance of questions

The aims of this chapter are:

- to consider the role of questions in designing and doing research with children and young people;
- to discriminate between *hypotheses* and research *questions*;
- to introduce the core research principles of reliability and validity;
- to provide a practical guide for formulating and asking reliable and valid questions in doing research with children and young people.

A small child who is asked the question 'What is a prime minister?' may offer the correct answer, an inventive one, such as 'somebody who marries people', or a comic one that has no logical relation to the question, like 'a blue thing you put into the oven'. The inability to predict the answer a child will give is a fact that, in addition to providing entertainment for adults, demonstrates that children's minds are special. More recently, researchers have been finding out more about the mind of adolescents, how they continue to develop and change in ways that help us to better understand, for example, their difficulties getting out of bed in the morning and their inarticulate 'whatevers' and 'it's not fair!'. The relationship between children/young people and questions is special in several ways: the questions you need to ask yourself when designing your research; questioning the assumptions behind your research questions; and questioning children and young people themselves. You may wish, for example, to explore the nature of a young child's relationship with their mother and to know, in particular, how they feel when their mother has to leave them. The way in which you will go about this investigation needs to be *designed* and this entails asking yourself the following questions.

- What is the basic research issue?
- What do I want to do?
- With whom do I want to do it?
- When do I want to do it?
- Are my intended methods reliable and valid?

Many basic research designs flounder because the research issue lacks a clear rationale that conveys a sense of the importance of doing the research in the first place. Thus, the following questions prove helpful: Why is this important? Who will be interested in the results? Having set up a basic design and addressed the rationale, it is wise still to challenge the theoretical and popular assumptions that may underlie it. The rationale behind this particular research issue could be based on the assumption that a secure mother–child relationship is essential for normal development. The researcher needs to consider the sources of evidence for this. Is it based on research data or clinical evidence? Is it based on popular wisdom, personal conviction or a political or professional ideal? Finally, we return to questioning children and young people themselves. To determine how they feel whenever their mother leaves them in hospital, they could be directly asked: 'How did you feel when your mum left you in the hospital?' A teenager may or may not be too cool to go beyond a 'dunno' type of response. Even when put to a primary school child, the usefulness of the answer will depend on the age of the child and also on the child's verbal abilities. Younger children are usually unable to cope and, in the case of preschool children, require the researcher to enter the world with which the child is familiar – the world of stories, dolls, puppets, sand and drawing.

Clearly, asking questions in designing and doing research with children and young people is a skill that needs to be cultivated, and an effective training programme will deal thoroughly with the issue at all levels of research. In the following sections, we will cover these topics in more detail.

The question of research design

The research tutor has just handed you the Guidelines for Research. How do you feel? Your heart may flutter with excitement, anticipation and adventure at this new challenge and opportunity to systematically investigate a topic close to your heart. Conversely, your heart may sink in panic and dread at the prospect of coming up with a topic and coping with new research skills. The best studies usually come from researchers who have a 'hunch', and those who start from this point are likely to feel positive about the ensuing challenges. The hunch may be something the researcher has observed about children when working in a school, hospital, home, or from the researcher's own experiences as a parent or child. Whatever the source of the hunch, it will be something that interests the researcher and consequently will be a source of intrigue and passion. It has been well said that the challenges of doing research are such that only researchers who 'fall in love' with their subjects to the point of total immersion will succeed! Deciding on the right questions and approaches will make the difference between an interesting study and a mundane one. Equally important is knowing why the question needs to be asked in the first place and how to do it. Therefore, before attempting to design and investigate the proposed question, researchers need to ask themselves questions, such as:

- Why is it important to ask this question?
- To whom will the answers matter and what can be done with them?
- What kind of question is it – one that can be objectively tested, a subjective enquiry or an exploratory problem?

Why is it important to ask questions about children and young people?

At the general level, any question on children and young people is important if only because of their importance in our lives. Furthermore, the climate for doing such research has never been better, with new policies encouraging easier access to children and young people and cooperation between individuals and agencies to understand and support their developmental needs. Over the past generation, technological advances, such as digital cameras, recorders, remote viewing, computer technology, mobile phones, the WWW and computing software, have transformed the opportunities we have for investigating a wider range of research questions effectively. Subtle qualities of relationships and split-second gestures are the kinds of behaviours that can be captured on camera, played and replayed and rigorously analysed on our computers, further increasing our power in doing research.

The type of research and analysis shown in Figure 5.1 has been around for a long time now. As well as the structured, experimental example shown here, researchers have taken cameras into nursery schools, playgrounds, day-care centres, primary and secondary schools. The pioneering work of Robertson and Robertson (1971) is a very good early example where an ethological approach to the study and analysis of child behaviour has been able to benefit from a more rigorously recorded evidence base using technology. Figure 5.1 shows selected video footage of live research, the quality of which allows a detailed investigation of behaviour and relationships either in naturalistic or free-flow settings or in experimenter-led, controlled tasks. The work of Simon Baron Cohen and colleagues (Howlin et al., 2008) into the understanding of emotions in children and young people with autism has thrived on the use of computing software that has both assessment and intervention capacities. The use of the WWW for online surveys is a promising tool for specific groups such as teenagers or those with developmental communication difficulties that make ordinary face-to-face questioning difficult or unmotivated. These innovations are also described in Chapter 9 in relation to consulting with and empowering children.

Figure 5.1 Video footage of live research that enables detailed behavioural analysis

Researchers are now well placed to ask previously inaccessible questions in greater quantities, better and quicker. Given the current climate of research conditions for researching children and young people, it is more a case of why not do such a study rather than why do such a study! Other good general reasons for asking research questions on children and young people include: the fact that their rapid growth enables us to observe developmental changes and monitor intervention outcomes within a fairly short time span; finding out about them informs us about adults; research on children and young people can help practitioners learn more about and improve their practice; and, finally, such studies often help to support or disprove a theory about the nature and development of children and young people. More recently, advances in methods for consulting with children and young people on their perspectives, as well as actively involving them as participant researchers, means that we are becoming more able to listen to their voices and to empower them. This topic is covered in some detail in Chapter 9 and the relationship between research, theory and practice is explored further in Chapter 2. The question may also be of personal importance to the researcher. Indeed, the *raison d'être* of the research question may be a direct result of a childhood experience of illness, abuse, adoption, emotional behavioural disorders, school experience or relationship difficulties. Perhaps most importantly, is that the research question should be important for children and young people themselves and lead to an improvement for them and the worlds in which they live. In fact, a research question should be important in all the ways described.

When a research question is not a question

People wishing to do research with children and young people come from many professional backgrounds – child health, education and social care being prominent examples. The associated academic disciplines of biology, psychology and sociology each have preferred approaches to asking research questions. In considering the nature of an attachment relationship, for example, a biologist might ask: Do stress indicators in saliva increase during separations between mother and child? A developmental psychologist might ask: Do insecurely attached children perform less well than securely attached children in tests of psychosocial functioning? A social worker would perhaps ask: What is the social history of this teenager who is insecurely attached to their adoptive parents? Clearly all of these are viable research questions but there are some important differences. The first two questions imply an objective test or experiment of some kind together with the use of specific tests and equipment. In research, these sorts of questions are referred to as *hypotheses*, which propose a relationship between two variables. An example could be attachment security and the child's performance on a test assessing the understanding of emotion. The nature of the proposed relationships will be based on theory, in this case attachment theory, which allows predictions to be made about the relationship and to be tested in an experimental and controlled setting. Generally, a prediction is a statement that a change in one thing (the independent variable) will produce an effect in another thing (the dependent variable). Thus, a change in security of attachment is predicted to produce a change in performance of the emotion test. The aim of this type of research is to explain *why* children behave as they do as opposed to merely describing their behaviour, and the findings, being based on assessment of many children, are relevant to all.

The question posed by the social worker requires a different interpretation. Here we are concerned with an individual young person with a unique history. It is a matter of asking questions rather than hypotheses, and these questions are subjective and aimed at describing *what* is going on with the individual. While questions can be highly generalized, as in 'What is this young person's social history?', they can also reflect an intention to use a particular theory. In this case, where does attachment theory inform our understanding of this teenager and how can we help them? The main difference in the two approaches is between seeking explanation and seeking understanding.

Table 5.1 illustrates the differences between research hypotheses and research questions, and Box 5.1 illustrates the evolution of a research question.

Table 5.1 Examples of research questions that are best posed as either hypotheses or as exploratory questions

Pose as hypotheses (seeking explanation)	*Pose as questions (seeking understanding)*
What parenting strategies *determine* emotional and behavioural difficulties in children?	What are the feelings and thoughts of children and parents *themselves* about how they get on together?
What are the social and environmental variables that *predict* child abuse?	What are the definitions of the parents and children themselves of *experiences* of child abuse?
What is the *relationship* between family disruption and child characteristics of age, gender and temperament?	What are the *perceptions* of children from broken homes about conflict and divorce?
Emphasis is on determinants, predictions and statistical relationships. These questions seek explanations for WHY children behave and develop as they do.	Emphasis is on description and interpretation of the participants' perspective. These questions lead to an understanding of WHAT is going on in the child's world, and the child guides the research.

Source: Adapted from Hatch (ed.) (1995) *Qualitative Research in Early Childhood Settings*. J. Amos Hatch, Praeger Publishers, 1995.

BOX 5.1

The evolution of a research question

Julie is on a teacher training course and wishes to work in reception classes. As an experienced classroom assistant she has noticed that very young children tend to have more behavioural disturbances than older children in reception. In addition, she has been concerned about recent government legislation that means that children can now join formal education classes as young as four years of age. She watches television debates and reads the national press. She is annoyed that nobody appears to be considering the long-term developmental effects of the new legislation on very young children who are, she believes, at a most critical stage in their development. She decides that this will be a good research topic and begins to formulate a number of research questions to discuss with her supervisor.

Julie must first of all question her assumptions and those of established authorities. The assumption underlying her point of view is that younger children are disadvantaged in some way. Can she say that this is true of all the younger children or are some individuals doing at least as well as the older reception children? At this point all she has is an opinion based on limited personal experience and a belief based on a theory that children go through critical phases of development. She needs to question these opinions and beliefs and find 'scientific' evidence to back up her views.

Julie consults a number of research journals to find out what is known about the adaptation of very young children to formal education. She finds that there has not yet been a systematic study of this kind, so 'scientific' evidence is unavailable. This is the rationale and importance of her study. Policy decisions are being made with the potential to damage the development of very young children while no investigations appear to be taking place to justify decisions. The answers to her question will have the potential to inform policymakers and practitioners who wish to minimize any potential threats to the children involved. This means that she has indeed found a topic worthy of further investigation but also that her study will be exploratory rather than adding proof to an established body of scientific research. This is the difference between asking the general question 'What are the effects, if any, of entry to reception classes on the behaviour of very young children?' and predicting a very specific outcome such as the hypothesis that 'younger children in reception class will manifest more behavioural and emotional difficulties than older children in reception class'.

Research design: the basic questions

Once the research questions or hypotheses have been formulated and deemed important, the researcher has to come up with a basic design that addresses *who* are to be the participants, *how many* participants to include, *what* exactly is to be done and *when?*

Who? Given the nature of the purpose of the study and the research questions or hypotheses, who should the participants be: babies, toddlers, preschoolers, school-aged children, adolescents, pairs of mothers and children, whole families or children from several age groups? Perhaps the study requires the participation of a particular group or a range of different child educare professionals such as social workers, childminders, mediators, nurses, teachers, doctors, psychiatrists and service managers. Should the study include only boys or also girls? Is it about fathers, rather than mothers, or are both equally important?

Another crucial question is *how many* participants to include. If you ask only 10 children to complete a questionnaire on personality and relate it to their academic performance, you would not be very confident that your conclusions are accurate. If, however, you do the same thing with thousands of children, you would be much more confident. Another requirement is to ensure that the sample is representative of the general population – in this case, to include a range of abilities and cultures. The example shown in Box 5.1 is appropriate for testing a hypothesis, the purpose of which is to make generalizations with the results and make predictions. However, large numbers are not so important when the purpose of the study is to describe what is going on in the world of a particular child or relationship.

What? What is to be done to or with the research participants? The purpose of the research may be to find out what happens when you subject them to particular treatments or conditions. If the aim is to test whether the young participants perform better in achievement tests after a schedule of self-esteem enhancement, then an *experimental* design is required. If the aim is simply to observe or measure the relationship between actual self-esteem and achievement tests then a *correlational* design is needed. Conversely, the study may focus on one particular child or young person with reading difficulties, the aim of which is to obtain rich descriptions of both the teacher's and the participant's view of their reading ability, supplemented by other school, medical and social records, and an exploration of teacher strategies that do and do not work for this child or young person. If this is the purpose of the study, then a *case study* design is needed. Each of these designs and others are described in detail in Chapters 6, 7 and 8 and the theoretical frameworks that support them in Chapter 3.

When? Do you need to assess the participants only once or more than once? A study addressing the relationship between current self-esteem and test performance need only be done once. A study comparing a child or young person's performance on tests after intervention requires at least two assessments: before the intervention and after the intervention. Some studies that aim to say more about developmental pathways will entail continuous assessment throughout childhood and adolescence: measures at 18 months, a presumed critical stage for longer-term outcomes, can be related to a variety of other measures at the preschool stage, primary school stage, at adolescence and beyond. These studies, which look at the same individual or group of children or young people over a long period of time, are known as *longitudinal designs*. An alternative, less time-consuming, approach is to study the same measures in children at different developmental stages. Thus, self-esteem and achievement scores in a group of primary school children can be compared with self-esteem and achievement scores in a group of adolescents. This is known as a *cross-sectional* design, which is efficient but unable to map the developmental pathways of individuals.

Table 5.2 summarizes basic research designs for studying children and young people. These designs are more commonly associated with large samples, but most can apply to individual case studies also. An individual can be studied longitudinally, and receive experimental interventions and correlations between a variety of measures, say school achievement, social hardship, health, attachment security and self-esteem.

The question of reliability and validity

Continuing with our hypothetical examination of self-esteem, let us suppose that you wish to assess self-esteem in teenagers who are disabled or who have

Table 5.2 A summary of basic research designs for doing research with children and young people

Design	*Features*	*Aim*	*Advantages/ disadvantages*
Cross-sectional	Children from different age groups assessed at the same time	To describe developmental age norms	Quick, efficient, economic. Not about individual development
Longitudinal	Same children assessed periodically as they grow up	To describe developmental changes for particular groups or individual children	Addresses continuity of development/drop outs, and participants know the test
Correlational	Various child/ youth assessments are taken at the same time and correlated	To examine the relationship between two or more child/ youth scores and tentative explanations	Easy to implement/ cannot imply cause and other potential variables
Experimental	An experimenter controls an independent variable or intervention	To test hypotheses which explain children's/young people's behaviour and development	Valuable for providing strong evidence of cause and effect in child development

been disfigured as a result of an accident. All existing measures, you think, are not specific enough about certain issues that you feel are particularly important, so you create a new version. How can you be certain that the instrument you have designed is accurate and truly assesses what you want it to? How can you tell how good any instrument is at assessing what it is supposed to do? To be confident about your instrument's accuracy, you need to determine its *reliability* and *validity*.

Reliability

A reliable instrument will give a consistent measure of the behaviour or construct in question – in this case, self-esteem. If we have children complete the same questionnaire on several different occasions and the outcome varies each time from low to high self-esteem, then we cannot be certain than it does indeed measure self-esteem or that self-esteem is a consistent construct in itself. Likewise, an instrument supposedly assessing intelligence quotient (IQ) does not tell us much about an individual's intelligence if it varies dramatically between tests every Monday morning for a month. Another way of ensuring reliability is inter-observer reliability. This is a procedure in which two independent assessors agree on the behavioural codes being observed or the score obtained in a particular instrument. The greater the correlation or agreement between the results obtained by the two independent 'observers', the greater the reliability of the behavioural codes or instruments. If the aim is to assess, by observation, the extent of a child's solitary play, an inter-observer test would look like the one shown in Figure 5.2.

It can be seen, at a glance, that there is a perfect correlation or agreement in this case. However, it is acceptable to have merely good or high levels of agreement or correlation because human behaviour always entails an element of subjectivity and inconsistency (*random error*). In addition, where several different behaviours are being assessed or where there are many participants, it is necessary to run an appropriate statistical test (see Chapters 6 and 7). Yet another measure of reliability is the *internal consistency* of instruments such as a

Child	Frequency of solidary play	
	Observer A	Observer B
1	5	5
2	2	2
3	6	6

Figure 5.2 Example of an inter-observer reliability test

self-esteem questionnaire. If the instrument has 10 items assessing body image, you would expect the teenagers who score high on self-esteem generally to score high also on most of the other items. In effect, an instrument is internally consistent when all items yield similar scores. Establishing the reliability of a research tool can be a complicated and lengthy affair, so novice researchers are advised to use instruments that are already accepted as reliable by the research community.

Validity

As a researcher you need to ask yet another series of questions about your data. Once the self-esteem or behavioural scores are in, you must ask: 'Do my data make sense?', 'Does this measure what it is supposed to measure?' If you had interviewed a group of professionals on their strategies for dealing with low self-esteem in teenagers and they spoke at length about what they do, in principle, because you know they seldom have the time to implement their strategies, then your method does not do what it is supposed to do. It does not have face validity. Similarly, if the group of confident teenagers all score equally badly on your measure of self-esteem, then you need to question the face validity of your instrument and its general usefulness as an index of self-esteem. It has been argued that controlled, experimental, laboratory-based research studies do not reflect the properties of the real world and real relationships in which the young participants live. This type of research is said to be low in *ecological validity* and researchers need to be interpreting their findings from this research for real life situations. Controlled, experimental research has high internal validity, however, because confounding variables are systematically controlled for. There is quite a lot of developmental psychology and family research done in quasi-naturalistic research settings such as the one shown in Figure 5.3. This shows a laboratory set-up that mimics a real domestic setting and has a built-in observation and recording facility. What do you suppose are the advantages and disadvantages of this type of research setting?

Ecological validity can be enhanced by doing more naturalistic research, in natural settings such as homes, schools, playgrounds, hospitals and neighbourhoods, and using familiar people such as parents, peers and professionals in the research design. In some cases, researchers become 'participants' themselves, perhaps by assuming a teacher, nurse or carer role.

Reliability and validity of methods may never be perfect. It is certainly possible for a highly reliable instrument to lack validity. Although it is more difficult to assess validity than reliability, by obtaining similar scores on a variety of instruments and measures that supposedly measure the same construct and by assessing whether various scores relate in meaningful ways, it is possible to improve

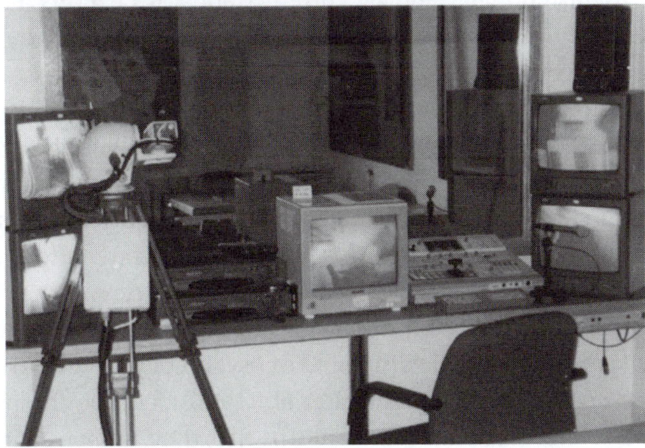

Figure 5.3 A laboratory domestic setting with built-in observation mirror and recording facilities

the validity of your research. This method is used most by researchers using a deductive model – that is, one that is theory-driven and requires hypothesis testing. An equivalent method called *triangulation* is used by researchers using an inductive model – that is, one that is driven by exploratory, subjective questions and by the participants' perspectives (deductive and inductive models are fully explained in Chapter 3). Triangulation enables researchers to capture, to some extent, the shifting realities of their participants. Case study triangulation entails obtaining more than one, usually three, perspectives on a given phenomenon. Research into agency thresholds in dealing with children and young people in need could include similar interviews addressed to fieldworkers, service managers and parents. Triangulation also occurs by using more than one researcher or a mixture of all of these.

The questioning of assumptions

It is ironic that a researcher, who has once been both a child and a teenager, needs to consider seriously questions such as: What is it like to be a child? How does a teenager think and feel? How can I find out? The feeling and thinking of childhood and adolescence are lost to the adult, at least in a direct sense, for all we have are memories of varying degrees of reliability and validity. Nonetheless, until the researcher has attempted to answer these kinds of questions, there is little point in researching children or young people at all.

The best place to begin is to challenge the assumptions we typically have. The researcher's own view of childhood and adolescence will be affected by personal experience as a child, teenager or parent, by professional training, identity and experience, by cultural views and by current trends or fashions. Caring professions, such as nursing and social work, naturally see the child or young person as an object of concern. The child or young person needs to be assessed and protected, and decisions will have to be made about their future. Honourable as this is, the downside is the disempowerment of the child or young person and the oversight of their own perspective. The assumption has long been held that children and young people are not able to contribute reliably towards discussions on their feelings, needs and future. This, in turn, has clearly affected the nature of the research questions that have been posed and a delay in the development of methods for speaking directly to them and eliciting their views. Certainly, researchers within the academic discipline of psychology have held assumptions about children and young people. Hill et al. (1996) describe the psychologist's view of them as 'objects of study'. This means that they too have largely ignored their point of view, subjective opinions and the methods that need to be used to obtain them. In effect, psychological research is done *on* rather than *with* children and young people.

Theories and hypotheses are generated by adults, standardized tests or controlled experiments are done on children and young people, and the data are statistically analysed. Such psychological research has achieved a great deal in improving techniques for studying children and young people (see Chapters 6 and 7) and should continue to do so in the future, for, as we will presently discuss, some questions need to be tackled in a controlled fashion. Professional assumptions can also influence our views of children and young people. Teachers are likely to see them as objects of learning and development. In addition, historical or cultural trends come into play. For instance, a teacher trained in the 'child-centred' 1960s would have perceived the child as an active player in the development of knowledge, requiring only the provision of an appropriate environment and the biological readiness to learn. Compare this with the early 20th-century view of children as passive recipients of reading, writing and arithmetic. Practitioner researchers, then, should critically consider how their professional identities and assumptions of children and young people may colour their research questions and methods. The child or young person is always so much more than it is professionally convenient to believe.

Schaffer (1998) gives specific examples of the fashions influencing our views of children, young people and their development. Child-raising methods, working mothers, separation from parents, divorce, and fathers as competent carers are all developmental issues that have been known to vary in emphasis over time and across cultures. Schaffer also warns of the danger of forming beliefs about children and young people based on the wisdom of established authorities. It often is the case that such wisdom is derived from a mixture of personal opinion, guesswork, folklore, work with clinical cases and experiences of raising their own offspring. Indeed, this is true, to some extent, of some of the most influential developmental theorists, including Charles Darwin, Sigmund Freud and Jean Piaget!

Questioning adults about children and young people

In some types of research it may be necessary to question an adult on the child or young person's behalf. This is likely to be the case when the child is too young or unable to speak, such as a teenager with communication difficulties. It could also be that it has been deemed unethical to raise particular types of questions with children and young people directly or that the researcher has a particular interest in the parent's or carer's relationship with the child or the perspective of the child. Another approach is to assess the parent's own experiences of childhood and adolescence and perhaps relate them to how they perceive and relate to their own children or teenagers. All of these approaches are important and relevant for anyone doing research with children and young people. Regardless of the focus of the main research question, a questionnaire or an interview with an adult or parent who knows the child or young person well can add a new dimension to the research. The techniques for interviewing parents and adults who care for or work with children and young people are discussed in detail in Chapters 8 and 9.

Questioning children and young people directly

The novice researcher about to question children or young people for the first time will have to deal with a number of myths that surround the whole process. Typically, these include assumptions about the child's or youth's capabilities. Notions that young children cannot be asked direct questions or chatted to are common, as are beliefs that they should not be seen alone or for any length of time. Nonetheless, in the context of the child's age, there are important issues that do need to be taken into account. Very young children or preschoolers do have limited communicative abilities relative to school-aged children and also to teenagers. In contrast, they are also surprisingly competent in ways not usually appreciated by researchers. The issues primarily concern the cognitive abilities of children, the validity of their statements and researchers' interpretations of their statements.

While reliability is important for specific measures, it is mainly validity that matters when verbally engaging with children and young people. The accuracy of their responses largely depends on their developmental capacities, including their ability to manage the demands of the research tasks used to pose the questions, to cope with one-to-one interviews or group interviews, and their understanding of the reason for the interview. The questioning of children and young people takes place in a variety of social contexts, such as clinics, classrooms, playgrounds, or the family home, which in themselves may have a direct effect on the validity of their response. Every effort should be made by the researcher to choose the context wisely, to understand the child's or young person's developmental and individual abilities in the design of questions and supporting materials, and to explain to the child or young person why they are there and what will happen. Researchers should present themselves in a friendly and reassuring manner and the child or young person should be allowed time to become familiar with a strange environment or new pieces of equipment or toys that are part of the research. Let us consider some kinds of questions a researcher might want to put to a child or young person.

Who? What? Where?

Very young children can identify people, objects and places either verbally or by pointing to them. They can distinguish self from others. Very young children, however, are prone to errors of classification, e.g. all male adults could be labelled 'daddy'.

Why? When? How?

Even though two-year-olds can make simple inferences about cause and effect and understand the permanence of objects, it is not until reaching school age that children are consistently able to respond to questions requiring explanations, such as 'Why?', 'When?' or 'How?'.

The past, present and future

Preschoolers are able to talk about present and past experience, but their concept of time is not fully developed. Order of recall and use of the past tense is not always easy for them. At around four years of age they are using past and future tenses but their notions of time are still associated with routines such as meals or television programmes. Their concept of time improves gradually once at school and they become able to deal with clocks and calendars.

Questions relying on memory

A related issue is the memory capacity of children. Like adults, a child's memory can be affected by other factors such as the circumstances around the event in question and associated emotional arousal. Children will not be comparable to adults until the end of the primary school years. Consequently, young children often need support in remembering, and this can be improved by using familiar toys and allowing the child to play or enact past events with the help of toys. This enables the researcher to clarify who or what the children are talking about.

Sensitive questions

The child's ability to distinguish fact from fantasy is important in questioning a child about a traumatic event, as is the researcher's ability to interpret what the child says and does. Even quite young children do not create a false picture. Three-year-olds are able to tell the difference between pretend play with materials and its real nature, and four-year-olds understand the difference between truth and lies and that telling lies is wrong.

Reporting on knowledge and beliefs

When using open questions or statements, nursery and early primary stage children tend to agree with the questioner, even if they do not know what is meant. They are capable of invention and can be distracted and literal.

Questioning adolescents

Problems can be anticipated in questioning adolescents due to overestimation and underestimation of their abilities to respond appropriately and poor attention to impact of gender and ethnicity on responses. Adolescent research does not often enough differentiate between stages of adolescence, namely early (10–14 years), mid (15–17 years) and late (18–20 years), and this can introduce intervening variables that can compromise the integrity of the research findings. For example, early adolescence is characterized by greater pubertal conflicts (Dashiff, 2001). Questioning adolescents in the real world is affected equally by all of the above issues. Research in clinics, homes and schools all present potentially high levels of distraction due to the imposition of regular routines (holidays, appointments, exams and associated increases in stress and study leave, lack of a regular private space free from intrusions, holiday periods, absences, poorly controlled classes, collaboration with professionals regarding the time allowed to work with adolescents). Obviously, it would be wise to plan to meet these eventualities in so far as it is reasonably possible. In health, social welfare and education research, youngsters may be concerned that their responses can be accessed by those who have power over them and consequently may expect to receive poorer care, support and understanding. Thus, attempts must also be made in the designing of adolescent research to provide privacy of responses.

In general, a model of good practice for questioning children and young people would entail:

- the preparation and use of clear, unambiguous instructions;
- the creative use of ability-appropriate materials, such as visual aids to memory;
- the careful choice of context;
- attention to impression management in one-to-one or group interview situations;
- skilled interviewing;
- avoidance of leading questions;
- obtaining the views of others for comparisons; and
- making it fun!

Interpretation of a child or young person's response

Problems in interpreting children's or young people's responses are related to social and cognitive factors. The fact that they are social beings, engaging with researchers and co-constructing the meanings of events, means that they are just as vulnerable to the social demands of the research situation as adults. Their self-reports are vulnerable to suggestibility and denial and are therefore influenced by the status of the interviewer as well as the context. Thus, children or young people who are interviewed in school are already in a power relation with teachers and have various rote responses in that context.

As Donaldson (1978) demonstrated, even very young children's abilities in learning tasks have been underestimated because of social presentation. For example, most children will assume their first answer is wrong if a question is repeated in a power relation. If they are interviewed at home, children and young people may be unlikely to be open about sensitive matters. For example, does the child or young person feel safe at home right now? In disclosing painful experiences, they may experience anxiety that either prevents them from speaking about it or causes them to deny it or change their minds. Fears of losing loved ones, punishment of self and others, and rejection are common. It is generally believed, however, that events that are important to the child or young person are fairly resistant to such distortion. They can respond differently to questions depending on whether or not they are asked in a one-to-one or peer group situation. There are advantages and disadvantages to each and these will depend on the individual and the issues being discussed.

Younger children tend to engage more easily if questioned in small groups or pairs. Groups are good for generating ideas, for finding key areas to follow up individually and for increasing confidence – and they can be more fun. However, gender composition can affect participation and the nature of the question is important, especially when it is more meaningful to some in the group than others (e.g. having a looked-after child or young person in a group of pupils being asked questions about family life). Some children and teenagers can dominate the group discussion. Individual interviews can be good where specific questions can be followed up in more detail and where there are any sensitive questions.

Problems of interpretation relating to cognitive factors are due to the overestimation and underestimation of the child or young person's ability based on performance. Even standardized tools can fail to take account of an individual's actual ability. All questioning of children and young people involves the use of the cognitive abilities of language, thought and memory. If the task is oral, then verbal skills are important. If the task is written, then literacy skills are important. Therefore, whether written or oral, account will need to be taken of the complexity of the language used and the demands placed on the child or young person. Chapters 8, 9 and 10 describe various designs used by a number of researchers in attempting to overcome these problems and the ethics of engagement and interpretation with children and young people in research.

Using drawings

Drawing is fun. Children of all ages tend to enjoy it and the activity is a good form of initial engagement for getting to know a child or young person. There is robust evidence, however, that drawings can be a reliable indicator of cognitive development. Spontaneous drawings of a man or woman reveal conceptual abilities in terms of which body parts are depicted and where they are located. It is also possible to learn about the child or young person's fine motor coordination. Many drawings have been researched and standardized on a developmental scale – for example, the Goodenough–Harris Drawing Test (Goodenough and Harris, 1963). Drawings are also believed to reveal the inner mind. The clues are believed to lie in the alterations of line quality, disguising of shapes and use of unusual signs or symbols. One of the easiest and most common drawing tasks is the 'draw a person, draw a tree, draw a house' task. This is shown in Figure 5.4 together with a case outline of the two children who drew the respective pictures. Child A's drawings are shown

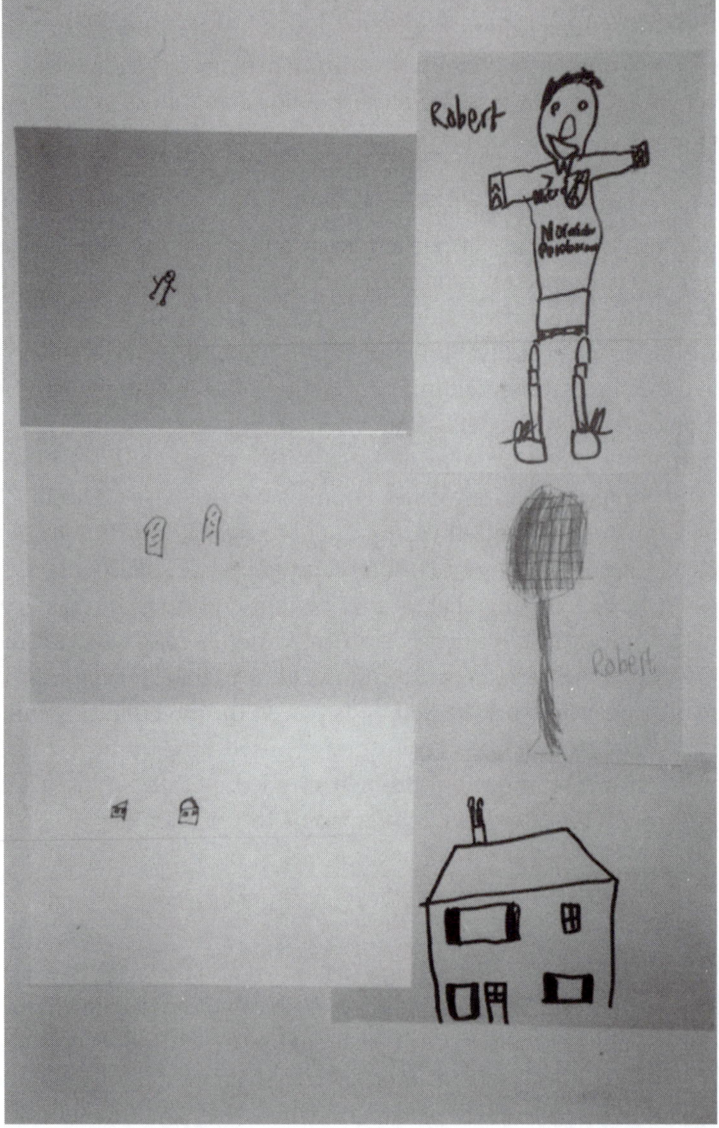

Figure 5.4 A comparison between a neglected child and a normal child on the 'Draw a person/tree/house' task

on the left. Child A is seven-years-old and has been physically abused. His parents have a history of mental ill health. He is rejected and bullied at school but do not have learning difficulties. Child B's drawings are shown on the right. Child B a happy, normal, seven-year-old. One is immediately struck by the impoverished work of child A in terms of size, detail and imagination.

There are a number of other possible indicators in drawings. Anxiety is believed to be represented through the intensity of line pressure, excessive shading, the size of the figure and rigidity of the drawing process, and abused children may include sexualized body parts or shaded-over body parts and sad or expressionless figures. Heavily scratched areas and repeatedly overworked lines across the body or torn hands may indicate physical abuse. Of course, drawings are particularly susceptible to false interpretations by the questioner and are mediated by fine motor abilities and the conceptual development of the child or young person in question. It is therefore crucial for such drawings to be used only by trained professionals and correlated with a variety of other sources of information. It is important to operate in an open, exploratory manner with young participants and their drawings (see Box 5.2 for guidelines on questioning children and young people and interpreting their answers).

BOX 5.2

Improving the validity of questioning and interpretation of answers

Improving validity: questioning

- Break complete events or issues into simple, manageable units for preschoolers who are unable to keep two concepts in mind at once. Use simple yes/no questions followed by more open-ended ones. Use familiar toys to clarify identities and demonstrate events. School-aged children can be expected to understand gradually and use more complex sentences.
- Children occasionally tell stories that parents know did not happen. In taking their capability to distinguish fact and fantasy and the possibility of denial into account, be prepared to accept an unclear conclusion.
- Ask the child if particular fears are affecting what they say.
- Take individual differences into account. Some children and young people may be learning-disabled or may prefer to reveal information slowly over longer periods of time.

Improving validity: interpretation

Verbal reports are more likely to be valid where:

- the child or young person uses age-related language;
- the account is relatively detailed for the child or young person's age;
- the child or young person displays appropriate emotional behaviour;

- younger children express emotional feelings behaviourally rather than in a detailed verbal account;
- a child or young person's report is consistent over time;
- hesitancy is evident during traumatic disclosures.

Source: Adapted from Reder, P. and Lucey, C. (1995) *Assessment of Parenting: Psychiatric and Psychological Contributions.* London: Routledge. Reproduced with permission of Taylor & Francis Group.

The child and young person's perspective and involving young researchers

This topic is developed fully in Chapter 9 but a particularly encouraging development is the realization that we can and should invite children and young people directly into the world of research by supporting them to become co-researchers or researchers themselves. This may mean recognizing the impact of their perspectives on altering our research agenda, using their strength of position and insider knowledge to enhance the validity of our interpretations by having them conduct some parts of our research, or having them do complete pieces of research by their own design. Improving children and young people's metacognitive abilities (or thinking about thinking) and the teaching of thinking skills are familiar territory now for teachers and it has also been long recognized that it is possible to teach them any subject in a meaningful way at any stage. The view expressed here is that research can and should be 'on the curriculum', and no doubt it already is, implicitly in an array of projects linked to other subjects. Although a full consideration of this development can be found in Chapter 9, it may be helpful to tease out some questions relevant to situations of partial involvement and deciding whether or not we should indeed involve children and young people as co-researchers. According to Kirby (1999), there are a number of questions we should ask ourselves in deciding whether or not it is appropriate to involve young researchers. The main questions are essential in any good practitioner research design and you should involve children and young people if you can answer as shown below:

• Is the topic worthwhile?	*Yes*
• What type of information is required (experiences, perceptions, knowledge)?	*Yes*
• Has a needs assessment identified an unmet need?	*Yes*
• Does the topic offer an evaluation of policy or service delivery and does it identify good or bad practice?	*Yes*
• How will the information be used?	*To empower the young researchers*
• Would other methods of obtaining data be more appropriate?	*No*

An appropriate decision to involve children and young people as co-researchers may bring certain benefits: for examples, less of a power issue between young researchers and young participants; better insider knowledge for obtaining and interpreting data; and positive role modelling for peers. On the other hand, a lack of maturity may mean discomfort with sensitive issues and a lack of confidence in negotiating with agencies; less monitoring of well-known confounders such as biased replies, social desirability; and low or poor responses to questionnaires and in interviews.

PUTTING RESEARCH INTO PRACTICE 5.1 – THE 'I'VE GOT A HUNCH' EXERCISE

This practical is to demonstrate further that you already possess a basic aptitude for posing research questions and hypotheses and designing approaches.

You may do the practical alone or your tutor will allocate you into relevant groups/pairs sharing an interest (e.g. education, health/nursing, social work). In these groups, discuss the following series of research 'hunches' in terms of:

- the type of study (qualitative, exploratory, experimental and so on);
- defining the problem to be researched;
- the importance of the question and practical applications of the answers;
- possible research questions or hypotheses;
- who the participants should be and their characteristics;
- possible assessments, materials and equipment;
- problems anticipated in doing the research;
- whether there is a researcher role for the children and young people involved.

Research hunches

- You are curious about the self-esteem of poor readers.
- You are concerned about the body image of children receiving surgery.
- You wonder how the birth of a new baby affects the behaviour of preschoolers.
- You are interested in the experiences of children who are bullies.
- You wonder how children feel about their parents' divorce and subsequent contact arrangements.
- You are interested in the child-raising practices of different cultures within your own country.
- You wonder how teenagers who are in the care of the authority feel about their experiences of being looked after.
- You are concerned about the number of adolescents in the criminal justice system who have unidentified literacy difficulties.
- You think that teenage girls getting pregnant while still at school lack attachment security to their own mothers.

References

Dashiff, C. (2001) 'Methodological issues in nursing research: data collection with adolescents', *Journal of Advanced Nursing*, 33 (3): 343–9.

Donaldson, M. (1978) *Children's Minds*. London: Fontana.

Goodenough, F.L. and Harris, D.B. (1963) *Goodenough–Harris Drawing Test*. San Antonio, TX: PsychCorp/Harcourt Assessment.

Hill, M., Laybourn, A. and Borland, M. (1996) 'Engaging with primary-aged children about their emotions and well-being: methodological considerations', *Children and Society*, 10: 129–44.

Howlin, P., Baron-Cohen, S. and Hadwin, J. (2008) *Teaching Children with Autism to Mind-Read: a Workbook*, 2nd edn. Hoboken, NJ: Wiley.

Kirby, P. (1999) *Listening to Young Children: the Mosaic Approach*. London: Save the Children.

Reder, P. and Lucey, C. (1995) *Assessment of Parenting: Psychiatric and Psychological Contributions*. London: Routledge.

Robertson, J. and Robertson, J. (1971) 'Young children in brief separation: a fresh look psychoanalytic study of the child', 26: 264–315.

Schaffer, H.R. (1998) *Making Decisions about Children: Psychological Questions and Answers*, 2nd edn. Oxford: Blackwell.

Recommended reading for further study

Robson, C. (2011) *Real World Research. A Resource for Social Scientists and Practitioner-Researchers. Chapters 3 and 4*. Oxford: Blackwell.

SIX

Quantitative research with children and young people: key concepts

The aims of this chapter are:

- to provide an overview of key concepts in quantitative research;
- to introduce common statistical procedures for data analysis;
- to discuss the key issues in interpreting test scores;
- to outline the main methods used in quantitative research designs.

Two primary school teachers in the same school both have a class of children at the same stage. One says: 'I have a terrible class this year. They have very negative attitudes to school and to their work, they are niggling one another constantly in the classroom and they are lazy and unmotivated.' The other teacher says: 'Mine are the very opposite – they are a great class, really cooperative, hard-working and with positive attitudes.' To see how valid their feelings are, they decide to put it to the test, to plan for some positive changes and to see if the changes have resulted in improvements. How would they go about it?

A social worker says: 'Far more of my caseload is now made up of really difficult child protection cases and emergency referrals. Three or four years ago I had a far wider spread, with a lot of cases that weren't so serious.' They decide to do some research on referrals of children and young people to their department to see if referral patterns are changing, so that working practices can be adapted to meet the changed demands. How would they set about this exercise?

A nurse in a children's hospital says: 'I think Ward A is a better place to be than Ward B. The children there seem to be better adjusted and to make faster progress. I think it's because Ward A is a lot brighter – it faces the sun most of the day.' A colleague replies: 'Is it not just that Ward B tends to have the more serious cases who have to be in for longer?' A third colleague interjects: 'But you have to remember that the main catchment area for Ward A is the posh houses up at Fairways[1], but for Ward B it is the Blackview[1] housing scheme where you get a lot of problems.' For their quality improvement plan of making the wards a better place to be they decide to start by investigating these hypotheses. How do they tackle this?

[1]Note: these are fictional names.

Questions of this kind can be reduplicated in every setting where people work with children and young people. They are part and parcel of the interest practitioners have in finding out more about what is really happening on their 'patch', and of the requirements everyone faces in improving the quality of services and provision. They are all essentially *quantitative research* issues. Ultimately, they are questions that are best answered with reference to *quantities* or *numbers*. They refer constantly to comparisons of amounts and levels, to concepts of 'more' and 'less'. They call for traditional research approaches, such as experimental methods, hypothesis testing and assessment of probability.

Quantitative research methods are a veritable 'snake pit' to the inexperienced and uninitiated (and often to experienced researchers as well!). This chapter, together with Chapter 7 on data collection, cannot attempt to be a manual of such methods, but what both chapters can do is to point to the key questions that must be asked, particularly in relation to work with children and young people, to outline some of the most useful strategies for dealing with these questions and to provide practical examples and illustrations. This chapter offers an overview of the quantitative approach, introduces the subject of data analysis and covers the important area of understanding and interpreting test scores. At the end of this chapter, some key texts are recommended as further reading.

For those who wish to carry out quantitative research the best advice is to *get advice*. It is best from the beginning of a project to have some guidance from someone who is steeped in the quantitative approach, and who can comment on technical issues such as your proposed sample size and your methods of data collection and analysis. This does not just apply to novice researchers. It is very common for experienced researchers in university departments to go and check with someone about how they intend to handle their data – usually the person who lies in bed reading about multivariate statistical analysis for pleasure (there's one in every department!). For those who do not have ready access to academic departments there are similar sources of advice in many of the settings where people work with children and young people. For example, all health boards have statisticians or researchers whose job includes tasks like advising the ethics committee on research proposals, dealing with service audits and preparing annual statistical reports. Likewise, local authority departments, such as social services, education or the chief executive's office, have people who compile results of national testing of children or analyses of population changes. These personnel are generally able to advise employees on appropriate methods.

Quantitative methods: an overview of key concepts

The three examples given at the beginning of this chapter cannot be answered without reference to a number of key concepts that are fundamental to the quantitative approach. These are:

- probability and significance;
- levels of measurement;
- sampling methods;
- types of research design and the core statistical concepts of measures of central tendency;
- the standard deviation;
- the percentile;
- the effect size; and
- the normal distribution.

These will be familiar concepts to those who already have research experience.

Probability and significance

Any hypothesis we generate about the difference between two groups of children or young people, or the comparative effectiveness of two different methods of intervention, will not be proved but rather supported or rejected at a certain level of probability. We want to avoid making either a *Type I error* – believing there is a difference when there actually is not – or a *Type II error* – failing to spot a difference when there actually is one. The accepted criterion is to go for at least a 95% level of confidence before deciding that there is a difference. This still leaves a 5% margin of probable error in our conclusion. This 5% (five in 100, or 0.05) probability of error is expressed as p, in this case, $p = 0.05$, or the '5% significance level'. Similarly, we would be more confident with a probability of error of less than 1% (one in 100, or 0.01), or less than 0.1% (one in 1000 or 0.001). These values would be expressed respectively as $p < 0.01$, or the '1% significance level', and $p < 0.001$, or the '0.1% significance level'. These three levels of significance – 5%,

1% and 0.1% – are the ones most commonly used in research publications, and as a form of shorthand they are often indicated by just putting one, two or three asterisks beside figures shown in results tables. For example, 16.54** would indicate that this score was significant at the 1% level.

Levels of measurement

Before we can decide how to test the significance of our findings, we need to know the *level of measurement* that applies to our data. This term tells us the relationship between what is being measured and the numbers used on any scale to record our measurements. Four of these levels are used: *nominal, ordinal, interval* and *ratio*. The *nominal* level refers to data where the numbers used to describe them do not have any numerical meaning but are simply codes for categories. For example, we might investigate how children and young people come to school and code them as number 1 for those who walk, 2 for those who come by car, 3 for those who cycle, 4 for those who come on the school bus and so on. These codes have no numerical relationship to one another. They are just categories, and represent nominal data.

Ordinal data tell us that the numbers used are related, but only at the level of the order in which they occurred. If 10 children sit a test or run a race they can be placed in rank order with the numbers 1–10, telling us who came first, second, tenth. This is a higher and more informative level of data than nominal, but it still gives limited information about how the numbers 1–10 are related to one another. We know that fifth was better or faster than seventh, and that seventh was better than tenth. All children might have scored high or run fast, or perhaps none of them did. The child who was second might have performed twice as well as the child who was third, while the child who was third might have been only a tiny fraction ahead of the fourth child. In other words, ordinal data tell us only about the rank order, but not about the magnitude of the differences between one rank and another.

Interval data are much more informative for researchers, and many statistical tests rely on having this level of data. An interval scale is one that is continuous, that has an arbitrary zero point and that has equal intervals on the scale to represent equal quantities of what is being measured. For example, in physical measurements, a Fahrenheit or Celsius temperature scale is an interval scale. It does not have a true zero, and therefore a reading of 50 degrees is not 'twice as much' as one of 25. Nevertheless, the intervals are equal. A rise in the reading from 8 to 9 degrees is the same interval as a rise from 78 to 79. Many test scores we encounter in working with children and young people, such as IQ tests, are based on interval scales. The test does not have a true zero, so it would be meaningless to say that an IQ of 140 is 'twice' an IQ of 70, but it is nevertheless constructed with a view to having equal intervals all the way along the scale.

Ratio data arise from interval scales with an absolute zero. To test how well preschool children can identify colours we might flash a range of colours on to a computer screen and test how quickly the right colour is selected when its name is given. This test of reaction time would provide ratio data. If we measure the response in seconds, a speed of two seconds would be twice as fast as 4 seconds, and 20 seconds would be twice as slow as 10 seconds.

Sampling methods

Having robust data to analyse using statistical tests does not depend only on the level of measurement but also on the nature of our sample. An important question is: 'How many?' If we only have a handful of participants in our sample it is unlikely that we will get very far with quantitative analysis unless, for example, we are looking at many measures taken for each child at several stages over a period of time. Small numbers are too prone to being unrepresentative and an extreme score will distort the data because it has a bigger proportional impact than it would in a large sample. So, in general it is a good idea when using quantitative methods to aim for including a good number of participants in our sample, if this is feasible. Even with experimental research designs it is possible to work with small samples. However, very small samples in quantitative research are subject to fairly brutal statistics, and large differences between groups tend to be required to show significant results. It is helpful to seek advice beforehand about what size of sample will be needed for the type of study you are planning.

In *random sampling* everyone in the population being studied has an equal chance of being selected. This could be done by having a computer generate random numbers, by using the random number tables found in many statistics books or, if the numbers in the population are relatively small – like all the children in a nursery – by putting their names in a hat. Much the same result can be achieved by taking a *systematic sample*, where every '*n*th' child in a list is selected, and where *n* is just any suitable number. For example, if you want to study a teenage club with 120 members, you could get a sample of 30 by taking every fourth name on the list. However, these methods might still fail to give an appropriate representation of different groups within your population, such as the number of males and females. This can be tackled by using *stratified sampling*, in which there is random selection of the right numbers from each group. This could either be *proportionate*, if you want a group with the same proportion of males to females as there is in the entire club, or *disproportionate*, if you perhaps want to study male/female differences by having two equal groups, no matter how many of each there are in the club.

Often researchers do not get the opportunity to be quite as representative as this, and they may therefore use other forms of sampling. If you are interested in studying the characteristics of young people who smoke you might opt for a *cluster sample* made up of all the smokers in a particular school or year group, on the assumption that they are likely to be fairly typical of smokers in general. Very frequently the participants in your sample may simply be an *opportunity sample*. In other words, you happen to be working with a group of young people and you ask each of them: 'Would you like to take part in a research project?'. A final popular method is *snowball sampling* in which, having interviewed your first participant you say: 'Have you any friends who might like to take part in this research?' The issue with these methods is to ensure that the sample turns out to be sufficiently representative. What if the smokers in your cluster sample or opportunity sample all come from a school that is in a very poor or very wealthy area? It may be that this is an important factor affecting the issue being studied. Or what if you are studying children's interests and your snowball sample ends up comprising the entire population of the school chess club? The aim has to be to try for a sample that is large enough to make the study viable and representative enough to reduce bias.

Types of research design

In quantitative research, *experimental* designs are popular – i.e. designs that manipulate one *variable* to see what effect it has on another. A variable is any factor that can change or vary. For example, if we want to test whether children's behaviour improves when we make more positive statements to them, we can manipulate the variable of 'number of positive statements' to see if it affects the outcome 'better behaviour'. The 'purest' form of experimental design is the *randomized controlled trial* (RCT), which requires a *control group* and one or more *experimental groups*. The control group is treated exactly the same as before, while the experimental group receives whatever form the manipulation of the variable takes, such as an intervention, treatment or change in approach. In the above example the experimental group would receive a larger number of positive statements than previously, while the controls would be just as before. For it to be an RCT, participants would need to be allocated to the two groups randomly. This can be done in simple ways in real-world child settings. For example, if you are a group worker and have a new programme to build citizenship skills in young people referred for committing offences, you might select 20 possible cases from which you will choose an experimental group of 10. You can then match them in pairs on important characteristics, such as sex, age and type of offences committed. Then you can put their names in envelopes and get a colleague who is not involved in the study to select one envelope from each pair to make up the experimental group.

However, it is often the case that the luxury of being able to make a random selection of participants for different groups is not available to us. If you are a practitioner in common child contexts like education, health care, social services or a voluntary organization, you may find a variety of practical or ethical reasons to stop you randomly selecting the children and young people who are to experience or not experience your new practice. In these cases a *quasi-experimental design* can be used. This differs from an RCT in that the allocation to the groups is not random. Nevertheless, every possible step is taken to ensure that the groups are well matched. In one of the five child research studies covered by MacKay (2006) the plan was to see whether secondary school children with reading difficulties would make better progress using a special teaching method. The learning support staff involved did not have the freedom of randomly assigning the referred pupils to different groups because of timetabling and other constraints. Instead, 12 pupils assigned to the group receiving the special method were matched closely with 12 pupils assigned to receive the normal package of learning support. The matching involved both finding pupils with comparable reading ages at the start of the project and taking account of the views of teaching staff about the reading abilities of the two groups.

For many people who are doing research with children and young people neither an RCT nor a quasi-experimental design will be possible, since it may not be feasible to have a control group at all, whether randomly allocated or otherwise. For example, there may be access to the study of only one group of children and young people, and all of them may require having the same treatment or approach. Suppose, for instance, that you are a health visitor and you want to evaluate the effect of a new intervention or an enhanced level of service delivery on the most vulnerable children on your caseload. Ethical considerations may prevent you from dividing your caseload into those who get the new treatment and those who are left without it, as it will tend to be assumed that it is going to be beneficial and that everyone should have access to it. You can still carry out quantitative research by doing an *outcome evaluation*. This is based on the idea of *gain scores*: you assess the children on a range of relevant factors before they receive the new treatment, and you assess them again afterwards, perhaps at various stages.

Outcome evaluations of this kind are not as robust research designs as experimental and quasi-experimental ones. They raise some obvious questions. Would the children have shown these improvements anyway? Have the changes come about because of the developmental maturity they have experienced through the duration of the pre/post period? Without a control group it is hard to answer questions like these. Nevertheless, outcome studies are very popular and frequently they are the only method available. There are also ways of getting good results from them. First, the general rule is: the larger the gain, the shorter the time and the more direct the measure, the more likely it is to be the effect of the intervention. Children who, in a short period, have shown a sudden increase in their scores on the very factors you are trying to change make a good argument for the case that your intervention was successful. Second, if you are using *standardized measures*, examples of which are described later, you can look at changes in standard scores using basic statistics like the *effect size*, also described later in the chapter. These can help to tell whether the changes that have been observed were to be expected.

One advantage of using an outcome evaluation is that you can apply it to a *single-case design*. There are many child practitioners who may not have access to large or even small groups of children or young people, but who have the opportunity to work intensively with an individual. This includes various counsellors, therapists and support workers. Even though only one individual is being studied, it is still possible to use traditional quantitative methods by looking at changes in a range of pre/post scores. An example of a single-case design studying the effects of a cognitive behaviour therapy programme on a boy with Asperger's syndrome (Greig and MacKay, 2005) is shown in Box 6.1.

BOX 6.1

Using quantitative measures in a single-case design

Greig and MacKay (2005) designed an innovative application, The *Homunculi,* for using cognitive behaviour therapy with young people with Asperger's syndrome, and piloted it with a 13-year-old boy. The programme was designed primarily to address mood disorders, such as depression, but also to address other features such as social impairments. The boy was assessed on a range of standardized measures before and after the intervention, allowing a comparison of pre/post scores for evaluating the effects of the programme.

Emotional state outcomes (Briere's Trauma Symptom Checklist for Children)

	Pre	Post	Mean	Effect size
Anxiety	19	5	6	3.7
Depression	21	6	7	3.8
Anger	15	10	9	1.0
Stress	25	8	8	3.2

Social competence outcomes (Spence's Social Skills Questionnaires)

	Pre	Post	Mean	Effect size
Parent report	0	5	15	1.60
Pupil report	0	4	16	1.26

Source: Greig, A. and MacKay, T. (2005) 'Asperger's syndrome and cognitive behaviour therapy: new applications for educational psychologists', *Educational and Child Psychology*, 22 (4): 4–15.

All of the above research designs involve the deliberate manipulation of one variable, such as the number of positive statements made (the *independent variable*), to bring about change in another variable, such as behaviour (the *dependent variable*). Some quantitative designs do not involve the attempt to change anything but instead look at how groups differ from or relate to each other. There is no generally agreed name for these designs, but they are often called *correlational studies*. They investigate whether there is a relationship between different variables. For example, we may study whether young people who do well in school have higher levels of motivation than those who do not. Discovering that this is the case tells us nothing about whether one variable causes the other one. All we can comment on is the extent to which these variables are correlated.

Core statistical concepts

Those who are not already experienced researchers are less likely to be familiar with a few core statistical concepts that are introduced here. All of these are essential to the interpretation of the test scores of children and young people, a subject that is covered separately later in this chapter.

Measures of central tendency

The first concept is *measures of central tendency*. When we see a range of scores children or young people have achieved on a test we are interested to know what would be a typical or average score for the group. This will tell us something both about the group and also about any individual's score – is it high or low? The most widely used and certainly the most useful measure of central tendency is the *mean (M)* or average score. This is found by adding all the scores together and dividing them by the number tested. The advantage of the mean is that it is the most sensitive and accurate measure of central tendency, it is the basis of the most powerful statistical tests for analysing data and it is easy to work out on a calculator. It also has one main disadvantage. It can easily be distorted by extreme or 'rogue' scores that are unrepresentative. For example, suppose we are interested in finding out how long seven children take to work out a simple puzzle. If the number of seconds they take are 4, 5, 7, 10, 10, 11 and 135 then the mean will tell us nothing of value about the group. It would be 26 seconds but that would not in any way be a typical score, as there is one rogue score or 'outlier' that distorts the whole picture.

The two other measures of central tendency will not be distorted in this way. The *median* is the middle value in the range of scores. In the above example it would be 10 seconds, a more representative score for the group. However, for most purposes, the median is less useful than the mean, as it does not take account of any of the other values in the data set. It is an appropriate measure for data at ordinal level – i.e. data that can be ranked but are not at interval level.

The *mode* is the most common score in a data set – the one that occurs most frequently. In the example above the mode would be 10. As such it can be useful in giving a very typical picture, and it is not distorted by extreme values. It can also make more sense than the mean if we want to refer to real situations. The mean number of children in a family in some countries may be 2.4, but it is certainly not typical! However, it is not a very useful measure if there is a small number of scores, and it can be affected by even one change in a score. For example, if the first two values in the above puzzle test were both 4 seconds then there would be two modes, 4 and 10, which would not tell us very much. Like the median, the mode does not make use of the other scores in the data set, but if data are at nominal level then only the mode can be used. If most of the children and young people referred to earlier walk to school, and the minority come by car or by other means, then the modal value is the score given to the group who walk.

The standard deviation

Knowing the mean or some other measure of central tendency allows us to put an individual score in context as being 'higher' or 'lower' than the average for the group, but it still leaves important gaps in our understanding of what a score really means. If we measure the body temperature of 100 children and young people, we will probably find a mean of approximately 37°C, with somewhat more than two-thirds of them in the range 36.5–37.5°C. If we found one with a temperature at 33 and another at 40 we would probably be going for a hot-water bottle and ice pack respectively (at the very least!) and thinking of calling a doctor. In contrast, if we measured how long these 100 children and young people could stand on one foot without falling over, we might again find a mean of 37 (in this case, seconds) but the range of scores covering two-thirds of them might extend from 6 seconds to over 1 minute. Therefore, even though the mean is the same at 37, a score of 6 could mean either that the subject is perfectly normal or that the subject is dead, depending on what is being measured.

It is here that measures of how scores are distributed around the mean are crucial, and neglect of these measures can lead to fatal miscalculations about the meaning of data. For example, it is meaningless to say that an 11-year-old child is doing badly with a reading age of 10 years. If almost every child at exactly age 11 is scoring between 10 years 9 months and 11 years 3 months, then a score of 10 years is not looking good. However, if about two-thirds of children at age 11 have a reading age somewhere between 9 and a half and 12 and a half (and this, in fact, is the case with reading scores), then a score of

10 years is a totally normal one. The best measure for interpreting what scores mean is the *standard deviation* (SD).

It is not within the scope of this book to discuss the underlying statistical rationale for these measures or the formulas for calculating them, all of which is fully covered in basic texts, such as the recommended books by Coolican (2009) and Salkind (2011). It is important, however, to know what measures like the SD signify. Where scores are normally distributed (that is, where they are not *skewed* or distorted by having a higher number of lower or higher values), the SD tells us how many of our scores fall in a given range. Most usefully, it tells us that around two-thirds of scores will be within one SD of the mean. Specifically, it is expected that:

- 68% of cases will fall within one SD of the mean (34.13% on either side);
- 95% of cases will fall within two SDs of the mean (47.72% on either side);
- 97% of cases will fall within three SDs of the mean (49.87% on either side).

For example, an IQ test is usually constructed in a standard way to give a mean of 100 and a SD of 15. Therefore, around two-thirds of the population will have scores between 85 and 115, but only 5% altogether will have scores that are either below 70 or above 130. In the case of body temperature the SD is very low, at around 0.4°C, so the scale does not have to rise very much before we decide that someone has a 'temperature', i.e. the score is sufficiently far away from the mean to suggest that it is abnormal. This is very important when interpreting test scores and is covered in more detail later.

The percentile

Another extremely useful measure is the *percentile*, or *percentile rank*. It tells us how many of our children and young people score at or below a particular point in a scale. A score at the 10th percentile means that only 10% of our population would have a score at this level or lower. At the other end, a score at the 90th percentile means that 90% would have a score at this level or lower. In other words, the 90th percentile takes us into the highest 10% of scores.

The effect size

If our research involves carrying out any intervention to bring about change, then we are ultimately interested in the question: 'Has there been an effect?' As noted previously in this chapter, in quantitative research we approach this question on the basis of probability and significance, by asking how likely it is that a change was due to our intervention and not just to chance variation. However, we may at times find that there has been an effect that we can demonstrate at the traditional 5% level of significance, but that the effect is nevertheless not important. Significance levels tell us that there is a statistical difference in the scores, but they do not tell us the size of the difference. We are therefore left with the question asked by all practitioners: 'Did our project bring about a difference that was meaningful and worthwhile?' We are not just asking 'could we measure a difference' but rather did it '*make a difference?*'. For example, it is possible with large samples to find that a very small change is statistically significant, but not really very important.

It is here that the idea of the *effect size* (EF) is invaluable. It is a standard measure of the magnitude of change. Several different measures of EF have been proposed but the most common is the amount of change measured in SDs. For example, if you carried out a programme to raise children's test scores on a test with a mean of 100 and a SD of 10, and the change in scores was a rise of five points, the effect size would be 0.5 – that is, half of one SD. If you raised it by 10 points it would be 1.0. The effect sizes given in Box 6.1 are an example of how one young person's scores changed in terms of the SDs published for the tests shown. We owe this measure of effect size to Cohen (1988), who has given helpful guidance on how to interpret the magnitude of change: 0.2 = small, 0.5 = medium and 0.8 = large.

The normal distribution

If we have scores for a large number of children or young people on almost any test or measure, whether it is height, weight, intelligence, reading ability, school attendance or time spent watching television each day, we will be able to show these scores graphically. In many cases, including all of the examples cited, the resulting graph will approximate to the *normal distribution curve,* which is bell-shaped. This curve is symmetrical, and the mean, median and mode fall in the central line. Figure 6.1 shows the normal distribution curve marked off in SDs, percentiles and other scores that are mentioned in the section on interpreting test scores.

Analysing the data

When you collect raw data in a quantitative study they need to be analysed using standard statistical procedures. As this book is not a statistical manual it does not attempt to cover the methodology required for data analysis. There are many basic texts dealing with this subject, such as the recommended book by Salkind (2011) and the study guide that accompanies it. While it is important to understand the statistical theory required for this task (one of the good reasons for asking advice from experts), it is no longer necessary for researchers to be able to

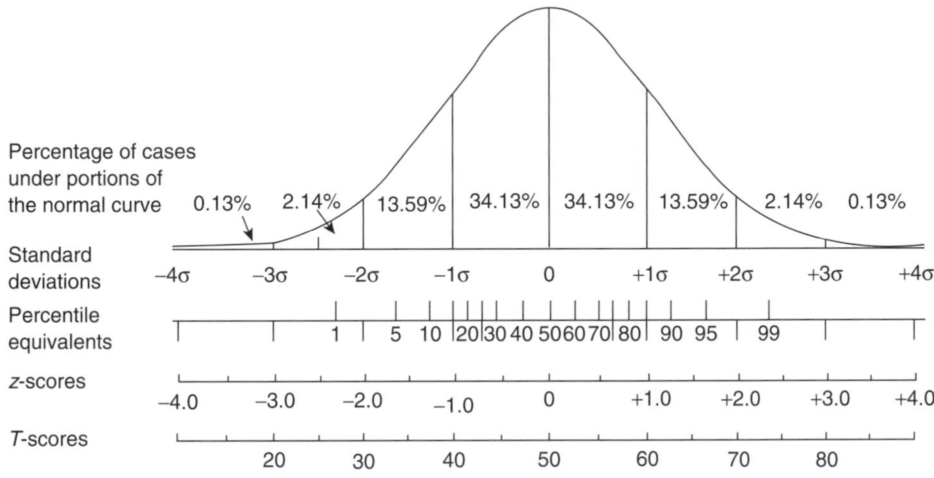

Figure 6.1 The normal distribution curve

work out the formulas and calculations themselves, as these are all now done for us by statistical software, such as IBM SPSS Statistics (www-01.ibm.com/software/analytics/spss/products/statistics/). For people who do not have access to SPSS, Microsoft® Excel®, a component of Microsoft® Office®, has a data analysis facility. (If the Analysis ToolPak is missing, instructions on how to load it can be found by clicking on the Help icon and typing 'data analysis' in the search box, then follow the instructions provided.) This facility will generate random numbers, do correlations and perform common statistical tests like student's *t*-tests and analysis of variance. There are also formulas in Excel for calculating means and SDs and for non-parametric tests like the chi-square test.

By way of introduction, three types of statistical procedure are referred to here. They provide a starting point for analysing data from many different kinds of research project, but again they should be supported by advice for those who are not experienced in statistical procedures. These are correlation, the student's *t*-test and the chi-square test.

Correlation

In everyday language when we say that two things 'correlate' we mean that they 'go together' and are related in a systematic way. If you have been following crime reports in the newspapers in which young children are involved while also taking note of the truancy rate at the school in which you work, you may notice a correlation between these two observations. Perhaps, as the truancy rate rises, so also do the number of reported crimes committed locally by children. This would be a positive correlation. Conversely, you may observe that as the truancy

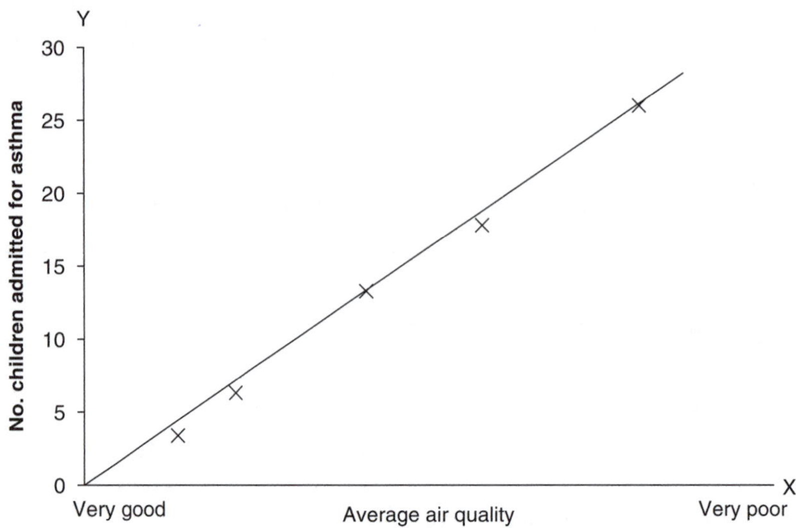

Figure 6.2 Hypothetical correlation between air quality and accident and emergency hospital admissions of child asthma sufferers

rate increases, the crime rate decreases. This would be a negative correlation. Of course it could easily be that there is no correlation, in that sometimes truancy and crime go together and sometimes they do not.

The relationship can be illustrated as in Figure 6.2. In this way the direct linear relationship between two observations can be seen. If there were a perfect correlation between them it would be possible to draw a perfect straight line across the graph.

The symbol for a correlation is *r*. It is measured on a scale of 1, with 1 being a perfect positive correlation, 0 no correlation and -1 a perfect negative correlation. Figure 6.3 shows various degrees of correlation and their *r* coefficient or score.

Correlation is worth mentioning here because of its usefulness in analysing observational data and in establishing the reliability or validity of observational schemes and codes (see also Chapter 5). It tests whether a systematic relationship exists between two or more variables. What can a correlation score or coefficient tell us and what can it not tell us? First, because there is likely to be a number of factors covarying we cannot say that X causes Y or Y causes X. A positive correlation between truancy rates and child crime in a particular town cannot be expressed as 'truancy *causes* crime'. Similarly, a positive correlation between children watching violent television and aggressive behaviour cannot be expressed as 'watching violent television *causes* children to behave aggressively', because it may also be said that 'aggressive children prefer violent television'.

The X–Y relationship may also be related in a systematic way to a third, unobserved variable: a positive correlation between attainment and head size in primary

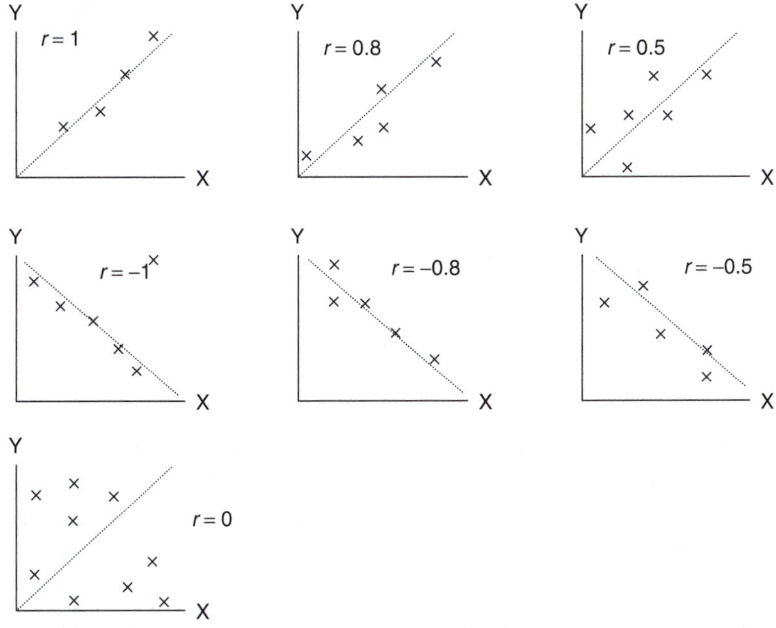

Figure 6.3 Hypothetical correlations and their r coefficient or score

school children is likely to be *confounded* by age. Finally, variables can be systematically related, such as the relationship between memory and age, but not show up as being related using linear correlation. This is because the data are *curvilinear,* i.e. they form a curve rather than a straight line, since many aspects of memory increase with age in childhood but decrease again later in life.

Some correlational studies attempt to improve internal validity by looking at patterns of correlation in longitudinal designs. The underlying assumption is that if one variable causes another, the first (say witnessing parental conflict) should be more strongly related to the second (say aggression) later in time than when the aggression was measured in the first place. In a sense, it is saying that causes should take some time to produce their effects. However, as correlation is only a method of agreement, it can only enhance the possibility of an explanation. Figure 6.4 shows an imaginary longitudinal (cross-lagged) correlation study. The important data are on the diagonals.

The student's *t*-test

The student's *t*-test (often abbreviated to *t*-test) is one of the most straightforward ways of comparing the results from two groups to see if they differ. We could take the example of the preschool children mentioned earlier whose reaction time in

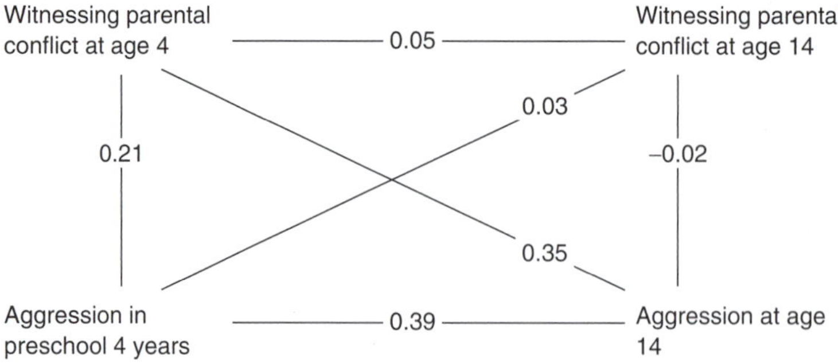

Figure 6.4 Hypothetical cross-lagged correlation data

identifying colours was measured. We might set up a programme in which an experimental group had a special programme to teach them colour recognition, while a control group did not receive the programme. Both groups would be tested pre/post. The scores could then be analysed using a '*t*-test for unrelated data'. In this case the scores of the two groups are independent or unrelated. Alternatively, we could test all the children first, and then give all of them the programme and test them again. This would call for a '*t*-test for related data', because the two data sets would be made up of related pairs of scores.

The *t*-test can be performed in Excel® using the '*t*-test: Paired Two Sample for Means' option under the data analysis tools for related data, or the 't-test: Two Sample' for unrelated data. The latter gives a choice of two tests, one 'Assuming Equal Variances' and the other 'Assuming Unequal Variances'. It is this choice that points us in the direction of the requirements that our data must fulfil for the test to be appropriate, so we must ask: 'What are the data assumptions for *t*-tests?'

The *t*-test, in common with the other most powerful statistical tests, assumes that the samples have been drawn from a normally distributed population. A simple check on the scores will indicate whether there are obvious quirks in them, such as being very much skewed towards high or low scores. For example, if a test is too hard then too many of our participants will score very low or zero (a *floor effect*), whereas if it is too easy too many of them will have the top score (a *ceiling effect*) and this will distort the distribution. Also, the data should be at interval level or above. Finally, in the unrelated *t*-test, if the sample size of the two groups is very different, the *variances* of the two sets of scores must not be significantly different. Variance is a measure of how much the scores vary – how widely they are dispersed (technically, it is the square of the SD).

It is these technicalities that highlight the need for advice or sound statistical knowledge. However, the *t*-test is very 'robust'. This means that it is very forgiving, and the assumptions can be violated to quite a substantial degree while still getting quite accurate outcomes.

The chi-square test

No matter how robust the powerful analysis tools like the *t*-test may be, often the data collected by practitioners doing research with children and young people will not meet the required assumptions. Many useful data sets produce data at nominal level, the lowest level of measurement. For example, we might want to investigate the views of young people on whether pupils should be required to wear a school uniform, on whether they want to go to university or on whether they believe the voting age should be reduced to 16. For a simple test of whether the numbers vary from what we would predict if the choices were random we can use the *chi-square test* (χ^2). This is based on comparing the observed frequencies of any choice with the expected frequencies.

In the example of the school uniform, if 20 out of 50 pupils are for it and 30 against, these are the observed frequencies. The expected frequencies, based on random choices, would be 25 for and 25 against. This would make a table with four *cells* as follows:

	For school uniform	**Against school uniform**
Observed frequency	20	30
Expected frequency	25	25

A more common example is when we are comparing the views of two different groups. Thus, we could ask the same questions of young people of high versus low socio-economic status (SES) and see if the responses differ. This is referred to as a *2 × 2 chi-square test*, and the table might now look like this:

	High SES (Observed)	**Low SES (Observed)**
For school uniform	15	5
Against school uniform	10	20
	High SES (Expected)	**Low SES (Expected)**
For school uniform	10	10
Against school uniform	15	15

In the SES example there are 25 young people in the high and 25 in the low SES group. Since a total of 20 were in favour of wearing a school uniform, we would expect that these would randomly have had equal representation from each group, that is, 10 in each. Since 30 were against wearing a school uniform, we would randomly have expected 15 in each group.

Although we are not concerned here with either the formula or the rationale for a test like this, it is relatively easy to find the results in Excel® by putting in the chi-square formula. This can be found by typing in 'chi-square' in the Help menu and selecting the CHITEST option, where there is a worked example. If the formula is entered correctly, you will see that that the figures in the first table are not significant ($p = 0.157$), but when the data are broken down by SES more high-SES young people in the hypothetical example want to wear a school uniform than low-SES young people ($p = 0.004$, or we would more probably just say $p < 0.01$).

Despite its appeal as a very flexible test that can use a nominal level of data and that is simple and effective, the chi-square test has some important limitations. It can only be used with frequencies (actual raw numbers in each category), and not with percentages, means, ratios or proportions. Also, it is not appropriate when there are very low frequencies in some of the categories. The general rule of thumb is that the numbers should not fall below five in more than 20% of the cells. So, if it is a simple chi-square with four cells, as in the first of the above examples, the lowest cell should have at least five in it.

There are, of course, many more sophisticated procedures for analysis of quantitative data, and the general rule is that it is best to use, or to be advised in the use of, the most powerful test that your data set will justify.

Understanding children's and young people's test scores

The above overview of quantitative concepts provides the essential basis for understanding and interpreting test scores. Many people who are doing research with children and young people gather background information that includes the results of standardized tests, such as tests of intelligence or educational attainments. There may also be tests that the researcher wishes to carry out with children and young people to obtain certain information directly. Test construction is based on a number of key principles and these apply to every type of test that gives some kind of score or quotient, whether it is of intelligence, personality, anxiety, depression, aptitude, attainment or height and weight. Standardized testing is on the whole a specialist area, and many of the tests are only available from the publishers to professionals who have recognized qualifications or experience in the use of the type of test in question. Nevertheless, the results of many of these tests will be available to a wide range of other practitioners, including people who are conducting research, so it is important to understand what they mean.

Understanding test scores can most easily be illustrated with reference to intelligence tests. These tests in general produce scores with which most people are familiar, as the concept of the IQ is well established in the public domain. Because they have often been misused, intelligence tests have generated considerable controversy. They also provide rather limited information on most of the population, except where scores are more extreme, such as very low test scores. At the same time they can provide useful background data for people doing research with groups of children and young people in cases where general ability might be a variable that affects the research outcomes. For instance, MacKay (1999) screened children for intelligence before selecting them for three groups of eight in an RCT investigating attitudes to reading. The test used was one of the two tests of ability illustrated in Box 6.2, Raven's Coloured Progressive Matrices. Children with extreme scores were excluded since the purpose was to study children of ordinary intelligence who were experiencing reading failure, rather than those where the difficulty might have related directly to a factor associated with intelligence, such as a general learning disability.

The IQ, as with similar standard scores, is based on the idea that raw score measures do not give as meaningful information about ability. For example, a very bright child aged four and a young person aged 15 with a severe learning disability might both have a 'mental age' of six years and therefore achieve similar raw scores on a test. While this gives a description of current performance it does not give an accurate picture of ability. This is done by finding the spread of scores in the population at every age range and converting these into a standard score that can be interpreted the same way for any age. As noted earlier, in the case of intelligence this standard score usually has a mean of 100 and a SD of 15.

It is these standard scores that allow us to interpret what an individual score means. This may be done easily by looking back to Figure 6.1 and relating it to the information given about the two tests that are illustrated in Box 6.2. A score of 70 (on tests with $M = 100$ and SD = 15) falls two SDs below the mean, and is between the second and third percentile. Sometimes you will see this expressed as a *z score* of -2.0 (a *z* score is simply the number of SDs above or below the mean). A few tests, including some extensively used ones like the British Ability Scales, use *T scores*, so it is useful to have a reference point for this scale also. You will see from Figure 6.1 that a T score is one that converts the raw scores into a scale with a mean of 50 and a SD of 10. Any T score can therefore be compared directly with any other score. It might seem somewhat arbitrary to have a scale like this, but it is based on a clear logic. It assumes for practical purposes that the normal distribution can be viewed as extending from five SDs below to five above the mean. The T score therefore represents the percentage of the total distance along the normal distribution from 0 to 100. It is for this reason that the mean is 50; that is, it is 50% of the distance along the distribution.

Interpreting low test scores

Referring to an intelligence test score of 70 draws attention to a further important point regarding interpreting test scores. A score that lies two SDs below the mean, approaching the lowest 2% of all scores, is regarded frequently as a 'cut-off' point where we may wish to look more closely at its implications. In IQ terms it has traditionally defined the level formerly described as 'mental retardation', but more widely referred to with terms such as 'learning difficulties', 'learning disabilities' or 'intellectual disabilities'. The main international classification systems for mental and behavioural disorders, which include things like autistic spectrum disorders and attention deficit (hyperactivity) disorder (ADD/ADHD), often refer to a 'clinically significant' impairment in such things as cognitive function or early language development. 'Clinical significance' is normally understood to refer to the point that falls two SDs below the mean. (Equally, if the area of concern was marked by high scores, such as high levels of anxiety or depression, the significant scores to look at more closely would be two SDs above the mean.) You will see from Box 6.2 that the current version of the Wechsler Intelligence Scale for Children, fourth edition (WISC-IV) now uses the description 'extremely low' rather than 'mentally retarded', in recognition of the fact that an IQ score falling under 70 does not in itself define that a child has a learning disability, although it is an important pointer towards fuller investigation.

The descriptions given in Box 6.2 for the WISC-IV, ranging from 'very superior' to 'extremely low', are generally useful for interpreting the meaning of any test score. Where you do not have a figure expressed in a standard scale you should find the information that allows you to relate it to the various standardized scores we have discussed here. It is meaningless in and of itself to say that a child has a reading test score of 27, and only partially more helpful to be told that this is a reading age of eight years. This tells you almost nothing about how well the child is doing, other than that if the child is age 6, 7 or 8 the score certainly looks fine. Only the data that will relate it to the normal distribution, such as the mean and SD appropriate to the child's age, will allow the score to be properly interpreted.

BOX 6.2

Interpreting intelligence test scores

The following are two of the most widely used tests throughout the world for children and young people.

The Wechsler Intelligence Scale for Children, fourth edition (WISC-IV)
(Wechsler et al., 2004)

This is a general intelligence test measuring the abilities of children and young people across four domains, each comprising several sub-tests: verbal comprehension (e.g. vocabulary, word reasoning), perceptual reasoning (e.g. block design, picture completion), working memory (e.g. digit span) and processing speed (e.g. coding). These domains can each be given a standard score and can be combined to give a composite full-scale IQ (in all cases $M = 100$, SD = 15).

Interpretation

The following table shows the official descriptions of the various bands of scores on the WISC-IV, but they are equally useful descriptions for interpreting any tests using standard scores of this type (or their equivalent point on the normal distribution curve).

130 or above	Very superior
120–129	Superior
110–119	High average
90–109	Average
80–89	Low average
70–79	Borderline
69 or below	Extremely low

Raven's Coloured Progressive Matrices (CPM) (Raven et al., 2008a)

Raven's CPM is a non-verbal intelligence test measuring capacity for productive thinking in children aged about 5–12 years (and for older, less able children and adults). It normally comes in book form and comprises 36 items in three sets of 12, in which the child must make the correct choice from several pieces shown beneath a larger design with one piece missing. These items progress through the stages of intellectual development, starting with distinguishing identical from different figures. For older children and adults there is a higher level of the test, the Standard Progressive Matrices (Raven et al., 2008b). Each can be combined with a separate vocabulary test.

Interpretation

The official descriptions of scores on the CPM are shown below. The standard measure used is the percentile, so again the scores can be related to all other standard scores in terms of the normal distribution.

GRADE I	95th percentile or above – 'intellectually superior'
GRADE II	75th percentile or above – 'definitely above average' (Grade II + if 90th percentile or above)
GRADE III	Between 25th and 75th percentile – 'intellectually average' (Grade III + if above 50th percentile; Grade III if below)
GRADE IV	25th percentile or below – 'definitely below average'
GRADE V	5th percentile or below – 'intellectually impaired'

PUTTING RESEARCH INTO PRACTICE – 6.1 INTERPRETING TEST SCORES

The aim of this practical is to give you some experience of interpreting scores on standardized tests.

You are doing a research project with a group of children who are all nine years old. Six of the children come from one school class. Some of the background information you have includes reading ages. The teacher says: 'This group of children range from those whose reading ages are so high they are at genius level, to those who are so low they clearly have major problems'. Do you agree with her?

The reading test in question has the following properties for children age nine years: $M = 53$; SD = 16. Here are the scores for your six children:

	Score	**Reading age**			**Score**	**Reading age**	
Alan	41	7 years	11 months	Karen	71	11 years	0 months
Anwar	53	9 years	0 months	Natalie	50	8 years	9 months
Benjy	35	7 years	3 months	Tasha	68	10 years	7 months

Here is one approach, using the descriptions in the WISC-IV as a guideline:

1 For each of the six scores work out where it lies in SDs away from the mean. (For example: Alan's score of 41 is 12 below the mean. The SD is 16, so he is three quarters of a SD below, or -0.75 SD.)
2 Look at the descriptions of the WISC-IV scores given in Box 6.2. For each band work out where it falls in SDs away from the mean. (For example, as the mean is 100 and the SD is 15, the 'borderline' band of 70–79 extends from -2 SD to -1.4 SD. Remember, you would need to get down to this level of score before it became low enough to look like it might be a bit of a problem.)
3 You can now compare your reading test scores with the WISC-IV bands, because they are both expressed in the same measurement of number of SDs away from the mean.
4 What description would you now give to the six reading scores? (For example, Alan's reading age of 7 years 11 months at age 9 years falls in the 'low average' band, and indeed is just marginally below the middle range of 'average' scores.)

Did you find any apparent 'geniuses' or 'major problems'?

(As a matter of interest, the data here are taken from one of the major standard reading tests, and in common with almost all tests, its results are frequently misinterpreted.)

References

Cohen, J. (1988) *Statistical Power Analysis for the Behavioral Sciences*, 2nd edn. New York: Routledge Academic.
Greig, A. and MacKay, T. (2005) 'Asperger's Syndrome and cognitive behaviour therapy: new applications for educational psychologists', *Educational and Child Psychology*, 22 (4): 4–15.
MacKay, T. (1999) 'Can endemic reading failure in socially disadvantaged children be successfully tackled?', *Educational and Child Psychology*, 16 (1): 22–9.
MacKay, T. (2006) *The West Dunbartonshire Literacy Initiative: the Design, Implementation and Evaluation of an Intervention Strategy to Raise Achievement and Eradicate Illiteracy: Phase 1 Research Report*. Dumbarton: West Dunbartonshire Council.

Raven, J., Raven, J.C. and Court, J. (2008a) *The Coloured Progressive Matrices*. Oxford: Oxford Psychologists Press.
Raven, J., Raven, J.C. and Court, J. (2008b) *The Standard Progressive Matrices*. Oxford: Pearson.
Wechsler, D., Kaplan, E., Delis, D., Fein, D., Maerlander, A. and Morris, R. (2004) *Wechsler Intelligence Scale for Children — Fourth Edition Integrated*. San Antonio, TX: Harcourt Assessment.

Recommended reading for further study

Coolican, H. (2009) *Research Methods and Statistics in Psychology*, 5th edn. London: Hodder Education.
Kremelberg, D. and Salkind, N.J. (2011) *Study Guide to Accompany Neil J. Salkind's Statistics for People Who (Think They) Hate Statistics*, 4th edn. London: Sage.
Salkind, N.J. (2011) *Statistics for People Who (Think They) Hate Statistics,* 4th edn. London: Sage.

SEVEN

Quantitative research with children and young people: data collection

The aim of this chapter is to provide an introduction to data collection in quantitative research.

Data collection

So far, we have devoted considerable attention to research design and the basic concepts and methods that are fundamental to data analysis. This may look like putting the cart before the horse, since obviously we first need to collect the data before we can begin to analyse it. However, the right time to become as familiar as possible with the design of the study and the issues that arise when we are analysing the data is before we have even thought of how the data may be collected. Far too many research projects have foundered because people have started at what appears to be the beginning – going out and gathering all the information – and then finding that their data are unanalysable.

This chapter covers several key methods used in quantitative research: observation, interviews, questionnaires and survey methods. Observation and interviews are also used extensively in qualitative research.

The impact of new technologies

Since the first edition of this book was published in 1999, new technologies have transformed the range of options available for the collection of research data. Previously, apart from direct fieldwork and document reviews, the available options were largely limited to sending questionnaires by post or interviewing people on a telephone landline. Now, most people, both children and adults, have immediate access to the Internet and email, make their telephone calls and send text messages on a mobile phone and are connected with one or more social networking sites. It has become routine to expect that responses to many matters that were once done on paper will now be done online. Research studies based on surveys are making increasing use of free or low-cost facilities, such as SurveyMonkey (www.surveymonkey.com/), for reaching large samples online. For doing research with children and young people, this opens up many new possibilities for data collection. While direct fieldwork and traditional methods of gathering information will always continue to have a central place, newer technologies offer attractive options for communicating with children and young people in a way that is likely to appeal to them. It has been estimated that up to 96% of people in developed countries own a mobile phone (Kuntsche and Robert, 2009), and even for young children a very significant proportion of every day is spent connected to digital media (Gutnick et al., 2011; Rideout et al., 2010).

In addition to creating a means of greatly increasing sample size for some types of research project, without a comparable increase in cost, the new technologies also open up methods for more immediate and potentially more accurate collecting and monitoring of data. Box 7.1 provides an illustration of the use of text messaging to increase engagement of youth with therapeutic interventions.

BOX 7.1

Reaching young people through text messaging

Mobile phones play a central role in the lives of young people and are being increasingly recognized as valuable tools in research and intervention. In an Australian study, Gareth Furber, Research Manager of Southern Adelaide Child and Adolescent Mental Health Services, Anne Crago, Youthlink Coordinator and their colleagues noted the difficulties faced in maintaining contact with vulnerable young people. The normal method of direct contact was home telephone numbers, and this limited the likelihood that young people would either answer or return calls.

Instead, the team exchanged mobile phone numbers and contact was made through texting. This gave the young people more of a sense of ownership of their communication with the team, using a medium that they found user-friendly. Texts were also used to send the young person a message in advance of a call so that they would have prior notice of the fact that the call was due, allowing them to feel prepared for it.

Over a seven-month period, a content analysis of all text messages was carried out. This revealed that the principal use made by the young people of the text messages was to respond to requests for face-to-face appointments. The study also revealed that the use of text messaging provided reassurances for the young person, allowing contact with the team to be on their terms, thus building a relationship of mutual trust and respect. Only a very small number of the messages sent by the young people (2%) involved inappropriate use of the service, by sending messages not directly related to the purpose of the contact.

The researchers concluded that text messaging is a valuable asset in supporting direct contact with young people, noting in an interview following publication of the study, 'If we can be where they are, we are far more likely to engage them' (http://reachoutpro.com.au/using-technology/interviews-with-professionals/using-sms-to-support-youth-services.aspx).

Source: Furber, G.V., Crago, A.E., Meehan, K., Sheppard, T.D., Hooper, K., Abbot, D.T., Allison, S. and Skene, C. (2011) 'How adolescents use SMS (short message service) to micro-coordinate contact with youth mental health outreach services', *Journal of Adolescent Health,* 48 (1): 113–15.

Observation

In a sense, all research involves observation. If the purpose of research is to improve our understanding of an individual, a relationship, a particular social group or culture, then that knowledge begins with observation. Observation means watching children or young people individually, in relationships, in contexts and asking:

- What do they see?
- What do they feel?
- What do they think?
- What do they do?

As a basic technique, observation underpins a variety of approaches to research. There are also a variety of observational techniques to consider, and these vary according to the age of the child or young person, their conceptual abilities, their relationship with the observer and, of course, the purpose of the research.

Observational techniques divide mainly into *participant observation* and *structured observation.* In participant observation the observer becomes part of the group being studied (Figure 7.1). This could include observation in adult settings to obtain data relevant to studies on children or young people, such as a social worker working in a social services agency to discover how referrals to such agencies are handled or an undergraduate working in a school to discover how teachers define quality of curriculum. Participant observation is essentially a qualitative method originating in the work of social scientists such as anthropologists. As our focus in this chapter is on quantitative methods, we focus on *structured observation,* in which the observer only watches and uses a structured approach to the recording and management of observed information. This could, for example, be a psychologist behind a two-way mirror watching the free play interactions between a mother and her infant while coding the behaviours that are observed. Or it could be a teacher who wants to observe if a new intervention increases the quality of their pupils' learning behaviour in class, such as more and better use of the library. Whereas the latter approach has an element of simulation about it, the naturalistic observation down in the real-life situation such as the home, playground or hospital ward is considered to be the method of choice for 'real-world' observational data.

Naturalistic observational techniques conducted in real-world settings are particularly helpful for doing research with younger children who may be unable to communicate any other way. However, there are other sound reasons why it is desirable to research children and young people of all ages and abilities in their natural environments, such as the home, school or neighbourhood, rather than subject them to experimental manipulations. For one thing children and young people are particularly reactive to strange people and strange situations. Even simple note-taking can be very off-putting and interfere with the information collected. Children and young people can become accustomed to professionals who work with them and the methods they use for accessing their thoughts and feelings. Professionals can often find that their young clients can refuse to talk to them or merely say what they think is expected. Observation therefore offers a simplicity that does not involve asking about thoughts and feelings. It is simply about watching and listening, and this minimizes problems with expression and interpretation. Another reason is children's and young people's vulnerable position regarding informed consent (see Chapter 10).

Choosing an approach

A key decision in observation is the choice of sampling method – what to observe and how to record it. There are many possibilities. Here we consider and discuss the following approaches:

- the target child method;
- time sampling;
- event sampling;
- the checklist method.

Target child method

The *target child method* was developed by Kathy Sylva and colleagues in the 1970s for investigating the behaviour of very young children in preschool settings and the approach owes much to the ethological methods used in the study of animals.

Figure 7.1 The challenges of participant observation!

Therefore, while it is naturalistic and observational, a prestructured format allows for further coding and quantification (Sylva et al., 1980). The observer will need a timing device that shows seconds, allowing minute by minute recordings of activity and language used. A typical observation would last 20 minutes. Figure 7.2 shows the layout of a *target child observation schedule*. Each number on the pro forma indicates 1 minute and the abbreviations used are to speed up note-taking. There are columns to record the activity, the language used, the type of task and the nature of social interaction. In this case, PRE refers to pretend play and PAIR means it is two children together rather than in parallel or in a group. Researchers can create their own codes of course, but in this case they are as follows:

- TC = target child
- C = any other child
- A = any adult (member of staff, parent, helper, student, researcher)
- > = speaks to

Date: 15 June 2012 Time: 10.05 Child's initial: AG Gender: F

Age: 3 years Date of birth: 15 June 2009

Setting: Nursery free play (dressing up, Wendy house, painting, climbing frame).

Ten children and three adults

Activity Record	Language Record	Task	Social
1. TC opens Wendy house curtains, smiles at C	Good morning, time to get up.	PRE	PAIR
2. TC watches C. C ignores her.	Come on, you will be late for school.	PRE	PAIR

Figure 7.2 Layout of a target child observation schedule

Notes: A: any adult; C: any other child; PAIR: two children together; PRE: pretend play; TC: target child.

As you can see, the target child method uses a structure involving an instantaneous, minute by minute record of activity, language, task and social context. It requires some preparation of the grid and coding system as well as some practice to become proficient. It is more constrained than a free-flow narrative account of behaviour. It is also time-consuming and information may be easily missed when compared, for example, with recorded or videoed material that can be subject to replay and microanalysis. This type of structured observation could nevertheless be applied to a video of such interaction, if the visual and sound quality is good enough to observe the behaviours of interest.

Time sampling

This approach does not require a running narrative of behaviours to decipher or activities to code but allows us to focus on one activity to discover its frequency, perhaps relative to other behaviours sampled, or its frequency in different contexts or at different times. The classic study in this area was carried out by Parten (1933) who used time sampling on the nervous habits of children. Time is sampled because a specified period of time is usually broken into equal periods of observation (such as every 1 minute, or every 5 minutes) that are followed by periods that are not observed or when some other type of behaviour is observed. If you are studying behaviour over a long period of time, time sampling is a more economic approach to coding, which can be very time-consuming. This method requires that the behaviour in question is directly observable and is unambiguous. Therefore, references to the child or young person's possible state of mind or emotion (looks sad or distracted or daydreaming) would not be appropriate with this approach. The researcher needs to have a very clear idea about the purpose of the study and the particular behaviour to be sampled, and an expectation that it will occur frequently enough in the given time to produce a meaningful pattern. For example, you may have some concerns about a young person's ability to

Table 7.1 Time sampling of a young person with suspected problems in concentration

Time (hh:mm)	*Actions*
09.00	Fidgeting in bags
09.01	Looking through jotters in the drawer, dropping them
09.02	Rocking in chair
09.03	Looking through bags
09.04	Watching others
09.05	Rocking in chair
09.06	Out of chair talking to another pupil
09.07	Fidgeting in bags
09.08	Asking teacher what to do
09.09	Fidgeting in desk
09.10	Copying pupil in next seat

focus in class. The time sampling method might indicate that you should record what the pupil is doing every minute on the minute. The observation schedule may look something like Table 7.1, and it would be likely that a checklist would be drawn up, in advance, of behaviours that indicate a problem of concentration.

Time sampling therefore is a method of observing a child or young person at fixed intervals over a period of time. It could be that the individual's particular behaviour may be of concern or interest, such as in the example above, or perhaps there is a failure in the formation of relationships around the child or young person. This approach allows the researcher to create a relatively accurate picture of what the child is doing with whom, how often and for how long.

Event sampling

Event sampling is a method that records specific events when they occur. The behaviour or the event that is to be recorded needs to be decided in advance and will be related to the research question. The thing to be recorded, therefore, needs to be clearly defined. The basic event sampling schedule will record the number of times the event happens, when it happens and how long it lasts. The kinds of things you may wish to record as an event could include: frequency of aggressive behaviour, behaviours that are symptoms of a health problem such as diabetes, incidents of quarrelling or attempts to make new friends. It is a useful technique when a child or young person can be observed over a substantial period of time, such as whole morning, day or week. The method will also work for a shorter period when an event occurs very frequently (attempts to make new friends at break times) or it occurs a lot but only within one particular context (e.g. only with foster carers). A typical event sampling schedule that records the situations when an individual falls out with another individual may look like the one shown in Figure 7.3. In

Event	Time	Duration	Event
1.	09.45	2.5 minutes	A is alone in the lounge and sits on a sofa. B enters, tells A that they are in their seat. A kicks the chair and runs out.
2.			
3.			
4.			
5.			

Figure 7.3 Event sampling schedule for the number of rows between A and B

this hypothetical case, the workers in a unit for young people are concerned that the rows occur mainly between A and B rather than between A and anyone else, because the older boy (B) is dominant and specifically targeting A.

This approach is good for any contained and well-defined event. It can provide greater understanding of the dynamics of the event and therefore how better to manage it. The method is best suited to observation of individuals rather than groups and the researcher will need to be vigilant and skilled at recognizing the precursors to the event itself.

The checklist method

A good example of the *checklist method* is to use a guide on developmental milestones for children, such as the classic developmental norms devised in the early 1970s by Mary Sheridan (2008) or a rating scale that measures the degree to which the child or young person is more or less the same as others on a particular item being rated, such as empathy. Table 7.2 shows an example of an observational schedule for developmental norms in a four-year-old child.

Table 7.2 Checklist sampling for developmental norms (behaviour is noted only if it occurs in a particular time frame, such as at age 4.5 years)

Sheridan's norms of child development (4.5 years)	*Yes*	*No*	*Comments*
1 Affectionate, confiding	x		Holds friend's hands and whispers
2 Likes to help with domestic chores	x		Readily agrees to help wash up and takes interest in how clean cups are
3 Tries to keep environment tidy		x	Messes toys and runs away when asked to tidy up
4 Engages in symbolic play	x		Asks imaginary friends to tea
5 Joins with others in symbolic play	x		Plays weddings with friends, each with a role
6 Shares toys	x		Not observed

Box 7.2 gives a further example of checklist sampling in the form of a rating scale.

BOX 7.2

An observational instrument from a study on the comparison of the anxiety-reducing potential of two techniques of bathing

Child identification code:

Date:

Behavioural cues:

While observing the patient/child indicate the category of behaviour as follows:

Body activation (circle one)

Severe anxiety	–	continual, non-purposeful activity or inactivity
Mild anxiety	–	some motions not purposeful, activity increase on mentioning pain/operation
No anxiety	–	gestures purposeful and appropriate

Facial expressions (circle one)

Severe anxiety	–	frowning, down-turned mouth continually
Mild anxiety	–	occasional facial expression of anxiety
No anxiety	–	content and pleasant facial expression

Vocalizations (circle one)

Severe anxiety	–	sighing, inappropriate laughter, 'I don't know', desperate, panicky, terrified
Mild anxiety	–	angry, depressed, uncomfortable, nervous, frightened
No anxiety	–	use of non-anxiety words: happy, optimistic, secure

Conversation (circle one)

Severe anxiety	–	expresses numerous concerns, worries, complaints, inability to focus on interview
Mild anxiety	–	occasional expression of worries, complaints
No anxiety	–	no expression of dissatisfaction and/or expressions of contentment

Source: Adapted from Barsevick, A. and Llewellyn, J. (1982), 'A comparison of the anxiety-reducing potential of two techniques of bathing', *Nursing Research*, 31 (1): 22–7. Reproduced with permission.

Combining methods

Time-consuming narrative information can also be completely removed from an observation schedule, if appropriate, using time sampling and combining it with activity sampling and a coded checklist. Table 7.3 shows how pure frequencies may be generated in a situation where the researcher wanted to know how much time a child or young person, perhaps with an attention deficit, spends off task.

Figure 7.4 illustrates how the target child method can be combined with event coding and natural time sampling where everything that happens over a specified period in broken down into events, codes and durations.

Using a pick-and-mix method can therefore generate a large amount of quantifiable data in a short period of time. There are a number of challenges, however. The success of the approaches requires diligent recording of data as the pre-designed schedule must be followed and this may not give an accurate account of the bigger picture, including why the behaviour is occurring.

Table 7.3 Time and activity sampling using a precoded checklist

Time (hh:mm)	*On task involved*	*On task uninvolved*	*Off task quiet*	*Off task disruptive*
10.00	✓			
10.01	✓			
10.02	✓			
10.04		✓		
10.05				✓

Note: Blank cell indicates that the behaviour is not observed.

Time onset	Time offset	Event (coded)[a]	Language	Social
09.15	09.18	PA + HA: TC pulls hair of C. They cry.	TC > C: I hate you	PAIR
09.19	09.20	VA: TC sneers at C.	TC > C: You're an ugly sissy.	PAIR
09.21	09.22	PA: TC pushes C on floor.		PAIR

Figure 7.4 Target child, event coding and natural time sampling combined

Note: [a]where possible, the events preceding and following an aggressive event.
>: speaks to; HA: hostile aggression; PA: physical aggression; PAIR: two children together; VA: verbal aggression

In choosing an observational approach, the researcher needs therefore to consider:

- How much time is available to observe?
- How long should each observation last?
- How well defined is the event or behaviour?
- How long should there be in between observations?
- Will this observational approach answer my research questions?
- Is there a coding system already available that suits the research purpose or do I need to create one especially for the research question?
- How do I know my observations are reliable and valid?

These last two questions are covered in the following sections.

Coding schemes

There are many research studies that have developed their own coding schemes for observing children and young people and they have also tested the reliability and validity of their categories. This is extremely helpful for novice researchers as it is quite a complex and time-consuming process. We have already looked at some examples of these that date back to classic studies (Parten, 1933; Sylva et al., 1980). Another classic is the Flanders (1970) interaction analysis (IA) coding system that was developed for analysing pupil and teacher behaviour in the classroom. Flanders created 10 categories of observable behaviour with which an observer would need to become familiar and practised before conducting an observational study. These are shown in Box 7.3. The recording method involved noting the number attached to each category, where each row represents 1 minute of time (20 3-second intervals) over a 10 minute period. This is shown in Figure 7.5.

BOX 7.3

The interaction analysis system categories and numbers (Flanders, 1970)

1 Teacher accepts student feeling
2 Teacher praises student
3 Teacher uses student ideas
4 Teacher questions
5 Teacher lectures
6 Teacher gives directions

7 Teacher criticizes student
8 Student response
9 Student-initiated response
10 Silence or confusion

Source: Flanders, N.A. (1970) *Analysing Teacher Behaviour.* Boston, MA: Addison Wesley.

Reliability and validity of coding

For a coding scheme, such as the IA one, to be reliable and valid, the creator would need to have very clearly defined behavioural definitions of each category so that another observer would have a very high agreement that a particular behaviour belongs in that category. For example, Flanders describes category 5 (teacher lectures) as follows: 'Giving facts or opinions about content or procedures; expressing his *own* ideas, giving his *own* explanations, or citing an authority other than the pupil' (1970: 34). This tightly defined behavioural category, and all the others, would have been 'piloted', perhaps in a less defined way initially and then refined to take out as much ambiguity as possible. This is known as *intra-rater reliability* or observer consistency, the aim of which is to make sure the same person consistently gets the same coding result each time the behaviour is categorized. The whole coding system would also need to be rated independently by another researcher. This is known as *inter-rater reliability.* The amount of agreement between the two separate coders would then be calculated (for a description of how to do the Cohen's Kappa calculation, see Robson, 2011). As you can see, the creation of a new coding system is no simple or easy matter. Nevertheless, as Robson (2011) has said well, the Law of

Minute	Coding
1	555 555 444 488 883 332 05
2	
3	
4	
5	
6	
7	
8	
9	
10	

Figure 7.5 Recording sheet for the interactional analysis system (IAS) (10 is shown as 0 here)

Maximum Perversity will be likely to ensure that no existing scheme will meet the requirements for addressing your research question! In this likely event, you would do well to heed the rest of his advice and make sure that your categories are:

- focused (what use will this data be?);
- objective (very clearly defined, as little ambiguity or inference as possible);
- non-context dependent;
- exhaustive (covering all observational possibilities);
- mutually exclusive (each item coded should only fit into one category);
- easy to record.

Observing a child in the natural environment will give research a 'real-world' edge to it. Data collection needs to be low-key and slick and can be aided in some situations by the use of concealed or discreet video cameras or digital recorders, well-designed, economic recording sheets and stopwatches. A well-designed observational study will also enable the researcher to record these real-life events as they occur. This direct experience facilitates the researcher's ability to understand complex individuals and situations and to build on theories. Observational methods, however, often do not adapt well from single individuals or simple settings to large groups or complex settings and this limits the possibility of making comparisons and contrasts.

PUTTING RESEARCH INTO PRACTICE 7.1 – OBSERVATION

The aim of this practical is to give you some experience of doing an observation of a child or young person, and scoring it up.

This practical is best done in a real-life situation or using a good quality video of children or young people interacting. A fairly common theme is attention seeking. You are free to generate your own research question (e.g. there is an increase in attention seeking in the child or young person when the parents are going through a divorce/adopting another child *or* there is an increase in inappropriate physical attention seeking when one or both parents do not visit a sick child or young person in hospital). If you are free to do so and can obtain permission, decide on your location: e.g. a playground, a special unit, a hospital ward, a local play park, corridors within a building. Here is a list of codes for you to use:

Physical attention seeking	**Code**
Tapping/patting	T
Standing in front of	SF
Looking into face	LF
Swinging about dangerously	S
Pulling	PUL
Pushing	PUS
Shoving	SH

Verbal attention seeking	Code
Please may I?	PL
Swearing	SW
Shouting	ST
Verbal demands (Give me!)	D
Saying the person's name	N
Screaming	SC

Use the observation schedule below to get you started. This is not a perfect instrument, but it is one that will make you think. Example times and events are given here to get you started but you obviously make your own arrangements.

	Time						
Category	10.00–10.10	10.20–10.30	10.40–10.50	11.00–11.10	11.20–11.30	11.40–11.50	**Totals**
SF	x						
LF			xx		x		
S						x	
Totals							

Discussion and reflection

When you have completed an attempt at the observation, discuss in pairs or in groups the following questions:

- What kind of sampling and recording is used here?
- In what way is this approach helpful and unhelpful?
- Given the specific research question you decided on, what were the limitations of this observation approach? What other approaches could have been used?
- What difficulties did you experience with the categories?
- What could have been done with the categories to improve them?

Interviews

Interviews are a very widely used method of conducting research, whether directly with the children and young people or with adults. As a method of obtaining children's own perspectives, it has much to offer and this subject is developed further in Chapter 9. A significant amount of what we know about children and young people is gained by well-designed and conducted interviews of adults who know them well – parents, teachers, carers, case workers, health visitors and peers being a few examples. Important issues that potentially influence children and young people via policies and practices can also be examined using interviews. Willing participants like being interviewed and the interactive nature of the procedure allows the researcher access to dimensions of information not otherwise available, such as non-verbal cues on feelings. The relatively free-flow interaction enables the researcher to pick up on important and emotive issues by gentle probing and to discover what matters most to the participants from the topics they raise themselves.

It is in their level of *structure* that interviews mainly vary. The extent to which they do or do not have predetermined questions leads to their being described as *structured, semistructured* or *unstructured.* A *structured* interview is much like an interactive questionnaire, where the researcher reads out set questions and records the responses. At the other end of the scale an *unstructured* interview gives maximum scope to the ideas generated by the interviewee and develops according to the topics that arise. In this situation the interviewer takes on the role of an informed prompter, giving sufficient guidance to keep the interview on track but not controlling the way it develops. The most commonly encountered format in research is the *semistructured* interview, which has questions or prompts covering set topics, but within that framework allows a lot of scope for the interviewee's own ideas to develop.

Choices about the level of structure for an interview should be guided by the purpose it is designed to serve. Interviews that aim mainly to obtain facts, or that look for views on a number of predetermined topics, will have more structure. Interviews that aim to tap into topics that are meaningful and important to the interviewee, and that will reflect the interviewee's authentic experience, will have less structure. Also, unstructured interviewing can be useful for an exploratory study in a new area. It can be used to generate the background information that will guide subsequent more structured approaches. Bailey et al. (1995) give the example of an investigation into what young people know about illegal drugs. The study begins with three long unstructured interviews to provide background on the kind of language young people use about drugs and the issues that are important to them. On this basis, a better-informed structured interview is prepared for use with a further 20 young people.

Table 7.4 Guidelines for designing and doing an interview

Designing it	*Doing it*
Get ideas on paper, arrange into themes and list in order of intrusiveness	State purpose, ensure confidentiality and right not to answer, and stop at any time, especially distressed
Turn into open-ended questions: What? When? How?	Choose setting carefully for privacy and intimacy
Ensure questions are clear, short and unambiguous	Make yourself useful, help in a field setting
Put in a logical order starting with easy questions, ending with hard ones	Be interested and non-judgemental Record interview, stick to agenda but allow interviewee some freedom
Avoid leading questions, technical terms, emotive language, negatives	Techniques to help: expectant pause/ glance; encouraging vocalizations; reflection and returning words used by interviewee; skilful probing
End with positive issues/questions	
Pilot interview	
Rewrite	

Each form of interview has its advantages and disadvantages. More structured interviews allow each person to be asked the same questions in the same way. This allows for more direct comparisons and is more amenable to quantitative methodology. However, they are less flexible than unstructured interviews and make the assumption that the researcher already knows what the relevant questions are and only has to ask for the answers. In many ways the semistructured interview can capture the advantages of both approaches.

Interviews take time and require detailed analysis, but a well-done interview is well worth it. Table 7.4 offers some general guidelines for designing and doing an interview.

Questionnaires

Questionnaires are a popular research tool because they can be quickly designed, administered to large numbers and easily analysed. They are an excellent way of obtaining both factual data, such as attendance rates at a school or hospital admissions, and also opinions. Perhaps it is the beguiling simplicity of the questionnaire that makes it so universally used by researchers – but beguiling it is, and there are many attempts at research that have ended up with unanalysable data and meaningless results because of flawed questionnaire design. Box 7.4 provides some salutary advice about compiling your own questionnaire.

BOX 7.4

Getting questionnaires right

Questionnaires are among the most common methods used by researchers – and the worst carried out. Bad questionnaires will effectively torpedo the whole project, no matter how much labour is expended on it. They usually end up with an item that says something like: 'If there are any other questions I should have thought of but didn't, please answer them here'. Many of these questionnaires seem to have been sent out when, for all practical purposes, they were still at their first draft. There is only one place for the first draft of any questionnaire – the bin. If you ignore this advice, your project will probably end up there instead. Here are some ground rules for those who are compiling questionnaires:

- Avoid any possibility of ambiguity. Assume that the person answering your questionnaire knows *nothing*. Explain and define your terms exactly.
- State precisely and comprehensively the information you require. Questions that ask me if I have dealt with many school refusers recently will tell nobody anything. Specify all you want to know – times, ages, dates. Does 'last year' mean last calendar year or last session? Your questionnaire is not a rehearsal: you don't get a second chance.
- Put the questions in a suitable form for quantifying the data afterwards. It may not be true to say that if it cannot be counted it does not exist, but for questionnaire data it is *mostly* true.
- Do not throw in every question you can think of and then wait to see if anything interesting turns up. This is the wrong way round. Decide the variables you are interested in studying and frame the questions to provide the type of information you want.
- Do not present the respondent with an impossible task. For example, I do not know and could not tell you how many primary age children in my service were referred to a psychiatrist in the past five years compared with the previous five.
- Do not ask for pieces of personal information you do not need. You will receive a lower return if you ask for children's names or other personal data if these are not essential.
- Try a 'dry run' first, even if only with a handful of colleagues. You will soon pick up the major flaws.
- Consider beforehand what steps you will take to maximize your return rate. For example, always state the date by which you wish to receive the reply, a few days after that send a friendly reminder and later make a phone call if possible. For the type of questionnaire that is sent to colleagues and other professionals, *a low return is always the fault of the researcher – not of the respondent.*

Source: Adapted from MacKay, T. (1987) 'Planning research in child guidance', *SALGEP Quarterly*, 6 (1): 3–11.

Researching children's attitudes

Questionnaires can be a good way of finding out about the attitudes of children and young people, and they can be designed to cover exactly the areas you are interested in. One such questionnaire, titled 'What you think about school', is shown in Figure 7.6. It was designed to assess attitudes to school and schoolwork on the part of the child, as well as the child's perceptions of parental attitudes. Three questions related specifically to attitudes towards reading and perceived ability

WHAT YOU THINK ABOUT SCHOOL
(Briggs and MacKay, 1993)

We want to find out more about what children think of school. Please put a tick in one box for each question. There are no 'good' or 'bad' answers. We just want to know what you think.			
1 I like coming to school	True	In between	False
2 My favourite time is playtime	True	In between	False
3 I think school is important	True	In between	False
4 I am often in trouble at school	True	In between	False
5 My parents think teachers are usually right	True	In between	False
6 It's a good thing to have lots of books at home	True	In between	False
7 I'm not very good at reading	True	In between	False
8 Homework is important	True	In between	False
9 My school is a good school	True	In between	False
10 I'm not very good at working with other children	True	In between	False
11 My friends think school is a waste of time	True	In between	False
12 My parents think school is important	True	In between	False
13 I wish I didn't have to come to school	True	In between	False
14 If I'm in trouble at school my parents usually take my side	True	In between	False
15 I haven't got a 'best' subject at school	True	In between	False
16 I do not like reading very much	True	In between	False

Figure 7.6 A simple attitudes questionnaire used with children

Source: MacKay, T. (1995) 'Reading failure in an area of multiple social disadvantage: response of a psychological service to a school's priorities' in: The Scottish Office Education Department, *Matching Service Delivery to Client Needs: Quality Assurance in Psychological Services.* Edinburgh: The Scottish Office Education Department. pp. 210–33.

in that subject. All but two of the questions were judged to have directionality (i.e. to suggest either positive or negative attitudes or perceptions regarding school and education). The remaining two were considered to be neutral ('My favourite time is playtime' and 'I haven't got a best subject at school'). A simple scoring system was devised to give a score of 0, 1 or 2 on each of the 14 relevant items.

However, testing attitudes with young children, especially using questionnaires, can present some major problems, as MacKay and Watson (1999) found to their cost. They tried to adapt the above questionnaire into 'What you think about school for younger children'. Instead of statements of the type, 'I like coming to school', all the statements were replaced with the type: 'Freddie the Fish likes coming to school. Are you like Freddie the Fish – do *you* like coming to school?'

The statements were read out to the children, who were five-years-old, in small groups by their teacher. For every statement each had a picture (in this case, Freddie the Fish). They were told: 'This side says YES and this side says NO.' They then had to put a circle round their choice.

The result was a disaster! As with any new questionnaire or method, the researchers carried out a quality check to see how it was being carried out. They entered the room at the point where a teacher was saying, 'Minnie the Mouse wishes she didn't have to come to school. Are you like Minnie the Mouse – do *you* wish you didn't have to come to school?' As she made the statement, she was unconsciously shaking her head in a disapproving fashion, and with one voice the children responded, 'Nooooo ... ooo', and circled the appropriate answer! The write-up in the journal article omits the details and just discreetly says, 'The pre–post attitude questionnaires proved unsuitable for meaningful statistical analysis.'

It is very important to avoid the 'social desirability' factor in questionnaires and other methods – in this case pleasing the teacher and being the same as the rest of the group. The above fiasco led MacKay (2006) to develop an innovative and successful method for testing young children's attitudes – but not using a questionnaire. Instead, some remarkably low-tech and readily available technical equipment was used (three jam jars!) as described in Box 7.5.

BOX 7.5

Testing young children's attitudes: the jam jar technique

How do you assess the attitudes of children as young as four or five without getting just the socially desirable response – the one the child thinks will be approved by the person asking the question? In this study the aim was to see if the early literacy skills of young children and their attitudes and beliefs about reading would be enhanced by getting them to make three bold declarations every day about becoming good readers.

The children had three glass jars (jam jars) set before them. Each jar contained a large and similar number of small white cards, designed to represent the responses made by other children to the same questions. Every question was presented to each child in the following manner:

- *These children don't like reading very much* (pointing to jar 1).
- *These children think it's OK* (jar 2).
- *These children like reading a lot* (jar 3).

What do you think about reading?

The child was then invited to post a card into the chosen jar and the choice was recorded. The direction of the questions was varied to avoid response set (e.g. always choosing the first jar, or the last one). Posting the cards in this way made the exercise appear more anonymous, and since children have high levels of group conformity it was clear from all the cards already in the three jars that the answers could safely be deposited wherever the children liked.

A score of 1 was assigned to the most positive response for each question, a score of 2 to the middle response and a score of 3 to the negative response. Before the intervention there was no difference in attitudes between experimental subjects and controls. After the intervention all children were tested again. All of the scores that had changed upwards from less to more positive and downwards from more to less positive were analysed by comparing actual changes with possible changes. This therefore took account of the fact that scores that were already at 1 could not change up, and scores at 3 could not change down. These overall change scores showed that the children who had made the declarations had developed more positive attitudes to reading ($p < 0.01$, chi-square test).

This simple jam jar technique proved highly effective. Of 54 children tested at age 4–5 years, only one was unable to engage with the idea of selecting a preferred jar.

Source: MacKay, T. (2006) *The West Dunbartonshire Literacy Initiative: the Design, Implementation and Evaluation of an Intervention Strategy to Raise Achievement and Eradicate Illiteracy: Phase 1 Research Report.* Dumbarton: West Dunbartonshire Council.

Standardized questionnaires

As well as questionnaires designed specifically for a research project, there are also many standardized questionnaires that are useful for researchers working with children and young people. Large numbers of different subject areas have ready-made questionnaires available from the catalogues of the main test publishers in the various disciplines of education, health and psychology. For example, the ones designed by Spence (1995) for social skills, social competence and related areas are useful, easy to administer and interpret, and very accessible. (They come in a photocopiable resource pack.) They also have the advantage of providing triangulation by allowing comparable information to be collected from different sources – parent, pupil and teacher. The results have been standardized on a mixed-age group of children and young people aged 8–17. Each item can be rated as 'not true', 'sometimes true' or 'mostly true'. Examples from the social skills questionnaire for pupils are: 'I listen to other people's points of view during arguments' and 'I control my temper when I lose in a game or competition'.

PUTTING RESEARCH INTO PRACTICE 7.2 – QUESTIONNAIRE DESIGN

The aim of this practical is to give you some experience of the issues involved in questionnaire design.

Think of a child research study that would be of interest to you and that could use questionnaires as a method. For example, you might want to find out how many children in a school or group are being bullied, what form it takes and how they deal with it. Or you might be interested in how young people spend their leisure time, or what they spend their pocket money on. Or again, you might want to know whether parents of children and young people with autistic spectrum disorders manage to organize family holidays, and if so, where they go, how they travel, what kind of accommodation they use, whether they eat out and whether they manage to get time to themselves. All of these questions lend themselves to questionnaires, some of which might be completed by the children or young people themselves and others by adults:

Construct a questionnaire that will answer your key questions. In doing so, follow the advice given in this chapter, such as the bullet points in Box 7.4. In your questionnaire include the following types of question.

- YES/NO questions.
- Multiple choice questions (e.g. selecting which box answers how often people go away on a family holiday, ranging from 'never' through to 'more than three times a year').
- Scalar questions (e.g. questions where the choice of answer is recorded on a scale, such as one of three points or one of five points).
- Open-ended questions (questions where people write in their own comments).

Look at your first draft and refine it through better drafts by asking key questions. For example:

- Is YES/NO unambiguous, or will people be saying 'it's sometimes yes and sometimes no'?
- Does your questionnaire include enough questions to get all the key data you require from it?
- Are there any questions that will not really contribute to your analysis and understanding?

- If you have used a three-point scale, does it have enough range to allow you to capture a variety of viewpoints? Or, if you have used a five-point scale will you just end up combining the first two points (e.g. 'little' and 'very little') and the last two points ('much' and 'very much')?
- Do your open-ended questions give enough scope to people to say other important things? Or are they so open-ended that they will just give information that you can't do much with?

Once you have a good draft, pilot it on a few children or colleagues – you'll soon find where the flaws are!

Survey methods

A commonly used method in education, health and social work research is the *survey*. A broad aim of survey research is to describe what is actually going on in a particular field of practice regarding a particular issue of some importance or to find out about consumer views of services. An example might be finding out what are the practices of local authorities in consulting with young people about the provision of leisure facilities in their community, or the views of young people regarding the provision of such facilities. Surveys can tell us about standards for comparing existing conditions and help us in determining the relationships that exist between specific events (Cohen et al., 2011).

In survey research, a large number of questions are devised into a questionnaire, rating scale or structured interview format. The survey can be totally structured, with fixed, alternative responses, or it may include open-ended questions that allow participants to express their answers in a more personal way. Surveys are designed to be administered to very large numbers of participants who are a representative sample of an even larger population: a survey given to every young person attending every club run by youth and community services in a local authority aims to represent the views of that entire client group.

In a classic study, Rutter et al. (1979) combined survey methods, structured interviews and classroom observation. The aim of the study, titled *Fifteen Thousand Hours: Secondary Schools and their Effects on Children*, was to examine how secondary schools in an inner London education authority area of six-miles radius differed in terms of academic achievement, attendance and delinquency. Variables considered important for differences included status and sex of pupils and organization of school environment (size, space, staff, class size, age and sites of buildings). The survey was conducted on how the 12 schools in the area selected measured up in terms of these variables.

As with all research methods, surveys have advantages and disadvantages, as illustrated in Table 7.5.

Table 7.5 Advantages and disadvantages of surveys

Advantages	*Disadvantages*
Particularly suitable for large samples	Response rates may fall to very low levels
Efficient in terms of time and cost	Very dependent on participants' motivation, memory and honesty
Very suitable for quantitative analysis	Level of structure may limit validity of more complex responses
Large volumes of data can be generated and multiple variables analysed	Questions asked may miss other important variables
Easy for respondents to complete	Sample may be biased by method (those who have email or a landline)
Highly structured, reducing complexity and ambiguity in results	Those who choose to respond may be unrepresentative of the total sample who received the survey
A wide range of approaches can be used – post, email, telephone, social networking sites	

Finally, the whole subject of doing quantitative research with children and young people – together with the statistical foundations to support it – involves entering territory that can at times be difficult and exacting for the most experienced of researchers. To conclude this chapter on the lighter side, Box 7.6 takes a tongue-in-cheek look at some of the telling statements found in student dissertations and research reports.

BOX 7.6

Reporting quantitative research: the art of dodging

'The results obtained from three of the participants were selected for detailed study.'
(The results of the others didn't make sense and were therefore ignored.)
'Results suggest that ...' *(The results were not significant.)*
'It is well known that ...' *(No evidence available.)*
'A representative sample of Scottish psychologists' *(Me and three friends.)*
'This aspect requires further research.' *(I can't make head or tail of it myself.)*
'A content analysis of 43 items identified eight distinguishable categories.'
(I looked at the cards and put them into eight piles.)
'Some of the scores from this group were extrapolated.'
(I lost the envelope I wrote this group's scores on.)
'Because of complicating factors this group was omitted from the analysis.'
(I couldn't sort out the mess so I scrapped the lot.)

'Full details of the statistical procedure will be found in Guilford's "Psychometric Methods".'
(I found the stats utterly incomprehensible.)
'This was a pilot study.' *(I messed up the whole project.)*

Source: MacKay, T. (1987) 'Planning research in child guidance', *SALGEP Quarterly,* 6 (1): 3–11. Originally adapted from Nisbet, J.D. and Entwistle, N.J. (1970) *Educational Research Methods.* New York: American Elsevier Pub. Co.

PUTTING RESEARCH INTO PRACTICE 7.3 – DESIGNING QUANTITATIVE RESEARCH PROJECTS

The aim of this practical is to explore some ways of answering research questions using the information given in this chapter.

Look back to the three examples with which Chapter 6 opens and consider the following.

- How would you set about planning a research project to answer each of the questions raised?
- What kind of data would you need?
- From what potential sources might you get it?
- What methods might be included (e.g. documentary sources of information such as referral records, observation, questionnaires, interviews)?
- What factors would you need to consider in analysing and interpreting your data?
- Would all of your data be quantitative, or would you also be able to enrich your projects with qualitative information (see Chapter 8) – rich descriptions from individual children or staff that convey the flavour of what is happening and what it means in their real experience?

References

Bailey, V., Bemrose, G., Goddard, S., Impey, R., Joslyn, E. and Mackness, J. (1995) *Essential Research Skills.* London: Collins Educational.

Barsevick, A. and Llewellyn, J. (1982) 'A comparison of the anxiety-reducing potential of two techniques of bathing', *Nursing Research,* 31 (1): 2–7.

Cohen, L., Manion, L. and Morrison, K. (2011) *Research Methods in Education,* 7th edn. London: Routledge.

Flanders, N.A. (1970) *Analysing Teacher Behaviour.* Boston, MA: Addison Wesley.

Furber, G., Crago, A., Meehan, K., Sheppard, T., Hooper, K., Abbot, D., Allison, S. and Skene, C. (2011) 'How adolescents use SMS (short message service) to micro-coordinate contact with youth mental health outreach', *Journal of Adolescent Health,* 48 (1): 113–15.

Gutnick, A.L., Robb, M., Takeuchi, L. and Kotler, J. (2011) *Always Connected: the New Digital Media Habits of Young Children.* New York: The Joan Ganz Cooney Center at Sesame Workshop.

Kuntsche, E. and Robert, B. (2009) 'Short message service (SMS) technology in alcohol research: a feasibility study', *Alcohol and Alcoholism*, 44 (4): 423–8.

MacKay, T. (1987) 'Planning research in child guidance', *SALGEP Quarterly*, 6 (1): 3–11.

MacKay, T. (1999) 'Can endemic reading failure in socially disadvantaged children be successfully tackled?', *Educational and Child Psychology*, 16 (1): 22–9.

MacKay, T. (2006) *The West Dunbartonshire Literacy Initiative: the Design, Implementation and Evaluation of an Intervention Strategy to Raise Achievement and Eradicate Illiteracy: Phase 1 Research Report*. Dumbarton: West Dunbartonshire Council.

MacKay, T. and Watson, K. (1999) 'Literacy, social disadvantage and early intervention: enhancing reading achievement in primary school', *Educational and Child Psychology*, 16 (1): 30–6.

Nisbet, J.D. and Entwhistle, N.J. (1970) *Educational Research Methods*. New York: American Elsevier Pub.Co.

Parten, M.B. (1933) 'Social play among preschool children', *Journal of Abnormal and Social Psychology*, 28 (2): 136–47.

Rideout, V., Foehr, U. and Roberts, D. (2010) *Generation M2: Media in the Lives of 8- to 18-Year-Olds*. Menlo Park, CA: Kaiser Family Foundation. Available at: www.kff.org/entmedia/mh012010pkg.cfm (accessed 6 March 2012).

Robson, C. (2011) *Real World Research: a Resource for Social Scientists and Practitioner-Researchers*, 3rd edn. Oxford: Blackwell Publishers.

Rutter, M., Maughan, B., Mortimore, P. and Ousten, J. (1979) *Fifteen Thousand Hours: secondary Schools and their Effects on Children*. London: Open Books.

Sheridan, M.D. (2008) *From Birth to Five Years: Children's Developmental Progress*. London: Routledge.

Spence, S. (1995) *Social Skills Training: Enhancing Social Competence with Children and Adolescents*. Windsor: NFER-Nelson.

Sylva, K., Roy, C. and Painter, M. (1980) *Childwatching at Playgroup and Nursery School*. London: Grant McIntyre.

Recommended reading for further study

Fink, A. (2009) *How to Conduct Surveys: A Step-By-Step Guide*, 4th edn. London: Sage.

EIGHT

Designing and doing qualitative research with children and young people

The aims of this chapter are:

- to discuss the nature of qualitative research and its benefits and limitations;
- to outline some of the main methods used in qualitative research designs;
- to give practical illustrations of how research with children and young people may use mixed quantitative and qualitative designs.

> If something exists, it exists in some quantity. If it exists in some quantity it can be measured. (Thorndike, 1905)
>
> If you can measure something, that ain't it. (Kaplan, 1964: 206)

These two quotations caricature the essential difference between the quantitative and the qualitative approaches to research. The notion of *quantity* refers to the amount of something – to questions of how much, how often and to what extent. *Quality*, conversely, refers to the essence of something – to questions about its nature and how it is experienced and described. However, the two approaches are not as opposed or even as distinct as these quotations suggest. Very many quantitative studies are supported and enriched by qualitative data, and many qualitative studies include some data that can be counted and analysed using traditional quantitative methods.

In some respects, the dichotomy between quantitative and qualitative methods is an artefact that is not entirely helpful. Most people who wish to do research with children and young people are practitioners whose concern is with *action research* rather than with 'pure' scientific research conducted in the university laboratory or other contrived settings. Action research, sometimes referred to as *participatory action research* (Reason, 1994), is a method of improving practice.

'It involves action, evaluation and reflection and, based on gathered evidence, changes in practice are implemented' (Koshy, 2010: 1). It is a continuous learning process in which new knowledge is both learned and also shared with those who may benefit from it. Action research is viewed as being so central to qualitative approaches that it is given a key place in many qualitative texts (e.g. Berg, 2009; Holloway, 1997). It enshrouds many of the basic principles of qualitative research in that it is carried out in natural, real-world settings, is participatory, constructs theory from practice, involves dynamic processes of change as it progresses, and aims for understanding of meaning and experience. Nevertheless, many action research projects use traditional quantitative methods.

It is most likely that in your research with children and young people you will use both quantitative and qualitative methods, so although this chapter focuses on qualitative designs it has examples of the mix of approaches that typifies most action research in the real-world settings of childhood and adolescence.

The nature of qualitative enquiry

Qualitative research strives for depth of understanding in natural settings. Unlike the positivist tradition, the quantitative tradition does not focus on a world in which reality is fixed and measurable but one in which the experiences and perspectives of individuals are socially constructed. It is 'a form of social inquiry that focuses on the way people interpret and make sense of their experiences and the world in which they live' (Holloway, 1997: 1). It grew out of a concern on the part of many researchers that 'research activities structured through the logic of quantification leave out lots of interesting and potentially consequential things' (Freebody, 2003: 35), not just in terms of research aims and content but also in terms of missing the richness of accounts of experience.

The roots of qualitative research are to be found in the social anthropology and sociology of the early 20th century. Anthropologists, such as Bronisław Malinowski (1922) and Margaret Mead (1928), carried out their classic cross-cultural studies in Melanesia and Samoa, respectively, and in doing so used methods of enquiry that aimed to develop deep understanding and provide rich descriptions of the lives and experiences of people in non-Western cultures. The 1960s saw the more formal development of qualitative methods and theories. A key contribution was the publication of *The Discovery of Grounded Theory: Strategies for Qualitative Research* by two sociologists, Barney Glaser and Anselm Strauss (Glaser and Strauss, 1967). It was their work that began to bridge the gap between theory and practice, to make qualitative research more systematic and rigorous and to establish qualitative methods in their own right rather than merely as exploratory tools for quantitative work (Charmaz, 1995; Merriam, 2002). By 1978 there was a separate journal devoted to qualitative methods, *Qualitative Sociology*. Later, the methods would become fully embedded in most of the professions working with children and young people, including education (Sherman and Webb, 1988), nursing (Morse, 1991) and psychology (Banister et al., 1994).

Qualitative research is a complex and varied field of enquiry, and the term should not be used so loosely as to refer to almost any research project that does not depend on analysis of numerical data, or that has not been conducted rigorously enough to produce such data. Richardson (1996) issues a number of 'health warnings' for those who would embark on these methods. They include the observations that qualitative research is a specialist area of expertise with its own language, that it is not to be taken as meaning 'easy research' and that it merits proper training and supervision. As a specialist field it has a number of defining features, the most commonly accepted of these are shown in Figure 3.6 in Chapter 3.

There have been many debates about what properly constitutes qualitative research. Kidder and Fine (1987) distinguish between 'big Q' and 'little q' approaches. 'Big Q' refers to strict qualitative methodologies that are inductive, that are concerned with the exploration of meanings and that seek to generate theory from data rather than starting with a hypothesis. 'Little q' refers to a wider range of less pure methodologies in which various types of non-numerical data are collected, often within the context of more traditional approaches.

This book cannot serve as a manual of either the 'big Q' or 'little q' methods of research. There are many comprehensive texts covering both general qualitative methods and specific methodologies. You will find some of these in the recommended reading at the end of the chapter. This chapter includes an account of a range of methods that characterize strict qualitative research. However, it also takes a practical approach in recognizing that most researchers are more interested in maximum flexibility in choosing methods best suited to their needs, rather than in debates about the purity of the research paradigm they adopt. In doing research with children and young people you are likely to find a variety of less pure approaches more useful.

Qualitative research designs: benefits and limitations

Qualitative approaches are particularly suitable for doing research with children and young people. This applies especially to those whose job is actually to work with this age group as opposed to researchers working in academic institutions who choose to do a child study. First, people who work with children and young people are already operating in a real-life, naturalistic setting. Indeed, they are much less likely to have ready access to the more contrived settings that often characterize traditional experimental methodologies. Natural environments such as the classroom or the playgroup are ideal arenas for research. Some of the rather 'unnatural' environments, such as the children's hospital ward, are also among the naturalistic settings in which qualitative approaches may be used. They are real-life situations that are naturally occurring, as opposed to artificial or contrived ones. Second, many people working with children and young people do so in individual or small group settings. They often do not have access to the larger samples typical of quantitative research, but, in contrast, they frequently do have access to small groups at a detailed and intensive level.

Third, children and young people represent an excellent source of the kind of data that are at the heart of qualitative research – rich descriptions in words and pictures that capture their experiences and understandings, rather than the cold, abstract findings that often derive from numerical analysis. Many research reports, including those that are largely quantitative, are enlivened by qualitative commentary of this kind, particularly when enriched by the actual words used by children and young people themselves. Sometimes a single comment from a child's perspective will convey much more meaning about the impact of research than a whole array of figures. The following extract comes from possibly the largest quantitative literacy study reported in the world, with almost 70,000 children and young people participating, but one that was enriched by qualitative data. It is the final part of a statement made by a young person who was not only a research participant but also a contributor to and communicator of the research, by providing an account of her experience of the research process at a dissemination conference:

> When all this started I couldn't read. I was a failure. Now I have a cupboardful of books at home. My favourite authors are Roald Dahl and J.K. Rowling. Now I am a success. (MacKay, 2006: 185)

A fourth advantage of qualitative approaches lies in the fact that a very large number of research projects with children and young people are carried out by people who are not ultimately reporting to the major research funding bodies. These major funders have traditionally been concerned with large quantitative studies based on inferential statistics. Conversely, child practitioners are often giving an account of their work to managers who themselves work in the caring professions – heads of establishments or services in education, health or social services. It is in these settings that most value is often placed on project reports that are enlivened by rich descriptions that highlight the participation and experiences of children and young people. Even some of the large funders, including those with a primary interest in research with children and young people, have in recent times moved towards funding a large number of small-scale research projects which, in their nature, are likely to be qualitative. For example, Koshy (2010) refers to the fact that in recent years the important role of small-scale action research projects has been highlighted in the number of small research grants made available in England and Wales by the Training and Development Agency for Schools and the Department of Education. She also refers to a similar trend in the USA.

A fifth benefit of doing qualitative research with children and young people arises from its very nature as participative research. A number of research journals, such as those of the British Psychological Society, no longer describe those who take part in research as 'subjects' but as 'participants'. However, while this policy gives out a good signal of respect and partnership, it is often the case in quantitative work, as shown by Table 7.1 in Chapter 7, that people are the subject of study rather than participants in a meaningful sense. Participation is more than involvement. 'Authentic participation means immersing people in the focus of the enquiry and the research method, and involving them in data collection and analysis' (Gray, 2004: 374). A theme of this book is partnership with children and young people, and encouraging research that involves true participation. In seeking to promote partnership and authentic participation of children and young people in the literacy study cited previously, MacKay (2006) used the five *context variables* (see Chapter 2) of vision, profile, commitment, ownership and declaration.

The entire project was predicated on a context in which everyone was fully committed to it and ownership was enjoyed at every level from researcher to the youngest pupil in nursery. Declarations were constantly made that this project was going to succeed and that nothing would stand in its way (MacKay, 2006: 87).

A final advantage of espousing qualitative approaches is that they have moved from the fringes of science, where they were once treated with suspicion as being less than scientific, to a position in which they are increasingly valued. There is evidence that qualitative research will become still more important and central in society in the future. A survey of the views of over 800 UK psychologists regarding future trends in research pointed to two developments (Haste et al., 2001). First, there would be an increased research emphasis on everyday life, quality of life and the whole person. Second, research would move increasingly from the laboratory to real-world settings. These holistic interests in well-being and in research conducted in natural settings are central features of qualitative approaches, and suggest that these approaches will become increasingly important.

Difficulties with qualitative research

At the same time, qualitative research also has its difficulties and limitations. Conducting real-world research requires a recognition that work must be done in 'complex, messy, poorly controlled "field" settings' (Robson, 2011), and those of us who do a lot of it know that real-world research with children and young people is usually even messier. MacKay and Watson characterized their group work intervention for early literacy – a mixed quantitative/qualitative study – as 'an excellent example of such messiness':

> The planned group work intervention for the experimental subgroup could not proceed because the group worker took ill; the home link teacher met with discouragement in her home support plan; the peer tutoring by older pupils in the Easter holidays did not get off the ground because of lack of response; one of the two researchers made a career change in the middle of the study; no sooner had the intervention begun than the school had to prepare for a merger with another school in the area; and in the middle of it all local government reorganisation took place, resulting among other things in the termination of funding and the necessity for a new grant application. (MacKay and Watson, 1999: 34)

These are the real issues that face practitioners seeking to do research with children and young people in the natural environments that dictate the need for qualitative approaches. They are seldom mentioned in published studies, since authors tend to smooth over the wrinkles as much as possible and not to highlight apparent flaws. However, these 'flaws' reflect the unavoidable challenges in this kind of research and they should not be a seen as a discouragement. MacKay and Watson (1999) go on to note, with regard to the above study: 'Nevertheless, the intervention was successful.'

Qualitative approaches are sometimes seen as a less rigorous alternative to quantitative research. This should never be the case, and much of what passes as qualitative is simply sloppy. It should not be a matter of saying, 'We couldn't get the numbers so we turned it into a qualitative study.' Qualitative, as noted in the 'health warning' from Richardson (1996), does not equate with 'easy', and indeed some methods of qualitative analysis are in various respects more difficult and more laborious than quantitative methods.

It is also the case that sometimes the data gathered for a project are left at the level of qualitative descriptions when they could more usefully have been categorized, counted and presented as quantitative data. It is a good maxim that if something can be counted it probably should be. Meaning, significance and trends can easily be lost in the midst of descriptions, and while rich descriptions will always enhance research findings, they should not obscure straightforward facts and figures when these will present a clearer account of research results. Finally, qualitative data are prone to being seen as weak and inconclusive, and never advancing beyond the exploratory level. It is here that the principle of triangulation is of particular importance (see Chapter 5). Triangulating the findings from several different perspectives, such as using multiple data sources for the same finding, can strengthen data that would be weak if presented singly but are robust if reinforced from different strands of enquiry. An example of triangulation is shown in the case study by Briggs et al. (1995) later in this chapter.

In summary, it may be said that qualitative research offers many persuasive benefits for those who are doing research with children and young people. So long as its difficulties and limitations are recognized it is a powerful approach that is likely to prove indispensable for everyone who is working in this field.

Qualitative approaches: an overview

Although we have been able to define key features and themes in qualitative research, it must be acknowledged that this is a complex area marked by few clear definitions, a variety of viewpoints on what constitutes qualitative enquiry, a lack of agreed terminology and a range of approaches that show considerable overlap. 'Qualitative is a slippery term, put to a variety of uses, and carrying a variety of conceptual associations' (Freebody, 2003: 35).

Four approaches are introduced here, selected on the basis that they are the ones most frequently referred to in basic texts on qualitative research methods. These are: *grounded theory*, *ethnography*, *narrative analysis* and the *case study*. While there has been a great deal of often strenuous debate, not only about the essential differences across these approaches but also about different schools of thought within each approach, the extent to which they overlap rather than be mutually exclusive will be apparent. A strict adherence to the technical specification of any one of the methods discussed may be a useful discipline for the student who is writing a dissertation or thesis and must show an informed understanding of a specific research methodology. However, it is much more common among practitioners and others who are doing research with children and young people to use a mixture of methods rather than to seek for a 'pure' methodology within one approach.

What all of the methods seek to do is to bring discipline and structure to qualitative enquiry in terms of how data are collected, analysed and interpreted, and how theory is constructed. All bring a different theoretical and practical emphasis, and each lends itself more to one type of enquiry than another. *Grounded theory* was one of the earliest structured approaches in qualitative research, and emphasized the value of not imposing preconceived theories and models on the data to be collected. It also brought considerable structure and formality to data analysis in a field that was often viewed as lacking scientific rigour. *Ethnography* stressed the need to understand the cultural context of the subject of study through aiming to become immersed in it. *Narrative analysis* focused on how individuals create meaning through the construction of stories and stressed the importance of researchers listening in depth to the narratives that made sense of their experience. The *case study* provided a means of obtaining an overall picture of a single entity being studied, whether an individual, a family, a group or an institution.

The overlapping nature of these approaches will be apparent from the many attempts made to demonstrate their common features. Thus, for example, Floersch et al. (2010) argued for the integration of grounded theory and narrative analysis, since together they provide a 'multidimensional understanding'; Pettigrew (2000) wrote of a 'happy marriage' of ethnography and grounded theory; and Taber (2010) saw the commonalities in ethnography and narrative analysis as an argument in favour of multiple methodologies.

The following sections in this chapter provide a brief account of each approach, together with an example of some aspect of its use or of its application to a particular research area. There is a key focus on the case study approach as offering a wide range of mixed methods that are accessible to those doing research with children and young people.

Grounded theory

Glaser and Strauss (1967) coined the term 'grounded theory' to convey the idea that theory emerges from or is grounded in the data. In the early days of qualitative research, when qualitative approaches were seen by many as being largely unscientific, grounded theory made a significant contribution to the field through its systematic methodology in the analysis of data and its development of a theoretical perspective. The fact that by the 1990s the two founders of this approach fundamentally disagreed as to what constitutes grounded theory highlights some of the difficulties and complexities associated with the still-developing field of qualitative research.

The starting point is the selection of a real-life situation as an area of study, and what is relevant to illuminating that area is allowed to emerge from the data that are collected. These data may be in a vast variety of forms, and are likely to include interviews and observation, with considerable emphasis placed on participants' own accounts of their experience. In addition, use may be made of many documentary sources, such as letters or diaries. Grounded theory is especially useful in situations 'where little is known about a particular topic or problem area, or where a new and exciting outlook is needed in familiar settings' (Holloway, 1997: 81). It is therefore likely to appeal to practitioners working in the constantly changing world of children and young people, where often researchers come up with interesting and innovative ideas.

Any brief overview of grounded theory will always be inadequate, as it has its own technical vocabulary and procedures, together with a large number of expectations regarding the precise ways in which data will be collected, organized and analysed. Among these are the expectation that there should not be a study of the existing research literature on the topic of study prior to the collection of the data and that interviews should not be recorded. For these reasons, many studies adopting a grounded theory approach do not adhere particularly closely to the more 'pure' methods followed by either of the two schools of practice that have developed from the founders. Nevertheless, it is one of the most widely used qualitative research methods, and any researcher who wishes to follow its methods closely will be rewarded by taking the time necessary to study it in depth (see the recommended book by Birks and Mills [2011] at the end of this chapter).

Coding

Data analysis in grounded theory goes on throughout the research and progresses by means of *coding* and *categorizing*. Coding is the key process, by which data are broken down into component parts. The approach taken to coding interview and other data in grounded theory is of general value across all research paradigms. Essentially, it replaces the general impressions the researcher forms of what is being said by participants with a more rigorous and systematic method of using all of the available data to allow core themes to emerge. Coding assists with the organization of large amounts of sometimes quite amorphous text, and assists in the discovery of key concepts and patterns that would be difficult to detect just by reading a transcript and seeking to make a summary of it.

Each separate idea is given a label, often using the words or phrases used by the participants themselves. The transcripts of interviews and observations, and the words used in documents, can be coded line by line, and large numbers of labels generated, so that the ideas are truly grounded in the data and not superimposed on it by pre-existing theories. For example, coding labels in a study of children who have moved to a new area or a new school might include descriptions such as 'missing friends' or 'feeling unsure'. The process generally begins with *initial coding*, by which numerous codes are generated to bring together statements that appear to be related. *Focused coding* then follows, by which the initial codes are reviewed and less useful ones eliminated. For example, codes that are associated with hardly any statements may be combined with larger ones, while codes with large numbers of statements may be subdivided. The process is an iterative one in which ideas are constantly reviewed and refined as the researcher works through the text line by line, and interview by interview.

As analysis progresses these codes are collapsed into categories, or themes, containing similar ideas. These might include 'socialization' or 'anxiety'. Ideally, the process of coding and categorizing proceeds until the point of *saturation* is reached, in which no further categories are emerging. The resulting categories are used to generate theory. For example, the data might illuminate particular stages through which children pass when they move home or school.

The transcript of a few lines of an interview with a primary school head teacher (Table 8.1) illustrates at the microlevel the way in which statements may be coded and then formed into broader categories. (This is taken from the interview excerpt shown later on in this chapter in Box 8.6 where case study methods are described.)

Table 8.1 Interview coding and categories

Text	*Coding*
Before it started *I was in despair* as there were so many children who were having *massive fights at lunchtime, and large gangs attacking each other.* In fact, underneath my office I kept the *bricks and stones and bits of wood that they had been battering each other with.* It was literally that bad.	Staff despair Children fighting Violence
It didn't seem to matter what we did, working with the parents or getting the parents up. It didn't seem to matter – *we just couldn't get these children under control.*	Failed attempts by staff Strategies involving parents Children uncontrolled
This was *a great worry*, as *it became so bad* that the school had what came to be called 'the OK Corral' and *all the children who couldn't behave, getting into trouble regularly – and there was a great number of them – they were herded into one area of the playground* and the *janitor's job was to look after them.* When staff went on in-service courses and said what school they were from *people used to laugh* and *members of staff got quite hurt* about the school's reputation.	Staff anxiety Deteriorating situation Disruptive behaviour Scale of problem Failed attempts by staff Strategies involving staff Public view of school Staff upset
Categories	*Coding*
Disruptive behaviour and violence	Children fighting Violence Children uncontrolled Disruptive behaviour Scale of problem
Lack of effective strategies	Children uncontrolled Deteriorating situation Strategies involving parents Strategies involving staff Failed attempts by staff
School's reputation	Public view of school
Negative impact on staff	Staff despair Staff anxiety Staff upset

Source: Briggs, S., MacKay, T. and Miller, S. (1995) 'The Edinbarnet Playground Project: changing aggressive behaviour through structured intervention', *Educational Psychology in Practice*, 11 (2): 37–44. Data archives: transcript not in the published report.

This was just a small part of one interview among many interviews with school staff and children. The overall picture that emerged, graphically illustrated at every level of detail, was of a school that had a bad reputation in the wider community and in which widespread violence and disruption were having a major negative impact on pupil and staff morale and well-being, while staff were in despair through lack of effective strategies to deal with the situation. The systematic approach to generating codes and categories from hundreds of individual statements allowed an accurate picture to be built up of the weight to be attached to the key themes emerging as being experienced by the staff and pupils.

Ethnography

Ethnography has a long history as the research method of anthropology. An ethnography is a description of a cultural or social group or system. The central feature of ethnographic research is that it aims for total immersion in the culture being studied, usually through participant observation. Ethnographers have been studying all aspects of child development and experience in varying cultural and social settings for a very long time (e.g. Mead and Wolfenstein, 1955; Whiting and Edwards, 1988; Whiting et al., 1975). One study involved research teams in different countries asking similar questions about child-raising practices and using similar methods across social settings (Whiting, 1963). Two examples of ethnography are given here, the first relating to the emotional experience of infants and toddlers in day-care centres, the second to teenagers in a skateboarding culture.

In a sociological study, Leavitt (1995) examined the emotional culture in day-care settings. Their study is a good illustration of how researchers using an ethnographic approach, while not having to go away and live in the culture they are studying as many anthropologists have done, still become sufficiently immersed in it to develop insights that are not available through other approaches. Through a period of seven years, on one day a week from when the children arrived in the morning until they went home at night, they became part of the lives of infants and toddlers in 12 settings across six day-care centres. As a participant observer they talked and played with the children, held and comforted crying babies, intervened when safety was threatened and generally helped out.

The result was a very powerful description and analysis of the everyday experience of young children in these settings. The emotional culture of the day-care centres was experienced through daily practices, including regulative norms, such as rules on crying, and carer beliefs regarding involvement and professional distance. Leavitt's analysis revealed troubling aspects of care in these settings, not in terms of meeting physical needs but in terms of responding to children emotionally. Often the issue of simply managing the children took precedence over meeting their emotional needs, leading to the children denying their feelings and suppressing their emotional expression. Leavitt concluded that important issues can arise in the care of very young children whose carers may be working solely to earn a wage, while being alienated from their emotional needs.

As this example illustrates, ethnography is a qualitative research approach that gives importance to the interpretation of actions and the contexts in which they occur. While many people who are doing research with children and young people will not have the time or opportunity to become immersed in the culture they are studying, ethnographic approaches may be very suitable to practitioners who are already immersed in child settings because they work in them every day. This often creates unique opportunities for carrying out research at a depth that could not be attained by visiting researchers coming in to conduct a study in settings with which they are largely unfamiliar.

Theory plays an important role in ethnographic research. Existing themes can inform and be tested in this kind of research. Leavitt's research was conducted within a symbolic interactionist framework and interpreted in terms of Marxist theory. Nevertheless, new theory can often emerge from ethnographic field notes, observations and interviews. Box 8.1 lists some of the ethnographic methods used for doing research with children at the preschool stage.

BOX 8.1

Some ethnographic methods used for doing research with preschoolers

- **The transmission of cultural values:** passive participant observation + informal interviews + formal interviews.
- **Spontaneous use of English at home (bilingual child)** as practice play for peer play at school: narrative play – tape recordings of play sessions + field notes by the mother.
- **The social and creative behaviour** of four 'highly original' children: observation + video + interviews.
- **Peers constructing their own culture**: participant observation of access rituals and friendship and description of field entry strategies.
- **Pretend play**: ethnographic interviewing + non-participant observation + analysis of children's writings.
- **Excellence of practitioners working with children**: life stories and narrative accounts of several excellent practitioners in different contexts; stories constructed from interviews, participant observation, written correspondence and autobiographical reflection.

Source: Adapted from Hatch, J.A. (ed.) (1995) *Qualitative Research in Early Childhood Settings.* Westport, CT: Praeger.

Ethnographic approaches lend themselves to the study of children and young people of all ages and in every kind of setting. They are not only suitable for structured contexts such as the classroom, the young offenders' centre, the children's home, the hospital ward or the youth club, but also for the completely informal and unstructured settings in which children and young people meet together and pursue their leisure activities. Box 8.2 provides an example of ethnography very different from the early childhood setting of day care – a group of teenagers in a large city skateboarding park. It illustrates the flexibility of the ethnographic approach in that, in contrast with Leavitt's study, it is not dependent on either participant observation or the need to devote very substantial amounts of time over a protracted period.

BOX 8.2

An ethnographic study of teenagers skateboarding

Seifert and Hedderson (2010) were interested in intrinsic motivation because of its critical role in development, learning and well-being. Intrinsic motivation occurs when individuals are engaging in an activity freely or autonomously because they find it enjoyable and rewarding in and of itself, as opposed to undertaking tasks under compulsion. It is fostered by contexts that nurture curiosity, exploration, challenge, mastery and interest. They therefore selected a spontaneous and natural context where young people seek to develop mastery of skills because they find it inherently enjoyable – a large city skateboarding park.

To provide a rich description of what it means to be intrinsically motivated, the research method they selected was ethnography. The fieldwork was carried out within a timescale that would be feasible for most researchers who wish to carry out a small-scale project with limited resources. The researcher (Hedderson) did not become a participant in the activity, although they spent considerable time interacting with those who were. They took on a role described as that of 'complete observer', becoming partially immersed in the venue, carrying out observations and taking notes. After six visits to the skateboard park, which represented about 8 hours of detailed observations, interviews commenced. They would pick out at random an individual to study and wait for an opportunity to make an approach. Often a skateboarder would approach the researcher and start a conversation.

Data were collected from 20 skateboarders, using mainly individual but also some group interviews. The interviews were semistructured and open-ended, and were conducted within a broader conversation about skateboarding. Questions about intrinsic motivation were derived from theoretical descriptions, and included a discussion of reasons for enjoyment of the activity, autonomy and control. The data were recorded in the form of field notes and jot notes, which were rewritten as transcripts. After an initial reading to develop an overall sense of the meaning, the participants' responses were broken down into units. This was done by extracting words or phrases conveying participants' thoughts and feelings about their experiences. These were clustered into sub-themes, which were then organized into higher-order themes – a process very similar to the use of coding and categories already described in relation to grounded theory.

To minimize bias and increase reliability, two researchers categorized the units and reached agreement on the themes. The themes were then compiled into a summary that was given to an independent group of skateboarders to comment on the interpretation. This group agreed that the summary was consistent with their own experience. Three main themes emerged relating to the factors that made skateboarding enjoyable: satisfaction and accomplishment; challenge; and freedom and autonomy.

As with most qualitative studies, this study was enriched by illustrating the themes with excerpts from notes taken during observations and from the responses of the participants. The authors concluded, within the limits of their methodology and the specific activity being investigated, that intrinsic motivation is more than freely choosing to engage in an activity for enjoyment, but that it appears to involve 'mastery of a challenge culminating in an intense subjective experience'.

Source: Seifert, T. and Hedderson, C. (2010) 'Intrinsic motivation and flow in skateboarding: an ethnographic study', *Journal of Happiness Studies,* 11 (3): 277–92.

Narrative analysis

Narrative analysis uses stories as data. It focuses on first-hand accounts of experience, and recognizes that people normally construe their lives in terms of they way they tell their own story. The method:

> refers to a family of approaches to divers kinds of texts, which have in common a storied form. As nations and governments construct preferred narratives about history, so do social movements, organisations, scientists, other professionals, ethnic/racial groups and individuals in stories of experience. (Riessman, 2003: 705).

When individuals or groups tell their story, it is a reconstruction and interpretation of the past rather than a factual account of it. The interest of narrative analysis is not in seeking to obtain an account of the past that is as factually accurate as possible, but in looking at the way those telling their story reimagine their lives.

A number of features characterize research that focuses on the role of narrative. It usually centres on life story research using oral or written history. It uses in-depth interviews with minimal structure rather than questionnaires, and in the course of the interview the researcher is essentially a listener who says very little and uses as few prompts as possible. A good example is provided in a study by Brooks and Dallos (2009) which explored young people's understanding of the development of their difficulties. The sample comprised five young women, all in the age range 15–17 years, who had been referred to child and adolescent mental health services. The narrative method was chosen in preference to other qualitative methods because the study aimed to elicit the developing stories the young people held about their lives, to explore their understanding of their experiences and what these experiences meant to them.

A single, broad, narrative-inducing question was used as a prompt to participants: 'Can you tell me about the important experiences that you have had that have led you to this point in your life?' The only additional prompts did not arise from any questions prepared beforehand by the researchers but rather served to elicit more information on points the young people had already raised – 'You mentioned _____; can you tell me more about what happened/how you felt?' Thus, the narratives were felt to give a very clear representation of what the young people themselves believed to be relevant or important with regard to their lives and how they made sense of their experiences.

Nevertheless, despite the fact that the researcher gives minimal prompts, narratives are always seen as being 'co-constructed' (even when the audience is oneself or an imaginary other), and the presence and prompting of the researcher plays a role in the story that is formulated for that particular context. An interview represents a relational context, and research participants consciously and unconsciously tailor their responses to fit that context, knowing that they are presenting themselves to a particular audience. Thus, stories are created and recreated in the midst of the shifting connections individuals forge among past, present and future as they seek to make sense of their experience.

The data for a narrative analysis study therefore encompass long sections of talk or written narrative. Over the course of single or multiple interviews, an extended account of human life and experience relating to the context being studied is developed. Narrative essays can also be obtained, and this could be done in large quantities, for example, from a whole class of children or young people. Field notes and transcripts of interviews and written productions are then analysed and interpreted.

As with the other qualitative approaches introduced here, narrative analysis has its own technical vocabulary, methodologies and varied schools of thought. Methods of data analysis can vary considerably from fairly simple intuitive approaches right through to very highly technical and formalized coding systems. A key part of the analysis is 'restorying' – the researcher's process of selecting particular features of the narrative data and then presenting these in the form of new descriptions of life experience (Cresswell, 2008). It is the process of reassembling the data into a different framework to elucidate underlying meanings and find new levels of significance relevant to the research topic. The example in Box 8.3 shows a simple approach to data analysis that was driven by theory and used a *thematic* approach.

BOX 8.3

Narrative analysis: 'An Asperger Diary'

MacKay and Carrison unearthed an unusually rich source of data for narrative analysis – the childhood diaries of a woman Goldy Carrison who was subsequently diagnosed with Asperger's syndrome. MacKay first encountered her in the course of his clinical work when she was referred to his national diagnosis and assessment service for autistic spectrum disorders. After being diagnosed at the age of 47 she subsequently attended for therapy, in the course of which she referred to her diaries. These proved to be a remarkably rich seam of detailed narrative covering her day-to-day life and thoughts from age 13 to 15. All were written in beautiful calligraphy, and they were so detailed that 18 volumes covered one single year. In that year alone there were over 100,000 words of childhood reflection on every aspect of her daily life and experience – her relationships with parents, peers and teachers; her all-absorbing preoccupations; the confused and frightening world of her sensory experience; her attempts to make sense of her emotions and the emotions of others; her quest for aloneness and her fear of being alone; her inability to make sense of a world of social conformity, in which girls were caught up in senseless activities centred on fashion, make-up and boys.

MacKay and Goldy moved on from a therapist/client relationship to become co-researchers. The aim was to carry out a narrative analysis of her diaries and 'restory' her life to look for meaning and significance in what had previously been simply a bewildering existence.

The approach to data analysis was theory-driven and thematic. The theory was that a confusing and disparate life story that seemed to lack coherent meaning could be reconstructed to make sense if analysed in terms of the diagnostic criteria that make up Asperger's syndrome. The thematic approach meant segmenting the narrative in terms of its dominant and recurring themes. Both researchers independently undertook the laborious task of working through the entire data set line by line and first identifying themes. Every segment of text that illustrated a theme was transcribed on to a spreadsheet. There was a very high degree of correspondence between the researchers in terms of the segments of text selected and the themes they represented.

The large number of themes identified were viewed as sub-themes, for collapsing later into higher-order themes (an example is given in Table 8.1). Sub-themes included fear of people, loneliness, obsession with art, sensitivity to touch and perfectionism. Higher-order themes included difficulties with social interaction, all-encompassing preoccupations and sensory sensitivity. The themes that emerged were then compared with the diagnostic criteria for Asperger's syndrome. The result was that what had previously seemed to be a childhood life story that was incoherent and baffling made sense to both researchers, in their respective roles as clinician and narrator when restoried as a coherent narrative of living with undiagnosed Asperger's syndrome.

Source: MacKay, T. and Carrison, G. (forthcoming) *An Asperger Diary.*

This example shows how narrative can be analysed in a way that is straightforward, intuitive and accessible. Narrative approached in this way can tell a powerful and credible story without having to rely on experience in using any of the highly technical coding systems. Table 8.2 shows a sample extracted from the analysis of selected text into sub-themes.

Table 8.2 Narrative analysis: deriving themes from text

Narrative	*Sub-themes*
I always seem to get on with people a year or two younger than myself better than with those of my own age, although most of them laugh at me – or I imagine they do – at school.	Peer relations
Main school is horrible – especially the cloakroom where there are loads of people. I *have* to get away from them.	Reaction to crowds
In exactly a week's time it is my birthday. I'd rather not think about it. I haven't decided exactly what I want to do. I s'pose the best thing I'd like to do is go for a long ride in the morning and paint in the afternoon on my own. And by 'on my own' I mean no parents either.	Special events; art; loner
Karen gave me notepaper, a book on lettering and … nail varnish! Oh well, perhaps it will be useful as paint or something.	Fashion and appearance
Birthdays, Christmases, holidays – oh how I hate them. Only art and dinner breaks are nice. I treasure my breaks alone in the art room.	Special events; art; loner
We then listened to Monteverdi's Orpheo opera which was horrible. Two people screeching on about how they loved each other (or it might have been that they hated each other – I don't know).	Lack of empathy
Nicky didn't do any of her art because of her grandma having a heart attack. I thought that if that happened to me, it certainly wouldn't stop me doing my art.	Art; lack of empathy
I was absolutely soaked as I didn't wear a jumper, but was keen to continue. By now the rain was pouring down and there was a high wind. I refused to go under shelter.	Sensory
Karen is correct when she says I have no feelings. My parents and relations for instance. I could never hug them or hold their hand. To be completely frank, I don't think I would care if Pa died. I might begin to feel sorry that I hadn't been very nice to him, but I force that thought back immediately and carry on without another thought. Above all, I would never even *dream* of crying.	Lack of empathy; atypical emotions

(Continued)

Table 8.2 (Continued)

Narrative	*Sub-themes*
I decided to try her bicycle. I lost control of the steering, my balance and my nerve – not that I had any anyway – and landed in the hedge.	Coordination
Now I am about to announce the Fact of the Year! Goldy Carrison has got a new shirt!! I didn't want it, but daddy bought it for me. I wore it yesterday to be obliging, and someone sneakily must have thrown my old one away, so I've got to wear this. It is black – which is convenient because I can wipe my paintbrushes on it without anyone knowing	Fashion and appearance

Source: MacKay, T. and Carrison, G. (forthcoming) *An Asperger Diary.*

PUTTING RESEARCH INTO PRACTICE 8.1 – DESIGNING A QUALITATIVE STUDY

The aim of this practical is to consider how a qualitative research project would be designed and how the data would be collected.

Chapters 5–8 have now covered the main issues relating to the design and methodology of a research project. Using the information you have studied so far, select a suitable topic of your own choice for a research project. This may be a practice topic or it may be an actual area in which you intend to carry out a complete research project. You may wish to select from a range of qualitative approaches, and you may also wish to include quantitative methods. Answer the following questions.

- How would you set about designing this study?
- What types of question would you ask and what would be the range of information you would need to gather?
- From what sources would you collect the information?
- What methods would you use to collect it?
- Would the topic of study seem particularly suited to grounded theory, ethnography, narrative analysis or a combination of approaches? For example, is this a topic that would be best researched by being totally immersed in the culture you are studying? Would there be advantages in becoming a participant/observer? Would you get the data you need by using semistructured interviews or would you gain more by using few prompts and getting lengthy narratives from your participants?

Case study methods

What is a 'case' and how is it studied? There are examples of case studies going back for more than a century. Our classic idea of a *case study* is probably exemplified by the work of Freud. Box 8.4 illustrates an extract from Freud's (1909) case analysis of a phobia in a five-year-old boy, little Hans. Fortunately there are alternative and more modern approaches to case studies. The case study approach is used by researchers from every discipline working with children and young people. It is a primary focus of this chapter because it provides a flexible way of carrying out a research project using a wide range of methods drawn from different approaches, both qualitative and quantitative.

BOX 8.4

Extract from *Analysis of a Phobia in a Five Year Old Boy* (Freud, 1909)

Other observations, also made at the time of the summer holidays, suggest that all sorts of new developments were going on in the little boy.

Hans, four and a quarter. This morning Hans was given his usual daily bath by his mother and afterwards dried and powdered. As his mother was powdering round his penis and taking care not to touch it, Hans said: 'Why don't you put your finger there?'

Mother: Because that would be piggish.
Hans: What's that? Piggish? Why?
Mother: Because it's not proper.
Hans: [*laughing*] But it's great fun.[1]

[1]Another mother ... told me of a similar attempt at seduction on the part of her three-and-a-half-year-old daughter. She had a pair of drawers made for the little girl and ... to see whether they were not too tight for walking ... passed her hand upwards along the inner surface of the child's thigh. Suddenly the little girl shut her legs together ... saying: 'Oh mummy, do leave your hand there. It feels so lovely.'

Source: Freud, S. (1909) Analysis of a Phobia in a Five Year Old Boy. From *The Complete Psychological Works of Sigmund Freud*, translated and edited by James Strachey, published by The Hogarth Press. Reprinted with permission of The Random House Group Ltd.

As a research method, the case study is an investigation of an individual, a family, a group, an institution, a community, or even a resource, programme or intervention. It is a study of any single unit or entity, however large or small, with clear boundaries. Some examples might include: the relationship between a mother and her terminally ill or disabled child; one child's strategies for coping with epilepsy at school; or a study of a child's care experience while their mother is in hospital. A survey on childcare workers, which solicits the practices and views of practitioners on the lack of an adequate practice framework for addressing the needs of the children of the mentally ill, can be enhanced by a case study of a family that nicely illustrates the whole situation. If a new practice policy is set up and interventions implemented by way of a special unit, this could be a case study on the process of change, in which views of managers, workers, parents and children are sought. Classic case studies in child research have included Ball's (1981) study of Beachside Comprehensive School and Lewis's (1961) study of the Sánchez family. The idea is to make up a total picture or a vignette that 'says it all'.

Since it is the unit of analysis rather than the methodology that defines a case study, there are no specific methods that are distinctive to this approach. Case studies employ a variety of methods including observation, questionnaires, standardized assessments, rating scales, in-depth interviews and other data sources such as narratives, documents and reports. They can therefore be combined with the other approaches described in this chapter – grounded theory, ethnography and narrative analysis. Indeed, although the case study is one of the main types of qualitative research, it very frequently includes traditional quantitative approaches. Its lack of a complex technical vocabulary and of any sophisticated or distinctive methodology of its own, its capability of being combined with other methods including classic quantitative ones and its suitability for the real-life settings in which most child practitioners work make it a very appropriate and popular choice for doing research with children.

One case study is described here in detail (Box 8.5) – the Edinbarnet Playground Project (Briggs et al., 1995). This study is very relevant to the contexts faced by child researchers for a number of reasons. It is a mixed study that includes a range of quantitative and qualitative methods, and is therefore very typical of a design likely to be useful to most practitioners. While the approach was imaginative and the outcome highly effective, the ideas and methods were all essentially very simple and accessible. Also, it was research in an important area: it addressed a real-life problem that had to be tackled in an innovative way. In addition, it was carried out without the need for much by way of additional resources, as the main resource was the work and commitment of the practitioners who were already involved in the situation. Another feature was that it highlighted the importance of some of the 'context variables' discussed in Chapter 2. Finally, it was research that *made a difference*. It not only illuminated a situation that required investigation but it also addressed it in ways that brought about lasting and important change.

BOX 8.5

The Edinbarnet Playground Project (Briggs et al., 1995): a worked example of a case study

Background: Briggs and MacKay were approached by the head teacher of a large primary school in a neighbourhood of multiple socio-economic disadvantage where they were working as educational psychologists. They were asked to investigate and find ways of solving a major problem – playground trouble. Every day at intervals and lunch breaks the playground had become a focus of conflict, bullying and aggression, and this was spilling over into disruption when pupils returned to their classrooms. Things had become so bad that the worst troublemakers were eventually confined to a particular area of the playground known as the 'OK Corral' under the supervision of the janitor.

Defining the problem: It was decided that a suitable starting point would be to identify as precisely as possible the extent and nature of the problem. Following a period of playground observation, teachers were invited to nominate pupils in their classes who had the greatest difficulties with their playground behaviour. Large numbers were identified, but most of them clustered within two year groups, the primary 4 and 5 classes (ages 8 and 9).

Planning intervention: To address the problem, a range of strategies was planned, with a central focus on a group work intervention. For this purpose a third colleague (Miller), a local social worker with experience of group work, was enlisted. The janitor, as the person with most experience of the difficulties at the point of occurrence, was given a key role in making the final selection of the 12 most troublesome pupils from the year groups in question. A meeting was held with the parents of the identified children, and regular planning meetings were also held involving school management, the researchers and a class teacher assigned to support the group work.

Two groups of six were run weekly for 10 weeks, each group lasting about an hour. The groups had closed membership to enhance group identity, and they aimed to build self-esteem, to explore issues such as honesty and trust, to promote increased awareness of the negative effects of current behaviour patterns for everyone, including the group members themselves, and to share in the investigation of alternative ways of behaving. To ensure that the focus was not exclusively on this group of 'problem children', the whole of primaries 4 and 5 participated in a bullying survey, the results of which were used as a basis for training sessions with the entire staff. Workshops were also run for the parents of all pupils in these classes. Weekly targets were identified for each child and teamwork was encouraged to help children to support one another in reaching the targets.

Data collection methods: Several methods of data collection were used – questionnaires, ongoing teacher ratings of pupil behaviour, playground incident records, semistructured staff feedback forms and staff and pupil interviews. All of these methods yielded qualitative data, but several of them also provided data that could be analysed by quantitative means. These data provided the basis of the published report but all of the various sources gave a vast amount of additional qualitative information that was of use in informing the intervention as it proceeded and in ongoing discussions with school staff and management.

Questionnaires: Before the intervention started all pupils in primaries 4 and 5 ($N = 90$) took part in a bullying survey designed for the project. This sampled their awareness and personal experience of bullying in the school and in the playground and allowed them to give their own descriptions of how it made them feel and what they had done in response to it. This served to highlight the extent of the problem, its effects on individual children and the key role the playground played as the main locus of bullying and aggression. Following completion of the project the same pupils completed a second questionnaire allowing pre/post changes to be assessed.

Behaviour ratings: Class teachers kept individual ratings of the classroom behaviour of the children attending the groups before, during and two months after the intervention period. This was done daily using a five-point scale ranging from 'very good' to 'very bad', together with descriptive commentary.

Playground incident records: The head teacher kept a record of all playground incidents reported to them for one month prior to the project. This exercise was repeated exactly a year later, well after the conclusion of the intervention, and allowed for longer-term follow-up. These records were a detailed description of the incident that had taken place. To assist in coding them, they were entered under one of three categories – 'niggle', 'serious' and 'very serious'. The researchers then gave each record a weighted score to reflect how major or otherwise the incident was. This therefore provided both quantitative and qualitative data.

Staff feedback forms: Most staff in the school returned semistructured feedback forms after completion of the intervention. These contained simple prompts to generate their views on the process of change taking place in the children and in the school as a whole as a result of the project. This allowed key themes to emerge from the perspective of staff.

Staff and pupil interviews: These were the data sources that provided the richest qualitative descriptions. Staff interviews were conducted at the end of the project with the head teacher and teachers in primaries 4 and 5. These were recorded, so that full transcripts could be analysed. The children in the groups were interviewed in pairs.

Results: These multiple sources of data provided the process of triangulation so helpful in small-scale projects. Questionnaire returns from pupils were strengthened by teachers' views on feedback forms and interviews and by their ratings of behaviour, and all of these could be compared with records of playground incidents and with the views expressed by pupils in their interviews. The quantitative analysis of questionnaires, behaviour ratings and incident records was conducted using simple methods such as chi-square tests (see Chapter 6), and showed persuasively that there was less of a bullying culture in the school, that the playground was a better place to play, that classroom behaviour had improved and that playground incidents had decreased. While these results produced the straightforward outcomes in terms of statistical significance, the really meaningful sense of what the project was like and what it had achieved emerged from the qualitative data. For example, one boy stated that what he enjoyed most about the group was 'learning to be good', while another commented that he was now playing team games like football whereas previously he only ever played combat games.

Conclusions: The simple ideas and methods used in this project provided a means of identifying the core elements of a problem situation, establishing an intervention to address it and collecting and analysing data to illustrate the quality of the process and to demonstrate the effectiveness of the outcomes. Following the published study, and two years after completion of the initiative, the head teacher was interviewed once more. She reported that the project had been a turning point that had transformed the school and its ethos and had turned the focus from controlling behaviour to promoting education and citizenship.

Source: Adapted from Briggs, S., MacKay, T. and Miller, S. (1995) 'The Edinbarnet Playground Project: changing aggressive behaviour through structured intervention', *Educational Psychology in Practice*, 11 (2): 37–44.

The case study described in Box 8.5 was very much in the tradition of 'participatory action research'. The school and its pupils were not subjects to be studied but collaborators in a process of investigation and change. It was *their* project. It demonstrated the importance of some of the *context variables* described in Chapter 2, particularly ownership. In identifying the factors that were seen as being vital to the success of the project, the authors noted that 'school ownership of the project was crucial'. By involving everyone at every stage, 'it was clear that the school owned the project and had a high level of investment in its success' (Briggs et al., 1995: 42). It was given the highest profile at all times, not just with the staff and pupils in the main target classes, but throughout the school. An anecdote from the head teacher illustrates this point. One day in the playground a girl was heard to say to one of the boys in the group, 'You can't do that any more – you're on the playground project.' A process was taking place by which the group members became such collaborators that they turned from being the playground tyrants to being its custodians as a place of peaceful cooperation.

One of the attractive features of this case study for practitioners who may feel daunted by more technical qualitative methodologies is that you can select simple but effective methods to gather and present your data. Indeed, sometimes a simple transcript of key themes from an interview will convey a more meaningful sense of the impact of a project than a series of data tables. Box 8.6 shows a transcript taken from the final interview with the head teacher. It provides insights that quantitative data could never convey. The transcript does not appear in the published study but is taken from the authors' data archives.

BOX 8.6

The Edinbarnet Playground Project (Briggs et al., 1995) Excerpt of transcript: final interview with head teacher

Before it started I was in despair as there were so many children who were having massive fights at lunchtime, and large gangs attacking each other. In fact, underneath my office I kept the bricks and stones and bits of wood that they had been battering each other with. It was literally that bad. It didn't seem to matter what we did, working with the parents or getting the parents up. It didn't seem to matter – we just couldn't get these children under control. This was a great worry as it became so bad that the school had what came to be called 'the OK Corral' and all the children who couldn't behave, getting into trouble regularly – and there was a great number of them – they were herded into one area of the playground and the janitor's job was to look after them.

When staff went on in-service courses and said what school they were from people used to laugh and members of staff got quite hurt about the school's reputation. Now it is quite different on courses as other people ask about projects like the playground project and this has been a boost for staff morale. I haven't been under stress such as I have been under previously.

One of the things that has come from the project is that I thought that nothing could be done, but I have a more positive view that children can change, and before I was never positive about this. I now see that there are things we can do, and I can see it going on here for a very long time.

Source: Briggs et al. (1995) data archives: transcript not in the published report.

In summary, qualitative research methods, or mixed methods that include a range of qualitative approaches, have a great deal to offer those who are planning to do research with children and young people. Qualitative findings enrich the data reported in every type of project, which are also usually illustrated and enlivened by selected quotations from interviews and narratives. Despite the health warnings given above about the fact that this is in many ways a difficult and technical field, even the novice researcher will find techniques, including some of those described in this chapter, that are relatively straightforward to apply with fruitful results. There is no predicting where a simple research project with children will lead, even though carried out with limited resources as part of the day-to-day work of a practitioner, if it is well conducted and relates to an important research question. The case study reported above had no research funding and was carried out in a school by practitioners just getting on with their job of 'making things better'. It led in its own small way to two other research studies opened up by its success – the Edinbarnet Reading Project (MacKay, 1999) and the Edinbarnet Early Reading Project (MacKay and Watson, 1999). These in turn led directly to the West Dunbartonshire Literacy Initiative (MacKay, 2006), a long-term study of mammoth proportions, involving a sample of almost 70,000 children and young people, with millions of pounds of research funding and bringing enormous benefits to a whole council area.

PUTTING RESEARCH INTO PRACTICE 8.2 – GATHERING QUALITATIVE DATA

The aim of this practical is to gain experience in the issues arising in gathering qualitative data.

This practical follows on from 'Putting Research into Practice 8.1' in which you were asked to select a qualitative research topic, plan its design and consider the methods you would use to gather data:

1 ***Designing and administering a semistructured interview.*** Semistructured interviews are used widely for generating both quantitative and qualitative data. Reread the section on interviews in Chapter 7 and the guidance on design given in Table 7.4 of Chapter 7. Design a semistructured interview that will generate qualitative data on your topic. This means that you will need plenty of open-ended questions that will give your participants the opportunity to express their thoughts in their own way, rather than having to choose from a limited range of responses. What are the main differences between the information you expect to obtain from the interview and the data a questionnaire on the same topic would give?
2 Once you have designed the interview, find a small number of participants on whom you can pilot it, even if only two or three. Ask their permission for the interview to be recorded so that you will have a full transcript to work from.
3 ***Obtaining a narrative.*** As a comparison with the semistructured interview approach, find one participant from whom you can obtain a narrative account relevant to your topic. Again, ask their permission for it to be recorded. Consider the main differences between the structure of your interview and your method of obtaining a narrative. Look again at the section in this chapter on 'Narrative analysis', and remember that a narrative is not just a set of longer answers to your interview questions. The topics in the narrative are largely generated by the participant and not by the researcher. Consider the single prompt question, with minimal further prompts, asked in the Brooks and Dallos (2009) study: 'Can you tell me the important experiences that you have had that have led you to this point in your life?' In short, use a prompt to orientate the participant in the direction of the topic you are investigating and let the participant generate their own account.
4 ***Compare and contrast.*** When you have collected your pilot data for this exercise, and have made transcripts of your material, look at the comparison between your interviews and your narrative. In what ways have they generated similar types of data? What are the key differences? What are their comparative advantages and disadvantages for the topic you are investigating?

PUTTING RESEARCH INTO PRACTICE 8.3 – ANALYSING QUALITATIVE RESULTS

The aim of this practical is to gain some preliminary experience in analysing results.

The task now is to carry out an analysis of the data you have collected in your interviews and narrative. The key idea is to be able to move from the overall impressions you have formed of what the participants are saying to breaking down their responses in a more systematic way into themes. It is not expected that you will use sophisticated or technical coding schemes at this stage:

1 ***Read the data thoroughly.*** The starting point is to read and reread your transcripts, together with any notes you have made during the process, so that you can move into the world of the participant and get a real feel for the data and the key messages that are coming across.

2 ***Cut and paste.*** The next task is to prepare for coding the data. This is essentially a 'cut and paste' job. It used to be a matter of literally cutting and pasting for many of us before the days when we could sit at leisure in a café or on a train and do it on our laptops. It can still be done this way for any who prefer to, or have to, work on hard copy, but it is very much less flexible and efficient. Whether you work from your computer or in hard copy, make sure you always work from a copy and leave the original transcript in one piece. First go through all of your text and highlight or underline every segment or unit of meaning. This may be a word, a phrase or a whole sentence. Essentially, it is any segment of the text that conveys a thought or idea relevant to your investigation. Look again at the two transcripts in the left-hand column of Tables 8.1 and 8.2. In Table 8.1 the whole transcript is shown and the italicized text shows what has been selected as units of meaning. In Table 8.2 the units of meaning have been extracted from the full text.

   Cut out every unit from the transcript and paste it into its own cell in a table (as in Table 8.2). Make sure that each unit is identified. This is most easily done by adding columns that number each unit and identify from which transcript it came.

3 ***Code the data.*** The next task is to make a preliminary coding of your data into themes. The column headed 'Coding' in Table 8.1 and the column headed 'Sub-themes' in Table 8.2 are examples of this. If one unit contains several themes, like some of the units in Table 8.2, copy these units as many times as you need until each time they appear they have only one theme in the column next to them. Now sort your units by theme (either using the 'sort' function or by shuffling your bits of paper into groups).

   What you will find at this stage is that several of your themes will group together into higher-order themes, like the 'Categories' shown in Table 8.1. Alternatively, there may be themes that are already too broad and that need to be subdivided.

4 ***Reliability and validity.*** It is very important in all research to find whether the way you have handled your text has reliability and validity (see the section covering this topic in Chapter 5). That is, would others have largely selected the same

segments of text and coded them in a similar way, and does it lead finally to a picture that meaningfully represents what your text is saying? The best way to check for reliability is to have someone else doing the same task independently and then compare your results. If you have a co-researcher working on the same project, you can then work together to achieve agreement on your themes.

This was the approach used to validity and reliability in the narrative analysis study of young people referred to mental health services:

> All the data were independently analysed by the researcher and sections of the interviews were independently analysed by colleagues. The independent analyses were then discussed, to strengthen validity and to ensure that the analyses could be 'recognised' by others, i.e. that the sense made of them could be shared by others'. (Brooks and Dallos, 2009: 105)

A similar approach was used in the ethnography study of skateboarding:

> First, two researchers categorised meaning units, which were compared to each other with refinements as needed, with agreement on themes being achieved. Second, the themes were compiled into a summary which was then presented to an independent group of skateboarders who were asked to comment on the interpretation. This second group agreed that the summary was consistent with their own experiences. (Seifert and Hedderson, 2010: 281)

References

Ball, S.J. (1981) *Beachside Comprehensive: a Case Study of Secondary Schooling*. Cambridge: Cambridge University Press.

Banister, P., Bruman, E., Parker, I., Taylor, M. and Tindall, C. (1994) *Qualitative Methods in Psychology: a Research Guide*. Buckingham: Open University Press.

Berg, B. (2009) *Qualitative Research Methods for the Social Sciences*, 7th edn. Boston, MA: Allyn & Bacon.

Briggs, S., MacKay, T. and Miller, S. (1995) 'The Edinbarnet Playground Project: changing aggressive behaviour through structured intervention', *Educational Psychology in Practice*, 11 (2): 37–44.

Brooks, E. and Dallos, R. (2009) 'Exploring young women's understandings of the development of difficulties: a narrative biographical analysis', *Clinical Child Psychology and Psychiatry*, 14 (1): 101–15.

Charmaz, K. (1995) 'Grounded theory', in J.A. Smith, R. Harré and L. van Langenhove (eds), *Rethinking Methods in Psychology*. Thousand Oaks, CA: Sage. pp. 27–49.

Creswell, J.W. (2008) 'Narrative research designs', in *Educational Research: Planning, Conducting and Evaluating Quantitative and Qualitative Research*, 3rd edn. Upper Saddle River, NJ: Pearson/Merrill Prentice Hall. pp. 511–50.

Floersch, J., Longhofer, J., Townsend, L. et al. (2010) 'Integrating thematic, grounded theory and narrative analysis: a case study of adolescent psychotropic treatments', *Qualitative Social Work*, 9 (3): 407–25.

Freebody, P. (2003) *Qualitative Research in Education: Interaction and Practice*. Thousand Oaks, CA: Sage.

Freud, S. (1909) *Analysis of a Phobia in a Five Year Old Boy. Pelican Freud Library. Vol. 8, Case Histories*. Harmondsworth: Penguin. pp. 169–306.

Glaser, B.G. and Strauss, A.L. (1967) *The Discovery of Grounded Theory; Strategies for Qualitative Research*. Chicago, IL: Aldine.

Gray, D. (2004) *Doing Research in the Real World*. Thousand Oaks, CA: Sage Publications.

Haste, H., Hogan, A. and Zachariou, Y. (2001) 'Back (again) to the future', *The Psychologist*, 14 (1): 30–3.

Hatch, J.A. (ed.) (1995) *Qualitative Research in Early Childhood Settings*. Westport, CT: Praeger.

Holloway, I. (1997) *Basic Concepts for Qualitative Research*. Oxford: Blackwell.

Kaplan, A. (1964) *The Conduct of Inquiry: Methodology for Behavioral Science*. San Francisco, CA: Chandler.

Kidder, L. and Fine, M. (1987). 'Qualitative and quantitative methods: when stories converge', in M. Mark and L. Shotland (eds), *New Directions in Program Evaluation*. San Francisco, CA: Jossey-Bass.

Koshy, V. (2010) *Action Research for Improving Practice: a Step-By-Step Guide*, 2nd edn. London: Sage.

Leavitt, R.L. (1995) 'The emotional culture of infant–toddler day care', in J.A. Hatch (ed.), *Qualitative Research in Early Childhood Settings*. Westport, CT: Praeger.

Lewis, O. (1961) *The Children of Sánchez*. New York: Vintage.

MacKay, T. (1999) 'Can endemic reading failure in socially disadvantaged children be successfully tackled?', *Educational and Child Psychology*, 16 (1): 22–9.

MacKay, T. (2006) *The West Dunbartonshire Literacy Initiative. The Design, Implementation and Evaluation of an Intervention Strategy to Raise Achievement and Eradicate Illiteracy*. Dumbarton: West Dunbartonshire Council.

MacKay, T. and Watson, K. (1999) 'Literacy, social disadvantage and early intervention: enhancing reading achievement in primary school', *Educational and Child Psychology*, 16 (1): 30–6.

Malinowski, B. (1922) *Argonauts of the Western Pacific: an Account of Native Enterprise and Adventure in the Melanesian New Guinea*. New York: Dutton.

Mead, M. (1928) *Coming of Age in Samoa*. New York: Morrow.

Mead, M. and Wolfenstein, J. (1955) *Childhood in Contemporary Cultures*. Chicago, IL: University of Chicago Press.

Merriam, S. (ed.) (2002) *Qualitative Research in Practice: Examples for Discussion and Analysis*. San Francisco, CA: Jossey-Bass.

Morse, J. (ed.) (1991) *Qualitative Nursing Research: a Contemporary Dialogue*. Newbury Park, CA: Sage.

Pettigrew, S. (2000) 'Ethnography and grounded theory: a happy marriage?', *Advances in Consumer Research*, 27: 256–60.

Reason, P. (ed.) (1994) *Participation in Human Enquiry*. London: Sage.

Riessman, C.K. (2003) 'Narrative analysis.' in M.S. Lewis-Beck, A. Bryman and T. Futing Liao (eds), *The Sage Encyclopedia of Social Science Research Methods*. London: Sage. pp. 705–9.

Robson, C. (2011) *Real World Research: a Resource for Social Scientists and Practitioner-Researchers*, 3rd edn. Oxford: Blackwell.

Seifert, T. and Hedderson, C. (2010) 'Intrinsic motivation and flow in skateboarding: an ethnographic study', *Journal of Happiness Studies*, 11: 277–92.

Sherman, R.R. and Webb, R.B. (1988) *Qualitative Research in Education: Focus and Methods*. London: Falmer Press.

Taber, N. (2010) 'Institutional ethnography, autoethnography and narrative: an argument for incorporating multiple methodologies', *Qualitative Research*, 10 (1): 5–25.
Thorndike, E.L. (1905) *The Elements of Psychology*. New York: A.G. Seiler.
Whiting, B. (1963) *Six Cultures: Studies of Child Rearing*. New York: Wiley.
Whiting, B.B. and Edwards, C.P. (1988) *Children of Different Worlds: the Formation of Social Behavior*. Cambridge, MA: Harvard University Press.
Whiting, B.B., Whiting, J.W.M. and Longabaugh, R. (1975) *Children of Six Cultures: a Psycho-Cultural Analysis*. Cambridge, MA: Harvard University Press.

Recommended reading for further study

Birks, M. and Mills, J. (2011) *Grounded Theory: A Practical Guide,* 4th edn. London: Sage.
Flick, U. (2009) *An Introduction to Qualitative Research,* 4th edn. London: Sage.
Gobo, G. (2008) *Doing Ethnography.* London: Sage.
Riessman, C.K. (2008) *Narrative Methods for the Human Sciences.* London: Sage.
Yin, R.K. (2009) *Case Study Research: Design and Methods,* 4th edn. London: Sage.

PART III

Special issues

NINE

Consultation and participation with children and young people in research

The aims of this chapter are:

- to provide an overview of recent practical advances for fully including children and young people in research and for obtaining their perspectives;
- to provide a practical guide for designing and conducting reliable and valid participatory research involving the perspectives of children and young people.

The first edition of this book, *Doing Research with Children* (Greig and Taylor, 1999), was the first of its kind and at that time researchers were yet to fully realize the implications of the need to consult with children and young people that arose from the Children Act 1989 (National Archives, 2012), the Children (Scotland) Act 1995 and the Children (Northern Ireland) Order 1995. We then called for more studies that sought to listen to the voices of children and young people, studies in which they participated, voiced their perspectives and which potentially empowered them. As well as a revision of the Children Act 2004 itself, and the guidance on children participating in research produced by the United Nations Children's Fund (UNICEF) in 2002, the ensuing years have witnessed the publication of a wealth of textbooks and journal articles devoted to doing research 'on', 'with', 'about' and even as 'co-researchers with' children. Furthermore, the development of the children's rights agenda has resulted in unprecedented attention, some of which includes: new international conventions; national bodies; regional and local initiatives; global bodies and charitable organizations. These developments have fuelled change through the new ideas about the rights and capabilities of children and young people. The resulting availability of research reports and guidelines has been particularly rich in the last five years and since the publication of the second edition of *Doing Research with Children* (Greig et al., 2007).

The role of research has been central to driving these new ideas and changes forward. Some of the best contributions have come from practitioner-researchers who have always, in the interests of good practice, sought to consult with and enter the worlds of children and young people in their professional practice. These workers have conducted research that has challenged how we perceive, relate to and work with children and young people and have raised our awareness of how oppressive accepted practice can be.

The United Nations Convention on the Rights of the Child (UNCRC) (UNICEF, 1989), ratified in the UK in 1991 and in Ireland in 1992, champions the liberty and welfare of persons up to the age of 18 in 41 articles relating to their provision, protection and participation. However, there is still no legal basis and the articles remain aspirational rather than enforceable. All states or countries that have ratified the 1989 UNCRC undertake the agreement to ensure that laws and policies will take the articles into account and report on such progress on a regular basis to the UN team of experts on human rights. The UK introduced the Human Rights Act 1998 to ensure that new legislation takes account of the UNCRC. Consequently, all those of us who work with children and young people are witnessing unprecedented levels of government and charitable projects, research, new frameworks and policies seeking to follow the guidelines for protection, provision and, importantly for this chapter, consultation and participation with children and young people.

The most important considerations for 'consultation and participation with children (up to age 18) in research' are spelled out in Articles 12 and 13 of the UNCRC.

Article 12 states:

1 States Parties shall assure to the child who is capable of forming his or her own views the right to express those views freely in all matters affecting the child, the views of the child being given due weight in accordance with the age and maturity of the child.

2 For this purpose, the child shall in particular be provided the opportunity to be heard in any judicial and administrative proceedings affecting the child, either directly, or through a representative or an appropriate body, in a manner consistent with the procedural rules of national law.

Article 13 states:

1 The child shall have the right to freedom of expression; this right shall include freedom to seek, receive and impart information and ideas of all kinds, regardless of frontiers, either orally, in writing or in print, in the form of art, or through any other media of the child's choice.

There are some important implications arising from these Articles for those of us who wish to do research involving consultation and participation with children and young people. Not only do we have to respectfully listen to them, we need to empower them to speak, act on it and use creative methods for effective listening.

These particular Articles are often quoted by authors who refer to the 'voice' of the child and our attention is drawn by them to the fact that many of the ways we have of perceiving, living, working and researching with children and young people actually subdues their 'voices'. Owing to assumptions about the validity of their contributions and adult authority, their views, opinions, feelings and wishes, are neither sought nor acted on. Children and young people are effectively silenced and ultimately oppressed by the adults who are in charge of them. The recent Education (Additional Support for Learning) (Scotland) Act 2004 has been instructing practice in Scotland since 2005 and not only highlights the need to consult with children in general but also with those who have learning and other difficulties. In consultation, we really need to be attentive, reliable and valid in the ways in which we listen to all children and young people, including the very young and those with additional support needs. Due consideration needs to be given to our methods for effective consultation and to what we do with our findings.

Another implication of Articles 12 and 13 of the UNCRC involves the process of participation. This is a task that goes beyond consultation as it is a process of engagement that is truly empowering for children and young people because they become partners in research, co-owners or co-researchers, who can initiate ideas and actions, make and contribute to key decisions and carry out key research tasks. In participation, we need to respect children and young people as experts in their own lives who have a unique and powerful contribution to make to the research. Finally, rather than merely paying lip service to children and young people, we need to have an ethos of consultation and participation embedded within a practice that also has a commitment to the demonstration of impact.

In this chapter we consider what is meant by the 'voice' of children and young people. We consider how we can ensure that youngsters of all ages and abilities are empowered to find and use their voices to speak, that we not only hear their voices, but we listen to them carefully, understand them and then act on them. We examine models, frameworks and practices to support the consultation and the participation of children and young people in the research process, from the first ideas through to dissemination. Finally, we explore some examples of the use of technology, such as software and online facilities, as an innovative means of promoting consultation and participation with children and young people.

Consultation and participation

Consultation: listening to the voice of the child

Ben Johnson's quip 'speak that I may see thee' pertains to the philosophical notion that it is language that reveals us most, and the understanding of any speaker is not just a question of *hearing* but of being compelled to *listen* to what is being said. Rodenberg, a voice coach, reflected on the empowering potential of her primary school teacher:

> I brought her a yellow flower once. She asked me why I liked the flower.
>
> 'Because it's yellow like the sun,' I said.
>
> 'How do you know it's yellow?' she asked.
>
> 'Because the sun gives it something,' I replied.
>
> 'How would you describe that something?'
>
> She went on in this fashion, re-inventing me with the Socratic method: seeking the truth by means of questions and answers. (1993: 27)

This Socratic form of consultation with a young person demonstrates how skilled engagement and communication moves beyond a simple question-and-answer format. It is about discovering the truth of a matter. Sadly, society has long made assumptions along the lines that all children, being incapable or at least less capable than adults, should be seen and not heard, especially in important matters that affect them. Furthermore, the fact that not all children are able, due to developmental stage or to a disability in the use of language in such a conventional way to develop ideas or opinions, or to express their views, thoughts or feelings means that some children and young people experience multiple barriers to their voices being 'heard'.

Kilkelly et al. (2005) reported the views of children regarding decisions being made about them. The majority of the concerns raised related to school. This is not at all surprising as this is where children and young people spend most of their time. The concerns raised by the research participants were mainly about not having their say in the decisions that were made about their school life:

> 'Pupils don't really have a say in school. Teacher's opinions always come first.'
>
> 'Some teachers get on to you without listening to what you are saying.'

As noted by Crichton and Barrett (2007), listening to, hearing and acting on what children say are three separate processes, all of which are essential in a model of researching *with,* rather than *on* children and young people. The rights-driven perception that children and young people are already valid citizens who can make valuable contributions to the processes of social change via a research agenda will avoid the appearance of consultation without real engagement (Lewis, 2010).

In 2001, the Department for Education and Skills (DfES) in the UK issued guidance by the Children and Young People's Unit entitled *Learning to Listen: Core Principles for the Involvement of Children and Young People* (DfES, 2001a). The guidance provides an official common framework for departments to develop tailored policies, action plans and effective practice for getting children and young people involved in the design, provision and evaluation of services that affect them (e.g. children using mental health, social and educational services such as residential schools). This is about empowering children and young people and it is likely to have been informed by the results of a major Economic and Social Research Council (ESRC) project, the purpose of which was to throw light on contemporary childhood (1995–2001) and as reported by Prout (2001, 2002).

The research agenda posited here is very much the traditional ground of sociology. However, in taking up the task, researchers immediately realized they had a major methodological task on their hands requiring them to embark on a creative programme of research in which children and young people are assumed to be social actors, both influencing and influenced by their social environment. This meant finding new methods for tackling areas such as children and young people as researchers, as strategic actors, the documentation of perspectives, and the exclusion and the voice of the child. The most recent revision of this guidance was in 2008.

Government guidance on consulting with children is now available in all countries of the UK and other states and countries that have ratified the UNCRC. Local authorities have information and guidance on their websites about their commitment to the rights of children and young people, and how to consult with them through participatory tools and processes. Specific UK departments such as Health, Education and Social Services have published statements and sponsored innovations designed to uphold these obligations to children and young people. Charitable bodies have also produced similar guidance and contribute, independently via research, to the process of evaluating the Government's progress in its humanitarian targets.

Participation: children and young people as citizens having their say

Education, health and social services that have recently taken forward initiatives relating to consultation and participation with children and young people usually refer to the revised 2008 DfES guidance definition of participation in their own publicity manifesto. The original (2003) consultation document describes 'participation' as follows:

> By pupil participation we mean adults, working in partnership with children and young people and valuing their views and encouraging them to:
>
> - become more active participants in their education, including evaluation of their own learning;
> - participate in creating, building and improving services to make them more responsive to their needs and those of the wider community;

- make a difference in their schools, neighbourhoods and communities;
- contribute to a cohesive community;
- learn from an early age to balance their rights as individuals with their responsibilities as citizens;
- and to develop, through the way they are involved, the knowledge, understanding and skills they will need in adult life.

> This means, in practice, opening up opportunities for decision-making with children and young people as partners engaging in dialogue, conflict resolution, negotiation and compromise – all important life skills ... (DfES, 2003: 3)

This definition has led to major initiatives, such as the development and evaluation of pupil councils and numerous toolkits to be used by a range of service providers, charities and government departments to ensure a working partnership with children and young people. However, a major consideration is: what are the implications for doing research with children and young people as partners in the research and as co-researchers? This is discussed in detail later on in the chapter.

Models of consultation and participation with children and young people

The most innovative and informative applications of methods of listening to and participating with children and young people that are now being used in research come from the arts and humanities, and sociology in particular. Nevertheless, the same basic methods have been around in the field of psychology for some time. They have been widely used in the everyday practice of applied psychologists, but are not well represented in the developmental psychology literature. In all fields, it is increasingly accepted that children are co-constructors of meaning and do have a valid perspective worthy of inclusion in research, even at very early developmental stages and despite apparent disabilities. A more detailed examination of the underlying psychological and sociological theories that underpin the research methodologies appropriate for the use of consultation and participation with children and young people are discussed in more detail in Chapters 2 and 3. In this section, we focus on major models that potentially inform our participatory practices with children and young people in a research context. This includes research in which the views of children and young people are sought; research in which children and young people play a significant role in conducting the research and participant-led research.

Crichton and Barrett (2007) critically reviewed a number of models for consultation and participation with children and young people. While some models emphasized the importance of the design and choice of tools, the difficulties of adult manipulation, the potential for tokenism, and the opportunities for different levels of child initiation, they also noted a significant problem with the models (Hart and UNICEF International Child Development Centre, 1992; Hayes, 2002; Shier, 2001), i.e. the lack of the representation of the wider social and historical context that affects how far all children and young people are able to truly participate. Clearly, drawing on the revised theoretical perspective of Bronfenbrenner (1992) (see also Chapter 2), Crichton and Barrett (2007) cited a model proposed by Hobbs (2006; Hobbs et al., 2000) that seeks to directly address the impact of power, authority, relationships and the construction of opportunities in the local context of schools in determining whether and to what extent children and young people can truly participate. Hobbs's model is shown in Figure 9.1 and it encourages professionals who work with children and young people in the real world to take more account of how these factors affect participation. In addition, we are encouraged to consider what tools, methods and approaches can best enhance true participation and promote the reduction of techniques that disempower the young participants.

Although this model refers specifically to the educational setting, it is equally valid in support of improving consultation and participation in health or social and other care settings. Figure 9.1 indicates a positive movement from participation to empowerment, where the model of working with children and young people is one that takes a critical account of the powerful interrelationship between the factors shown. That is, to gauge whether the young participant is being effectively engaged and consulted with to any extent, it is necessary to examine:

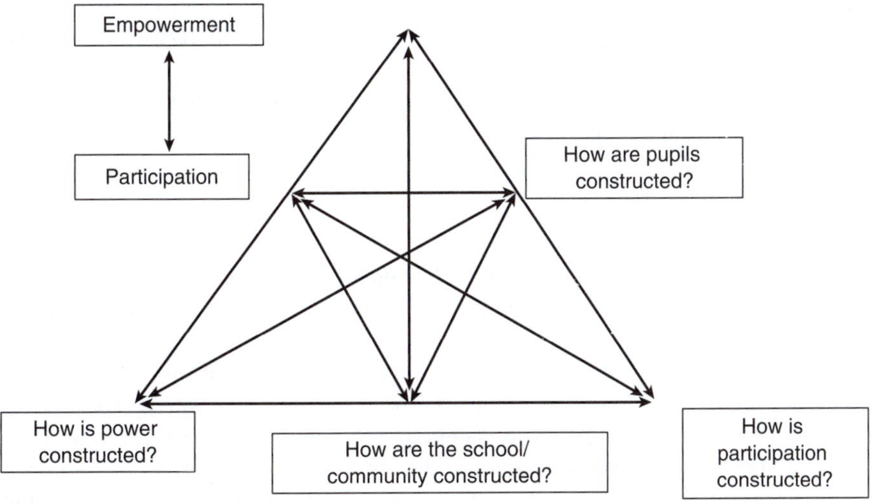

Figure 9.1 Hobbs's (2006) model for consultation and participation with children and young people

- how the young participant is constructed in terms of actual age, stage, abilities, and by constructions of them by others in power;
- how participation is constructed in terms of the ethos within local contexts, services and cultures;
- how the service provider is structured and run, including policies on participation if any;
- how power is constructed and the ways in which children and young people are related to within a setting by the service provider;
- how participation is addressed via tools, i.e. the tasks, activities and approaches used to supposedly empower and engage the participants.

Let's take the hypothetical, worked example of two school settings working with disabled children and young people.

School number one is located within a large inclusive education authority that is passionate in its response to the legislation on the views and rights of children and young people. This is reflected in local policy and project work that extends into all of its care settings, across disciplines, and has links with other community, voluntary and partner agencies. Projects include multi-agency working parties for the revision of local policies to reflect the necessary changes. Accessible documentation is put together that declares the local ethos and manifesto for upholding the rights and dignity of children and young people and for obtaining their views and participation and acting on them. Commitments are made to monitor such developments and the demonstration of impact on children and young people themselves. The school policy reflects these commitments and follows recommended guidance for the ethical and effective consultation and participation with the children and young people who use the school setting. There are awareness-raising events for the school staff and others. The school routinely uses well-designed, participatory tools and procedures to both facilitate and evaluate the success of participation and consultation and to demonstrate the actual impact on the matters that affect the children and young people.

School number two is set within a hospital where disabled children have to be educated for prolonged periods of treatment and rehabilitation within the hospital setting. The educator in charge of the school is an ex-nurse who retrained to be a teacher. Both they and the hospital hold a medicalized view of the way the child is constructed. In the case of disability, there is an ethos of a within-child deficit and education programmes are dictated by the demands of medical treatment and routines. It is a situation where the doctor and diagnostician know best and the delivery of education is not treated as a separate concern from the general hospital policies, procedures and practices. Therefore, there is not a policy specific to the education of disabled children and there are no tools, practices or procedures for consulting with children and young people about either their treatment or their education. Although the hospital does have a legal department, its primary function is to ward off and manage hundreds of complaints about treatment, and new legislation on the rights and views of the child, where there is no actual legal requirement to address them, are way down the list of priorities in terms of policy and practice.

PUTTING RESEARCH INTO PRACTICE 9.1: THE WIDER CONTEXT

Consider both schools above in the light of the triangular model presented in Figure 9.1. Discuss the following questions in groups/pairs.

- In what ways do the schools differ along the dimensions of the model?
- Why you think these differences, including social and historical/cultural factors, exist?
- Can these differences be changed?
- What needs to happen to lessen the differences between the two schools?

An important implication of this particular model of participation is the importance of the ethos of the wider context: the practice setting; the local authority in which it is placed; the national ethos and the levels of support and awareness made available to make it a practical reality. The best we can do is to mindfully manage and reduce power imbalances and create new platforms from which the voices of children and young people can be truly heard.

A consultation model for multidisciplinary meetings with children and young people

Conducting consultation exercises with children and young people in the interests of improving service delivery has become established practice in many areas and services across the UK. The Office for Standards in Education (Ofsted)/ Education Scotland (formerly, Her Majesty's Inspectorate of Education [HMIe]) now routinely consults directly with young participants in relation to their views about the quality of services they receive. In England and Wales, the Every Child Matters (DfES, 2004) agenda is explicit about the need to consult with children and young people in multidisciplinary contexts, as is the Scottish equivalent, Getting it Right for Every Child and Young Person. Woolfson et al. (2006, 2008) described a model for making more routine consultations within a practice more meaningful and reliable. They identified eight key strategies for supporting young participants as follows:

1 Participants should be fully informed about and prepared for the meetings.
2 Participants should attend meetings only with adults whom they already know.
3 Participants should be asked their preference for who attends a meeting.
4 Participants should have a choice in how they express their views in a meeting.
5 Participants should be given evidence of being listened to during a meeting.
6 Participants should always understand the language used during a meeting.
7 Participants should be involved in decision making during a meeting.
8 Participants should receive written feedback after a meeting.

Other important features of the implementation of this model is that it takes account of the centres' ongoing practices and resource; that the model is embedded within a practice in a real-life context and that there is a mediating adult who ensures that all eight strategies are applied before, during and after the meeting. While this particular model evolved around seeking the views of secondary school-aged participants with additional support needs in the educational context, these meetings are most likely to be multidisciplinary. Therefore, it is an adaptable model across disciplines and it is compatible with other guidelines (see National Youth Agency, 2006; Sinclair, 2004), other ages and stages (Cremin and Slatter, 2004 at the preschool stage; Hoppe et al., 1995 at primary stage) and for those with communication difficulties (Street, 2004). Woolfson at al. (2008) argue reasonably that this model of consultation will also work well with younger participants as well as those with more severe and complex learning difficulties.

Methods and frameworks

There are now many participatory tools and processes that seek to reduce the traditional power imbalance between children and young people and the adults who are engaging in research with them (O'Kane, 2000). In general, these methods aim to be child-friendly, fun activities, involving joint analysis and learning. They use respectful dialogue and processes over a period of time, allowing participants to select their own agenda. Participants are also allowed to have some control of the pace of some of the activities, and are supported with some structure such as prompts and examples that will facilitate the generating of new ideas.

Traditional techniques are a good starting point for aiding consultation and participation and these include interviews, focus groups, questionnaires, adaptation for ages and stages, and settings and structured and multi-sensory or multimodal methods, especially with the under-fives, in which views are not so much written or directly spoken but expressed via role-play, puppets and participatory games (Children in Scotland, 2002). Using methods such as pictures, photographs and words with children aged 3–5 and some aged less than two years, MacNaughton et al. (2007) identified the main difficulty for the youngest children to be that of the dominance of adult-oriented communication in early years settings. Behind this was a cultural assumption that this group of children have nothing of value to contribute and that this leads to practices that disable the confident expression of opinions in the young children themselves and if they are able to articulate such views, these views are not taken seriously. As Flewitt (2005) noted, the youngest children use a range of 'voices' via multimodal expression and we need to be mindful of child-based ways of encountering children's perspectives in their own communication territory. Sensible consideration also needs to be given to the citizenship of the youngest children.

The very youngest children and those with severe and complex learning difficulties, including communication difficulties, are perhaps the groups that have challenged researchers the most in terms of enabling, hearing and listening to their perspectives. In a review of research, the Joseph Rowntree Foundation found that many professionals mostly fail to consult with or involve disabled children in matters affecting them quite regardless of legislation and guidance on the rights of children and young people. The 'Ask Us' project, funded jointly by the Children's Society and the Joseph Rowntree Foundation, and following on from the Department of Health's National Disability Reference Group for the 'Quality Protects' initiative addressed this directly. A large reference group of children and young people with severe disabilities were included in a study aiming to ascertain their perspectives on matters such as: what they enjoy; what they want more of; their experiences of being consulted and of participation; and what they understand by 'inclusion'. They used a range of methods including photos, songs, videos, questionnaires and drawings. The researchers found evidence in their approach that their 'participants' had definite viewpoints. They wanted to be the same as other children, to go where they go, do what they do and feel the same buzz as them. They wanted to be respected, consulted, listened to and to have their say in things that do affect them and to be a definite part of the community.

Participation with younger children: the Mosaic Approach

The Mosaic Approach (Clark and Moss, 2001) is a multi-method process that can be flexibly used particularly with the youngest children but it can also be adapted as a participatory tool for adolescents. The Mosaic comprises a number of separate tools that can be put together to address the puzzle of the research question. These tools are 'listening' tools that are both verbal and visual. They include: photographs taken by the children of places and things of importance to them (in specified contexts such as nurseries or neighbourhoods); guided tours of the setting being studied that are documented in a variety of ways (videos, drawings,

Table 9.1 Pieces of the Mosaic for the 'What is it like to be at this nursery?' scenario

Tool	*Questions*
Observation (narrative accounts of researcher)	What is happening here? What do body language, vocalizations, expressions contribute to the narrative?
Child conferencing (short interview schedule) Why do children go to nursery?	Why do children go to nursery? What do adults do? What are the best/worst activities? What are the best/worst people/places? Open question
Cameras (cheap, disposable) for children to take their own photographs	What are your favourite things to photograph? Why did you choose these things?
Tours (child leads and chooses the means to document)	Tell me about/show me all the important places
Mapping (of the site, perhaps using the photos or drawings)	Observe, ask, listen, tape-record, map-making
Role-play (using preselected toys depicting the nursery world and story-stem techniques)	Tell me what is happening in your story now? Then what happens?
Parent and practitioner perspectives (short interviews)	What do you think is a good/bad day for your child at home/nursery?

maps); mapping; talking about the meaning of documents or materials produced; interviews or conferencing and observation. Thus, it is an eclectic use of both traditional and new techniques in a way that acknowledges both the context and the child as a co-constructor of meaning. Table 9.1 provides an overview of the tools of the Mosaic Approach and some considerations with regard to their use.

The Mosaic Approach is based on participatory rural appraisal methods that aim to access the views and empower those who live in impoverished, rural communities. Elements of the approach have been adapted for use with older groups of children in social services research (O'Kane, 2000), in health education research (Morrow, 2001) and in addressing risks and coping in mental health research on adolescents (Punch 2002a, 2002b). Typically, these studies seek to empower young people through research so that they might influence both service delivery and policy developments that affect them. Table 9.2 summarizes a number of research studies in terms of the questions being asked, the tools and procedures.

Participation: a framework for working with groups and older children

Those researchers conducting participatory interviews with children have found that both individual and group formats can be helpful. To explore this topic further,

Table 9.2 Summary of participatory methods used with children and young people

Study question and study population	*Tools*	*Procedure*
Do levels of social support in the community have an important effect on well-being?	Freely written/ taped accounts	Answer questions on: Who is important to me and why? What is a friend? What are friends for? Where do I feel I belong?
One hundred and two 12–15 year olds in two London schools (Morrow, 2001)		What happens when you are not at school? How long have you been friends? How long have you lived here? What are your future aspirations?
	Photographs	Choice of what is important to photograph. Control of cameras. Explanatory captions of the photos for discussions.
	Maps, group discussions	Drawing local maps. Newspaper articles on the antics of young people in their area for discussion.
What are your views on the decision-making processes that affect you?	Decision-making chart	Areas of concern and degree of decision-making perceived (none, some, a lot) along two axes and coded. Large visual poster and stickers.
Young people in the care of the local authority (O'Kane, 2000)	Pots and beans activity	Six statements given that are to be rated on a scale of 1–3, e.g. 'how much you like meetings', and six pots given for each statement. The child gives each pot/statement 1, 2 or 3 beans. If it gets 3, they say why. If it gets less, they say what needs to happen to get the other beans.
	Diamond ranking exercise	Nine statements identified in a focus group discussion are put onto little diamond-shaped cards and arranged in the shape of a diamond, the top representing the most important and the bottom the least important.
How do children aged 8–14 negotiate independence as they grow up?	Drawings	Freely done for engagement and later used in discussion and for information.
Children in schools in rural Bolivia (Punch, 2002a)	Photographs	As above.

(Continued)

Table 9.2 (Continued)

Study question and study population	*Tools*	*Procedure*
	Spider diagrams	This is a larger circle with key question in it (e.g. 'places I go'), that is given several 'legs' along which the name of a place is written, and a 'foot' at the bottom of each leg. In the foot, the child puts the number of times that the place is visited.
	Diaries	Capture everyday activities and routine aspects to life.
What are the coping behaviours for mental health problems?	Worksheets	Ability-appropriate, based on life in the community, places, likes/dislikes, schoolwork and chores.
Eighty-six young people in mainstream and residential schools (Punch, 2002b)	Interviews: Individual	More private, sensitive topics, completing tasks.
	Interviews: Group	More general themes and perspectives.
	Secret box	Overcoming inhibition by having problems written and posted into a sealed and shuffled box, so respondent remains anonymous on secrets that have never been told to anyone.
	Themed discussions on mental health topics	Video clips from soaps; problem page letters, common phrases.
	Ranking of worries task	Identify 20 worries and put them into big worry, middle worry and little worry piles.
	Coping spider diagrams	The big worry circle and coping legs (see also above).

we turn to a study by Hill et al. (1996), which was one of the first to address the glaring gap in research addressing the voices of primary school-aged children.

The general oversight of the usefulness of qualitative methods for doing research with children applies particularly to the 5–12-year-old age group. Typically, researchers have focused on preschoolers and adolescents because they are presumed critical phases in child development. To this end, Hill et al. (1996) explored qualitative methods that can be used to hear the voices of primary school children. The children's perspectives on their emotions and well-being were explored by adapting qualitative strategies used by practitioners such as social workers and teachers. The result of this research provides an excellent and flexible framework for those who wish to interview children. The paper recommends two principal methods of engaging with children: focus group discussion and individual interviews.

The optimal focus group size is five or six with a small age range, and for some purposes same-sex groups may be a viable option. Children should receive clear explanations of the group's purpose and format, with a limited number of themes planned for exploration. Questions should be put in a straightforward, open-ended manner, with the provision of a discussion overview from time to time. An important role of the interviewer is to facilitate productive peer interaction for all group members. The discussion agenda set by Hill and co-workers had the following limited themes:

- purpose of the research;
- listing of feelings children have;
- explaining emotions;
- the relative importance of different feelings;
- persistent negative feelings and responses;
- children's problems and worries;
- responses by others to children's concerns;
- adults' feelings and what could promote children's well-being.

These group discussions were conducted in the children's schools and individual interviews either at home or in school. The individual interviews used some of the same techniques and emerging themes of the group discussion but were able to explore particular emotions in greater depth with individual children. In this case, the researchers felt the children were more relaxed in the school setting than at home. Table 9.3 summarizes the variety of methods used to engage the children in both group and individual contexts. The preferred modes vary according to the age, context and individual child.

For consulting with children about the strength of their thoughts or feelings, there needs to be a conceptual understanding of the notion of a scale such as 1–5 or 1–10. Researchers often use visual versions of this, such as a 'feelings thermometer' (0 = no anger; 10 = very angry) or a series of faces showing increasing levels of happiness (e.g. a smile getting bigger on each successive face) and the child can then point to which face they think is like them.

Participation: toolkits

One of the effects of the rights agenda and associated response of the UK government is a proliferation of comprehensive participatory toolkits that are available to download for free on the WWW or to purchase as a publication. These

Table 9.3 Methods for obtaining the perspectives of 5–12-year-olds on their emotions and well-being

Group interviews	
Introductions	Researcher and children make name labels and say a bit on self.
Brainstorming	Naming and noting all feelings thought of for discussion focus.
Visual prompts	Outline faces showing different emotional expressions; Mr Numb the Alien with no feelings for children to explain meanings of feelings named; Pictorial vignettes: four pictures showing two friends fighting and making up (discuss likely cause and resolutions). Picture of a couple rowing while washing and drying up (discuss family tensions).
Role-play	Act out situations where a child is unhappy/fearful/worried and an adult is sought to help. Gives information on typical adult interventions. Needs careful preparation and debriefing.
Self-completion (worksheet)	Gives quantifiable data. Provides help for less verbally articulate children.
Questionnaires	Sentence completion: 'I am sad when ________.' Fantasy wishes: 'List three things that would make you happier'. Simple chart: indicates who the child would ask for help with worries mentioned.
Drawing	Entitled 'This is a child who is feeling ________ because ________.'
Individual interviews	
Introduction	'About myself' sheet. Likes/dislikes (e.g. food, pop stars).
Eco-map	Important people: 'Easiest to talk to', 'best helpers', 'most fun' also used in later discussion on specific emotions noted.
Outline faces	As in group.
Sentence completion cards	On intense feelings: 'I feel really safe when ________', 'The saddest I ever felt was ________.'
Role-plays	Researcher pretends to be a child seeking help from a friend: situations extracted from prior group discussion
Questionnaire	As in group.

Source: Adapted from Hill, M., Laybourn, A. and Borland, M. (1996) 'Engaging with primary-aged children about their emotions and well-being: methodological considerations', *Children and Society*, 10 (2): 129–44. Reproduced with permission.

kits have been produced by a range of bodies such as charities for children and young people, specific government departments, local authorities and independent authors. They are so widely available now that a simple search on a computer for the keywords 'participatory toolkits', will yield a plethora of resource links both nationally and internationally. Indeed, they are so numerous it is beyond the scope of this chapter to review them. In essence, these kits tend to begin with definitions and declarations about the rights and voices of children and young people. They often report examples of consultation or participatory research with extensive examples of techniques used to gather information from the young participants. Many have designed evaluative and other tools to address outcomes and specific questions. Many include basic techniques that are widely used in all kits and that have been around for some time, including those summarized in Tables 9.2 and 9.3. Table 9.4 describes some fairly typical participatory tools that are available in such toolkits.

Over the course of the last 10 years, published official guidance and creative participatory toolkits have proliferated. Those recommended for vulnerable children and young people include 'In My Shoes' (IMS) (Calam et al., 2000), the 'All About Me Profile' (National Society for the Prevention of Cruelty to Children, 2008) and the SEN toolkit (DfES, 2001b).

Computer software and online participatory toolkits

The use of information technology and the WWW is yet another mode for enhancing the participation of children and young people in research and other projects. In this section we describe some examples of these approaches.

IMS (In My Shoes) is a computer package that aims to support children, young people and vulnerable adults in expressing their points of view about their experiences as service users, including potentially distressing events or relationships. According to the website (www.inmyshoes.org.uk/In_My_Shoes/Introduction.html), extensive testing shows the package can be used in a wide range of circumstances, including interviews with children and young people:

- who may have been abused;
- who have difficulties in expressing emotions;
- who are hard to engage;
- who have developmental delay or difficulties.

IMS has also been used for interviewing adults with learning disabilities. The programme is a structured, trained adult-facilitated interview that uses sound, speech and video. Through a series of modules, participants are encouraged to share information on their experiences and emotions with different people at home, in education and other settings. Forensic considerations have been central to its development and the focus is on facilitating communication about the subject areas, with leading questions being avoided. The programme involves two days of training for the adult workers who sit alongside the child or young

Table 9.4 Examples of specific participatory tools from toolkits (based on website guidance such as Learning South West, Unite and Dynamix)

Activity	*Method*
Circle with chairs	Everyone stands in a circle with enough chairs for the participants minus one. One person, who is in the middle of the circle, makes a statement and those children who agree stand up and change chairs. The person in the middle tries to get a vacated chair. This then leaves someone without, who then stands in the middle. This 'new' person in the middle makes a statement and the game progresses. If no one stands up, meaning no one agrees, people in the circle applaud because this illustrates individuality.
Expressions	Everyone stands in the circle and one person says 'Show me what (type of emotion such as anger) looks like' and everyone in the group physically represents the idea. This can be varied to include degrees, i.e. 'show me a 1', 'show me 5', 'show me 10' (more or less intensity).
Degree of conviction	This activity highlights that decisions are not always black and white and everyone is entitled to a point of view. Everyone stands in a large circle with a chair in the centre. One person makes a statement, and everyone walks the distance to the chair that represents the level of their agreement. Standing at the outer edge means they disagree while touching the chair means they totally agree. Standing in between the chair and the outer edge by varying degrees indicates the level of conviction. Discussion can take place around where people are standing.
Puzzle art	Boards are put together prior to an activity and a large image is created across these boards related to the main theme (e.g. friendship). Boards are separated and given to each small group as a piece of a larger puzzle, and participants draw/write their feelings about a particular piece of the jigsaw they have (being a friend, helping others, how to make friends). Following the small group activity, each group presents and describes their piece of the puzzle to the whole group and the puzzle is put together.
The fishing game	Cut a fish shape out of a card. Write a word on each fish (could be used for rule development, discussion of issues, behaviour, choices). Attach a paper clip to each fish and make a fishing rod with a dowel, length of string and magnet. Each participant gets to 'go fishing' and voices their opinion about the word they fish out.

Activity	*Method*
Decision tree	Draw a tree on a sheet of chart paper. Write the question at the top of the tree in such a way that it may be answered with either a yes or no. Below the question, write yes on one side of the tree and no on the other side. Under the yes and no, ask the children to list all the possible consequences of each decision. Ask the children to consider all the consequences and come to a decision. In cases where the question is not a 'yes/no', use several branches for the different options and consequences listed for each. Again, the consequences are carefully considered and a decision may be made.
Walk in someone else's shoes	Cut out two pairs of shoes, each a different colour. Ask two children or a child and adult each to stand on one set of shoes. Stand in another's shoes to explore how other people feel, for example, children with disabilities, children living in rural areas, and so on.
Diamond ranking	Following an 'brain storming' discussion, everyone in the group selects nine ideas that are the most important and copy them onto a ranking sheet with the most important idea at the top, the least at the bottom, and other ideas grouped in the middle, resulting in a diamond shape like the one shown below. Everyone shares their rankings and contributes towards a discussion of each idea: strengths, weaknesses, obstacles, motivation. The group should try to reach a consensus for decision making. ______ ____ _____ ____ _____ _____ _____ _____ _____
Decision board	This activity can be used to explore children's views on the issues involved in decision making. A grid is used with specific decisions along one axis and significant people on the other. Using the traffic light system, children can evaluate who has the most say in each of the decisions made. Traffic light stickers represent a rating scale: Red for 'no say', yellow for 'some say' and green for 'most say'.
Needs in context	This requires a large map, photos that show the area, a ruler, coloured chalk, newspaper and large sheets of paper. With a map of the area, get children or young people to use photos, newspaper cuttings or drawings to show different areas on the map.

(Continued)

Table 9.4 (Continued)

Activity	*Method*
	They should show what they think about each area, highlighting issues in parts of the town/setting, but also what is good about the areas and about provisions that are situated there.
How? How? How?	This activity is for encouraging participants in developing project ideas and how they could deliver their vision. They should start with one question to explore how an issue can be developed and potentially reach a solution to a series of barriers, e.g. How can young people have a greater say the service? After each answer comes another How?
Balloon, basket, ropes and clouds (a form of visual representation)	This activity supports project planning. It requires a graphic representation of a balloon, its basket, its ropes and the clouds (poster or worksheet or drawing on a board). On the balloon – write issues and factors that will be needed for the proposal to fly. In the basket – write the names of people or organizations who can help and support your aims. On the ropes – what will hold it back, before the balloon/project has started? In the clouds – what could push the balloon off course (once the project has started)? Making it fly – above the balloon write factors that will make things happen and work. Supports? Could it be blown off course? How? What can make it fly? What could hold the project down? What could blow the project off course?
Onions	This task is to ensure a group understands a complex issue by investigating all angles and perspectives while making sure that there is a recognizable thinking trail: In the centre of a circle write in the issues that the group will look at. Ask the group to write down their initial thoughts, such as why they think the issue exists, on Post-its and then stick them on the second inner circle. Then invite them to look at other Post-its and ask them 'Why?' In the next circle ask participants to write down their responses and stick them down. Repeat.
Prioritizing	This task is to facilitate decision-making and prioritizing. Nine priorities are written up on Post-it notes/A4 paper and the diamond formation (see diamond ranking) to be drawn on to the flip chart. Ask each group to arrange their top nine ideas (they

Activity	Method
	can add any to the above list if they want to) in a diamond formation with the priority at the top, two in second, three in third, two in fourth and their lowest at the bottom. They need to reach a consensus as a group and can move the ideas around until they reach an order with which they all agree.
Posters	This task is about finding out what concerns young people about their circumstances and what negatively impacts on their well-being without requiring anyone to write, taking individual concerns and representing them as a group response, using a poster. It requires large sheets of paper, A3 or larger, glue and scissors, lots of magazines/newspapers/ postcards/ pens/stickers, and so on. Using everything from pictures out of magazines to felt-tip pens, children or young people work alone or in pairs and are invited to select images/ words that express the difficulties/barriers they are facing. Bring individuals or pairs together into small groups to discuss the posters. One young person from each group is selected to take notes on the discussion and then feedback the three main concerns brought out by the exercise (they do this by keeping a tally chart of the themes raised). The main group reforms and a large collective poster is made. This is done by inviting each group in turn to put up on the main sheet representing one of their top three issues. Once there are no new issues the main poster represents a collective view of barriers and difficulties.
Solution tree	A participatory exercise whereby young people identify problems/issues of concern to them and then think of their own solutions to these issues. It requires a tree, either drawn or cut out of flip chart paper or wallpaper, leaf-shaped Post-its, Blu-tack. Young people identify the problems/difficulties they are experiencing. (Using a 'problem wall' is also an effective way of doing this.) Young people put all the problems into themes. Each branch on a solution tree needs to correspond to a theme. Young people explore what the barriers/problems are in each theme and then look at all the themes in turn.

(Continued)

Table 9.4 (Continued)

Activity	*Method*
	They then write on the leaves all the solutions (a different solution on a new leaf) and then stick these to the branches that correspond to the theme.
Video	This mode allows young people to feedback on issues affecting them without having to write. An advantage of this approach is that you do not have to be in a room. You can take the camera to places where young people hang out and film the context as well as the discussion. Video can also be used to help young people show their environment. For example, they can film their play area before talking about it. It requires a digital camera, preferably with a touch screen that can be turned around to face the group, a monitor to hook the camera to for quick group feedback and some paper and pens for participants who want to plan what they have to say. The camera is handed over to the young people who take it in turns to talk into the camera and hold the camera. This initial session is about becoming familiar with the equipment. Allowing the young people to watch what they have produced will allow them to see when things do and do not work. You can help them with their questions on how to improve the picture. The second time round encourage the young people to think about what they want to say into the camera. Maybe a key theme came out while they were 'getting to know the camera' or maybe you want to ask them to speak to a particular individual or maybe they want to have a discussion. Nonetheless, film this. Maybe they want to draw up a storyboard of the themes they will discuss and in which order before filming. If a storyboard has been used, no editing will be necessary. The film can be used to highlight issues at subsequent meetings with the permission of the young people.
	Timelines can be used to unearth information (possibly forgotten) that direct questioning may not. A timeline helps to provide a context to information given by young people. It is also a good way of looking at what happened to them. Think about the project/idea and how that developed. Get people to go back to the problem wall after talking about the

Activity	*Method*
Timelines	past and place what they want to see happen in the next few years of the project. What do they want to have achieved by when? How can situations that have come about be solved? What actions can be taken in a particular time? This activity needs long and clean tables, accessible floor space, coloured paper, pens and pencils, stickers/glue. Place the paper to represent different time periods in the young people's life and the project. This can be illustrated with large events, then get the young people to write on the paper.
Colour Jacuzzi	This activity is useful to understand young people's ideas, motivations and issues that affect them in their settings. It requires coloured paper. On a blue sheet write 'Blue – Royal Colour' and ask: If you were ruler for a day, what would be the first thing you would do (to improve your area)? On a green sheet write 'Green – Money Colour' and ask: What do you plan to do for money? On a red sheet write 'Red – Turn off Colour' and ask: What is a real turn off in your area/setting/situation? On an orange sheet write 'Orange – Motivation Colour' and ask: What motivates you? What helps you be more creative?
Evaluation: graffiti wall	This task allows participants to feedback on the session anonymously using a flip chart/wallpaper, pens and some masking tape. Place a large paper wall somewhere in the room with plenty of different coloured pens nearby and encourage people to get up and write their views on the wall at any time during the session.
Evaluation: love/hate change	This is a similar task to the 'Graffiti wall' above which collects feedback in a structured manner. It requires Post-its, pens, and a diagram drawn onto a piece of flip chart paper for Love, Hate and Change options: Giving each participant three Post-it notes, ask the group to answer the following questions on separate Post-it notes: What did you think was good about the session? What did you think was bad? What would you change?

(Continued)

Table 9.4 (Continued)

Activity	*Method*
	Ask them to stick all their good, bad and changes on different parts of the Love, Hate, Change diagram.
Evaluation: Vote with your feet	One end of the room is described as 'very good', the other end is 'not good' and the space in between denotes expressions, according to where young people stand in relation to the two extremes. The facilitator can ask questions, such as 'What was the workshop like?', and young people stand in a place in the room that they feel best represents their thoughts on it. This is then discussed.
Evaluation: circles	This activity requires photocopies of blank circles, pens and pencils. The object/subject of the evaluation, e.g. an information leaflet, is discussed. The group first discuss what a good leaflet would look like, what would it contain. The chosen criteria are then represented on the edge of a segmented circle. Each section is coloured in to represent how closely the leaflet fulfils the criteria. A variation of this method can be used to evaluate a session. Ask the group members to outline the essential qualities of a good session. Put these statements on the wall and invite members of the group to place a happy smile or a sad smile under the statement. The group can then discuss: 'Why do you think some people have put sad faces next to the "length of session" statement?' Young people can then discuss 'hypothetically' without necessarily revealing themselves.

person to assist, guide and interact with them using a structured interview process. Consequently the process is not about the child or young person alone with the computer in a question-and-answer session. The usefulness of the programme has recently been addressed in a number of independent publications (Barrett, 2007; Cousins, 2006; Glasgow and Crossley, 2004).

Online consultation is a growing area that is being developed as a participatory research tool. There are a number of good reasons to consider the use of interactive information technology in participatory research. Computer networking is potentially vast and fast, holding the promise of large and quick data sets. Computers are highly accessible both at home and in schools and offer some choice in space and time for participants. Children and young people tend to be computer literate, using them as well as mobile phones extensively for social networking. Therefore, it is a mode with which they are comfortable and one they enjoy using. There is no paperwork and no tangible researcher to deal with, making it potentially more private, less pressured and convenient, perhaps even improving response rates. With good software, the young participants could design and analyse their own online surveys and questionnaires. It may serve to put the young respondents at greater ease and decrease the pressure for socially desirable or expected responses in the absence of an actual interviewer. There is also some evidence that respondents will more readily provide sensitive information on an anonymous computer survey rather than in other modes (Mann and Stewart, 2000, cited in Oliver, 2007).

Oliver (2007) describes how one Scottish local authority, in collaboration with a university's department of computing, developed a questionnaire that could be completed by children and young people online. Participation in Consultation On-line (PICO) enables questionnaires to be easily designed and adapted depending on specific research questions and the target respondent. So far this approach has been useful for widely gathering the views of thousands of children and young people about their experiences of school including:

- Learning with Care (2007), a project in which the views of children looked after by the local authority completed online questionnaires about how schools could improve their attainment;
- Homework Project (2006), using a PICO questionnaire, in which all primary pupils gave their views about homework;
- Behaviour and Discipline Survey (2005), using a PICO questionnaire to gather the views of pupils and staff on behaviour, discipline and school ethos.

For information on an online survey of pupils on their views on pupil councils look up the 'Having a Say at School' website (www.havingasayatschool.org.uk). For a more detailed introduction to using the WWW as a research tool, the recent book by Dolowitz et al. (2008) provides accounts of how online resources can help with research projects, including hints and tips on how to use the WWW effectively. Chapters cover: topic development, search engines and directories, ethics, collecting data online using surveys and forms, data analysis, plagiarism and citations.

A framework for participation as researchers

The decision to engage children as active participant researchers is often justified in terms of a whole range of potential benefits (see Jones and Welch, 2010 for a detailed discussion). These include the potential for:

- learning about the process of research and associated thinking and practical skills – children and young people as learners;
- increasing the political impact of any outcomes of the research – children and young people as campaigners;

- improving the reliability and validity of the knowledge gained about the world of children and adolescents – children and young people as the best experts in their own lives;
- improving efficiency and value in services that children and young people use – children and young people as consumers or users of services;
- improving protection via respectful dialogue with children and young people – children and young people are vulnerable, they are in danger of oppression and need to be empowered as valid and active citizens.

Research projects, whether conducted entirely by adults, entirely by children and/or young people or some form of collaboration, all face the same challenges if it is to be considered to be good, reliable and valid research (see Chapters 5, 6, 7 and 8). In this section the focus is on the process of participation of children and young people as researchers or co-researchers. The process of engaging in research has features that are relevant to all researchers, regardless of age and collaborative status. These are to do with good research practice and involve various stages from the generation of the initial idea and project planning, to identifying research questions and aims, to data gathering and analysing data, reporting and disseminating findings. Table 9.5 shows a breakdown of the various general levels and stages of research in which children and young people can potentially participate in a research project (Davis, 2009; Kellett, 2005; Kirby, 1999).

The above framework is a useful one to consult when considering the levels of participation on any given research topic. While the aim is to encourage children and young people to be researchers or co-researchers, and to give them some control and choice in terms of their participation (who, what, when, how), it has to be done appropriately. Common sense must prevail at all times. For example, the age and abilities of the potential participant will make some tasks and types of participation more or less difficult. Perhaps the most obvious example is giving the young researchers control over any available budget. This may well be possible in some well-considered examples, but it will need careful consideration within context.

PUTTING RESEARCH INTO PRACTICE 9.2 – CHILDREN AND YOUNG PEOPLE AS CO-RESEARCHERS

Study the case summary below.

1 Using Table 9.5 discuss with your partner/group the good choices that have been made regarding young people as co-researchers.
2 Discuss the possible reasons for making these choices.
3 Discuss what difficulties and limitations the researchers may have encountered because of the choices that were made.

Table 9.5 Potential participation of children and young people as researchers or co-researchers

Stage and level of participation	*Decisions and planning*
Stage 1: project planning	Who should be 'in charge' – adults or the children and young people – in making decisions about the overall project, including: deciding who should form the steering group and who should be part of the actual research team; the design and planning of a pilot study; the project budget; the methodological approach, including tools for data collection and analysis; the main aims of the research, including titles and topics; the actual research questions and objectives; and participation, roles of individuals or groups of children and young people.
Stage 2: gathering data	In what ways should the children and young people be involved in collecting information from children and adults, such as teachers, parents, social workers, health workers, community workers, and so on? As the main researchers collecting all of the relevant information. As partners to the research collecting some of the information. As peer researchers collecting only information from peers. As research participants responding to adult researchers.
Stage 3: analysis of data gathered	To what extent should the children and young people be involved in the analysis: to make key decisions about the analytical approach; to check the analysis of the adult research team; to solely interpret the meaning of the data; to collaboratively interpret the meaning of the data with the adult research team.
Stage 4: reporting findings	Which reporting tasks should the children and young people be responsible for in terms of demonstrating the research outcomes and their impact: to choose the form of reporting (published and written report, presentation, video, drama, and so on); to choose the key messages for funders/stakeholders; to propose main changes to policy as required; to author/co-author the research report; to check or validate the research findings.
Stage 5: Policy development/ campaigning	In what ways should the children and young people be involved in influencing society and government responses to the research findings: to choose the method of dissemination; to deliver messages to key parties (local service provider, authority or central government); to deliver messages to the media; to deliver messages to parents or community; to deliver messages to other children.

CASE EXAMPLE

Co-researching with young people living in a young people's centre

The research problem

The research was set up in response to reports regarding the needs of looked-after children and young people as it was found that they have poor life outcomes and are not involved in matters to do with their own care.

Research aims

To redress the power imbalance by engaging directly with the children and young people in care as co-researchers using participatory methods.

Participants

Six out of eight residents took part in some of the activities. A group of four (two male, two female) took part on a more regular basis. Three young people moved away during the project. Several participants had learning needs and materials had to be differentiated.

Participatory process

- Aid informed decision making by giving them appropriate information and a choice of participation.
- Set the agenda for working together.
- Use participatory techniques.
- Involve the children and young people in the sharing of information gathered and in dissemination.
- Obtain feedback on their experiences of co-researching.

Methodology

Permission was obtained from the Centre Manager following discussions and information leaflets for the staff. Researchers went to the Centre for dinner with the participants and issued clearly written information booklets that explained the purpose of the research and an outline of activities they may be asked to be involved with. These were left behind for the participants to consider in their own time.

Participatory process and techniques

Context

Regular tea-time visits to the Centre over three months with planning around the commitments of the participants, taking place in an informal manner in a large living area.

Agenda

Within the larger purpose of the study – educational experience – the participants were asked to identify the issues that mattered to them and that should be co-researched together. Sessions were aided using participatory toolkits such as 'Spice it Up!' (Dynamix, 2002), which has a range of methods and activities for engaging participants. These included:

- Post-its for information gathering (good for moving and grouping);
- diamond rankings for prioritizing ideas (most to least important issues);

- 'top ten' tips – for consolidating the information gathered;
- the 'world's worst' – exploring issues in the negative extreme;
- the 'cotton bud debate' – a method of giving everyone an equal chance of speaking;
- how, how, how – a way of looking at issues in more depth;
- time spent planning sessions so that they would be fun but also have flexibility and responsiveness to the unexpected in sessions;
- discussions recorded in the visual form of mind maps (other approaches, such as recordings by audio and transcription were too time-consuming in this situation);
- visual map provided joint focus for interaction and the use of computers on mind-mapping software and with flip charts;
- activity evening out of the Centre in a local community hall with a range of activities planned (see Dynamix, 2002), and a social break and informal discussions;
- regular review of discussions, checking of understanding and feedback, often done with the aid of computer presentation.

Dissemination

Participants themselves consulted on what should happen to the information gathered (e.g. sharing with Centre staff, managers, teachers, leaflets for other children and young people in their situation, production of a DVD).
Co-construction and presentation of findings at a residential child care conference that was also presented to Centre staff.

Evaluation

The use of a target chart (Dynamix, 2002) to obtain the participants' views about power, control and enjoyment with four of the young people. Discussion with participants about their responses and comments on the target chart. Ratings of views of informed choice, being listened to, being able to say what they wanted to say. Views on impact.

For further examples of case studies where children and young people have had roles as researchers see Burton et al. (2010) and Tisdall et al. (2009).

Source: Chick, H. and Inch, W. (2007) 'Co-researching with young people living in a young people's centre', in *Seeking and Taking Account of the Views of Children and Young People: A Psychological Perspective.* www.itscotland.com/pdp/. pp. 37–57.

A general framework for a participatory ethos

Doing research 'on', 'with', 'about' and even as 'co-researchers with' children and young people is never done in a cultural or contextual vacuum. As a reader you may be a teacher, nurse, social worker, nursery nurse, psychologist, student or a youth worker, to name only a few possibilities. In these positions, we too are embedded in a social context that impinges not just on the ability of the youngsters we work with to fully participate in our research, but also on us. Our own views, the culture and ethos of our government, of our local authorities, of the contexts and settings which we share with children and young people, including families and homes, hospitals, schools, units, and so on is crucial in determining the extent and quality of participation we can actually offer. As we discovered in our theoretical discussions in Chapter 2 and in the participatory model of Hobbs previously described, we can improve our own position on this by seeking to understand the issues and improve our own practice. We can strive to empower the voice of children and young people by enhancing participation, especially through research that demonstrates the power of their views and voices in making change possible.

The final framework to be discussed is one that can be used in our own professional practice for the evaluation of our own services, systems or practice. How participation-friendly are you? How participation-friendly is your research? How participation-friendly is your service? We can also use it when attempting to work with children and young people in a participatory project within particular settings such as schools, wards, residential units and clinics. How participation-friendly is that setting? It is a useful framework that is relevant for doing research 'on', 'with', 'about' and even as 'co-researchers with' children and young people because it addresses the reason we would choose to do the research in the first place: to empower the participants to have a say and to demonstrate impact through change. It helps us to understand where there is a weak link in the participatory chain that can be highlighted through research. Figure 9.2 illustrates these important questions and checks that need to be made in evaluating our own participation friendliness.

PUTTING RESEARCH INTO PRACTICE 9.3 – COMMITTING TO A PARTICIPATORY ETHOS

Revisit the case study in 'Research into Practice 9.2'. Using Figure 9.2, discuss with your partner/group, how the researchers have demonstrated their commitment to a participatory ethos.

Critique of methods for consultation and participation

Over the last decade, the proliferation of methods and tools for consultation and participation with children and young people has been extraordinary. It has been mainly due to research fuelled by the rights agenda that we have moved very rapidly from the situation of a few key, pioneering research studies on listening to children, to a megastore of easily accessible riches, many available free online. The WWW has undoubtedly also played a part in this and it will continue to revolutionize the ways we work and research with children and young people

ORGANISATIONAL ETHOS OF PARTICIPATION

- Participation of children and young people is a core feature of policy/practice.
- The reasons for involving children and young people are clear.
- Clear values underpin the inclusion of children and young people in your work.
- Clear objectives for children and young people, services and professionals are given.

CO-PARTICIPANT ETHOS

- Child/young person is respected as a source of unique expertise.
- Importance is attached to spending time with the child/young person to build relationships.
- Be aware of what is going on with them in their lives at home and other contexts and how this might impact on their involvement in the research.
- Demonstrate interest, respect and active listening.
- Provide feedback and reality checking on understanding.

PRACTICE ETHOS ON POWER AND CONTROL

- Is participation part of the service development plan?
- How can children get involved in planning such objectives?
- How do you support them in knowing how their views can have an impact?
- Do you have clear information for them to help them make informed decisions?
- Is this in a format that is easily accessed by them?
- Are there clear and genuine participatory options?
- How does the service deal with confidentiality?
- Are there choices for timings, locations and taking part?
- Do children and young people take part in setting the agenda?
- Are you obtaining a view of what matters to them and what they want researched?
- Do they have a say in the activities they engage in?

APPROACHES

- Use various tools/multi-sensory to include all ages, tastes and abilities.
- Joint focus of attention on activities that are flexible and creative.
- Provide examples for them to work from.
- Use all dimensions of giving control (where, when, who, eye contact).
- Be transparent about the information gathered
- Give interactive and ongoing feedback.
- Provide feedback and evaluation that is clear for them and others.

IMPACT

- Empowerment
- Self-esteem
- Belonging
- Mastery
- Demonstrate a response to the child's view.
- Be realistic about what can be achieved.
- Involve children and young people in dissemination where appropriate.

Figure 9.2 Summary of a participatory ethos in practice: a checklist aid for taking account of the views of children and young people (Kirby et al., 2003; MacKay et al., 2007)

in dramatic ways in the next decade. The field is not without its difficulties and debates, however. It is now generally accepted that children and young people should be respected as citizens, even those who are very young and those with disabilities, and that they do have a valid point of view that can be accessed using appropriate participatory tools and processes. Whether or not doing research with children and young people, as actual researchers or co-researchers, should be regarded as an absolute right, one that is truly liberating, is not universally agreed, and whether or not there are actual rather than supposed benefits for children and young participants who do participate as researchers has scant evidence either way (Hill et al., 2004).

It is questionable the extent to which a researcher, working within many ethical, legal, institutional and practical constraints, can be truly participatory. As we have explored throughout the chapter, the constraints of real-world research ensures that we have to make judgement calls in terms of what is realistic given any contextual constraints and the purpose of the research (Davis, 2009). These include things like research questions, ethics, budgets, time and the expectations of stakeholders. According to Lansdown (2001), effective participatory research has a minimum standard of:

- real relevance to the participants;
- the capacity to make an impact;
- adequate time and resources;
- realistic expectations of the participants (clear and agreed targets and goals);
- values of trust, respect and equity; and
- training and support for the participants to contribute to the planning.

Consultation is often confused with participation, and although there are overlaps, they can be quite different and serve different purposes when applied to children and young people. Although all research participants may want to change policy and practice, again the literature suggests that this is rare except where the findings are uncontroversial and do not give rise to conflicts of interest (Tisdall, 2009). It is acknowledged that it is important to have a balance between empowering children and not placing too much responsibility on them in making decisions that they have insufficient experience to deal with (Aston and Lambert, 2010; DfES, 2001). This is true of any task in consultation and participatory research.

The specific studies briefly reviewed here demonstrate that, with appropriately designed tools, children and young people can be keen, constructive commentators on their perspectives of everyday life at home, school and beyond. In addition, they can collaborate in data production, and contribute to research design and its implementation. Researchers have also demonstrated the importance of critical reflection on the effectiveness of these tools and have responsibly disseminated both the advantages and disadvantages of use in each case. Clark and Moss (2001) found that their Mosaic method informed service evaluation, promoted a climate of change, dialogue and the development of participatory skills. It was less clear, however, that the agenda was not resource-driven by adults, or that the children had sufficient privacy, or that any given culture would be in a state of readiness to promote 'listening'. This will take time, training and will compete with curriculum agendas.

Classic participatory tools of tours, maps, photos, and so on do generate useful data, but without the support of other methods, they may not be truly emancipatory. There can be practical problems with camera use, ranging from the ethics of introducing a gadget in a poor community that will not be available after the research, to children taking shots of the wrong things or photos not turning out at all, and finally to sabotage. Drawings, worksheets and diaries are all easily obtained by individuals and larger groups and mostly enjoyed. However, these tools mostly depend on the quality of adaptation of concepts being explored to match the abilities of the participants. Not all children like drawing and some just cannot do it. When there is a mismatch between the task and actual abilities in literacy and other academic skills, there will also be missing and incomplete data. Participants and their parents may feel burdened by tasks that go home with them, eating into other work and leisure tasks.

Well-designed worksheets and diaries are very useful for generating data and insights, but it will take time to get the design right (Punch, 2002b). Figures 9.3–9.8 illustrate a tongue-in-cheek attempt of the first author to give a lot of freedom in the collation of the perspectives of two children, Claire aged 12 years and Gemma aged 6 years. The girls were given a digital camera and asked to photograph the things that were important to them when they had a sleepover at their aunt's house. Once the photographs had been taken, the girls were asked to say why they chose to take the photographs they did.

Figure 9.3 Two sisters, aged 6 and 12, tell their story of visiting with their aunt using photographs

Getting started

Figure 9.4 Getting started

Claire: 'I asked my aunt to take pictures of me trying to get Gemma to choose things to photograph but all she was interested in was her dolls and taking pictures of Barbie, yuk! Then she went into a huff when I tried to show her how to take pictures with it. I decided to do it myself, but she did join in by following me around and annoying me!'

Favourite views

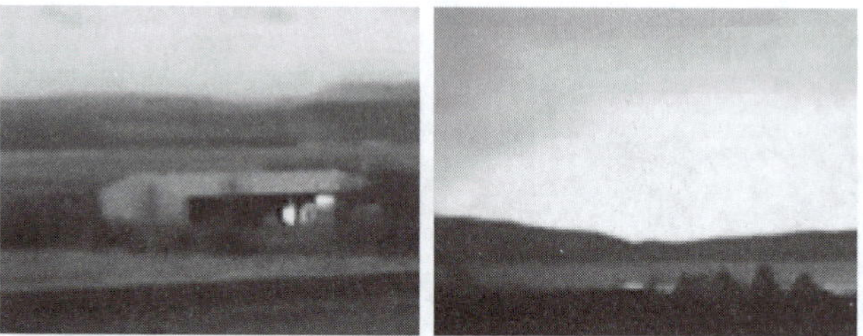

Figure 9.5 Favourite views

Claire: 'These are not very clear pictures but there are lovely horses at the stables that can be seen from the garden, out exercising. I love to watch them. And from my bedroom window I can see the farms, the sea and the lights across the sea on the land at the other side. My house is in a busy street.'

My bedroom

Claire: 'I like to sleep in this room because this was Granny's room when she stayed too. I miss Granny so much since she died last year, she really loved me

Figure 9.6 My bedroom

very much and was kind. Mum and Dad have made my own room at home a lot like this one because I liked it so much, I even have the same bed, only it's bigger!'

Bedtime

Figure 9.7 Bedtime stories

Claire: 'I took this picture of fairy stories because at night my aunts would come into my room and we would read some of the stories in Scottish dialect. I like scary stories and my favourite one is *The Strange Visitor:* My aunts know a version of this by heart because Granny taught it to them when they were little girls. It's scary and really good fun. I especially like the bit that goes "muckle muckle"!'

Figure 9.8 Breakfast time

Claire: 'A special breakfast treat just for me when I stay at my aunt's is fresh-baked bread with melted butter and honey toasted into it. It tastes really nice. My aunts gave me the nickname Honey Child because I liked it so much. It makes me feel special.'

It is not difficult to guess what the pitfalls of this type of research involving children and young people might be. It is also possible to see the potential for powerful statements, and if we can manage the pitfalls and plan carefully, some lasting data that make a real impact could be obtained.

With respect to participatory interview techniques, the focus group method is good for giving confidence to individuals within the group and allowing the children or young people to set part of the agenda. The individual interview context is, of course, both more private and intimate. It is not difficult to imagine the many research situations in which this approach is vital. Furthermore, used in conjunction with a prior focus group, the discussion could go a long way on establishing a rapport with an anxious child via group support, acceptance and an emerging structure of issues to be explored in greater depth with individuals. While group interviews have proved very useful for obtaining perspectives, they do have some drawbacks. They are difficult to tape-record and transcribe (who is saying what?) and impossible to record in note form whether you are leading the group or merely observing. Group activity also leads to group effects, with some voices being heard more than others (Hill et al., 1996).

Finally, the use of technology, such as computers, mobile phones and software brings many challenges as well as benefits. Without doubt, common sense tells us that these modes of participation are bound to be more interesting and fun for children and young people. However, without the actual evidence base, it cannot be assumed that they do indeed remove social desirability in response, improve intimacy, reduce failures to respond or increase the number of responses, as participants could be submitting multiple questionnaires or being put off with other limitations in technology. These approaches have much potential but are not universally practised, and not equally well supported for all participants. It is nevertheless an important growth area and the answers to many of these evidence questions shall no doubt be forthcoming in the near future.

Conclusion

The studies reviewed earlier in this book could be described as those which take a standard research tool such as questionnaires and interviews (see Chapters 7 and 8), adapt them creatively to address the research purpose and to ensure appropriate levels of task demands on participants, and which have the specific aim of obtaining valid perspectives. It is not, therefore, the tool in itself that is innovative, but the way in which it is used. In the cases reported, tools have been used in a qualitative, inductive and participatory manner in the search of understanding and empowerment of voice. This cognitive-developmental approach to consultation and participation in research with children and young people is very important (see also Clark and Stratham, 2005; Lewis and Lindsay, 2000) and is also addressed in Chapter 5. This helps to inform us about getting the tools right for the job of seeking valid perspectives. The use of a social constructionist model and framework approach to consultation and participation is one that places the children and young people in a highly influential context. This is also important as it is this consideration that often dictates the parameters within which we can offer some level of participation and impact. In Chapter 10 ethical considerations are explored in more detail with respect to reasonable expectation when collaborating with young research participants.

PUTTING RESEARCH INTO PRACTICE 9.4 – DESIGNING AND CONDUCTING A STUDY USING A PARTICIPATIVE RESEARCH APPROACH

This activity aims to provide you with experience of designing and conducting a study using a participative research approach to consulting with children and young people.

Consider the relative roles of adult and participant researchers. You may find the frameworks within the chapter helpful. Choose one of the following research questions and plan methods of data collection and analysis.

- What do secondary school pupils think of the ways they are supported with mental health issues at school?
- What are the views of children and/or young people who regularly attend reviews (e.g. children with special educational needs or disabilities; children who are fostered or looked after by a local authority)?
- How do young homeless teenagers taking part in housing projects feel about the project and its impact on their lives?

Remember to use a range of age- and interest-appropriate techniques that empower the participants in terms of expressing their views and facilitating an impact.

Recording interview data will require permission from individuals and their carers.

References

Additional Support for Learning Act (2004) *Education (Additional Support for Learning) Act 2004: Consultation on Draft Code of Practice, Draft Policy Papers and Draft Associated Regulations: Response Booklet.* Edinburgh: Her Majesty's Stationery Office.

Aston, H.J. and Lambert, N. (2010) 'Young people's views about their involvement in decision-making', *Educational Psychology in Practice*, 26 (1): 41–51.

Barrett, W. (2007) 'Evaluating the use of in my shoes as a participatory technique for seeking and taking into account the views of children and young people, in *Seeking and Taking Account of the Views of Children and Young People: a Psychological Perspective.* Available at: www.itscotland.com/pdp/. pp. 25–36.

Bronfenbrenner, U. (1992) 'Ecological systems theory', in R. Vasta (ed.), *Six Theories of Child Development: Revised Formulations and Current Issues.* London: J. Kingsley. pp 187–249.

Burton, D., Smith, M. and Woods, K. (2010) 'Working with teachers to promote children's participation through pupil-led research', *Educational Psychology in Practice*, 26 (2): 91–104.

Calam, R.M., Cox, A.D., Glasgow, D.V., Jimmieson, P. and Groth Larsen, S. (2000) 'Assessment and therapy with children: can computers help?', *Child Clinical Psychology and Psychiatry*, 5 (3): 329–43.

Chick, H. and Inch, W. (2007) 'Co-researching with young people who are looked after and accommodated in a young person's centre', in *Seeking and Taking Account of the Views of Children and Young People: a Psychological Perspective.* Available at: www.itscotland.com/pdp/pp. 37–57.

Clark, A. and Moss, P. (2001) *Listening to Young Children: the Mosaic Approach.* London: National Children's Bureau.

Clark, A. and Stratham, J. (2005) 'Listening to young children: experts in their own lives', *Adoption and Fostering*, 29 (1): 45–56.

Cousins, J. (2006) 'In my shoes: a computer assisted interview for communicating with children and vulnerable adults', *Adoption and Fostering*, 30 (1): 89–90.

Cremin, H. and Slatter, B. (2004) 'Is it possible to access the 'voice' of pre-school children? Results of a research project in a pre-school setting', *Educational Studies*, 30 (4): 457–70.

Crichton, R. and Barrett, W. (2007) 'The contribution of psychological/sociological perspectives to an understanding of effective participation', in *Seeking and Taking Account of the Views of Children and Young People: a Psychological Perspective.* Available at: www.itscotland.com/pdp/. pp. 12–24.

Davis, J. (2009) 'Involving children', in E.K.M. Tisdall, J.M. Davis and M. Gallagher (eds), *Researching with Children and Young People: Research Design, Methods, and Analysis.* Los Angeles: SAGE.

DfES (2001a) *Learning to Listen: Core Principles for the Involvement of Children and Young People.* London: Department for Education and Skills.

DfES (2001b) *SEN Toolkit.* Annesley: Department for Education and Skills.

DfES (2003) Working Together: Giving Children and Young People a Say. Available at: www.education.gov.uk/consultations/downloadableDocs/239_2.pdf (accessed 26 March 2012). p. 3.

DfES (2004) *Every Child Matters.* London: The Stationery Office.

Dolowitz, D., Buckler, S. and Sweeney, F. (2008) *Researching On-line.* Basingstoke, UK: Palgrave Macmillan.

Flewitt, R. (2005) 'Is every child's, voice heard? Researching the different ways 3-year-old children communicate and make meaning at home and in a pre-school play group. *Early years*, 25(3): 207–22.

Glasgow, D. and Crossley, R. (2004) 'Achieving best evidence: a comparison of 3 interview strategies for investigative interviews in a forensic population with mild learning disabilities', in C. Dale and L. Storey (eds), *Learning Disability & Offending.* Chichester: Pratis Nursing Practice International. pp. 35–44.

Greene, S. and Hill, M. (2005) 'Researching children's experience: methods and methodological issues', in S. Greene and D. Hogan (eds), *Researching Children's Experience: Methods and Approaches.* London: SAGE.

Greig, A.D. and Taylor, J. (1999) *Doing Research with Children.* London: Sage.

Greig, A.D., Taylor, J. and MacKay, T. (2007) *Doing Research with Children.* London: SAGE.

Hart, R.A. and UNICEF International Child Development Centre (1992) *Children's Participation from Tokenism to Citizenship.* Florence, Italy: UNICEF International Child Development Centre.

Hayes, B. (2002) 'Community, cohesion, inclusive education', *Educational and Child Psychology*, 19 (4): 75–90.

Hill, M., Laybourn, A. and Borland, M. (1996) 'Engaging with primary-aged children about their emotions and well-being: methodological considerations', *Children & Society*, 10 (2): 129–44.

Hill, M. Davis, J., Prout, A. and Tisdall, K. (2004) 'Moving the participation agenda forward; *Children & Society*, 18: 77–96.

Hobbs, C. (2006) Consulting with Children. PDP start-up conference keynote presentation, Pitlochry, May 2006.

Hobbs, C., Todd, L. and Taylor, J. (2000) 'Consulting with children and young people: enabling educational psychologists to work collaboratively', *Educational and Child Psychology*, 17 (4): 107–15.

Hoppe, M.J., Wells, E.A., Morrison, D.M., Gillmore, M.R. and Wilsdon, A. (1995) 'Using focus groups to discuss sensitive topics with children', *Evaluation Review*, 19 (1): 102–14.

Jones, P. and Welch, S. (2010) *Rethinking Children's Rights: attitudes in Contemporary Society*. New York: Continuum International Publishing Group.

Kellett, M. (2005) *How to Develop Children as Researchers: a Step-By-Step Guide to Teaching the Research Process*. London: Paul Chapman.

Kilkelly, U., Kilpatrick, R., Lundy, L., Moore, L., Scraton, P., Davey, C., Dwyer, C. and McAllister, A. (2005) *Children's Rights in Northern Ireland: Research*. Belfast: Northern Ireland Commissioner for Children and Young People in association with Queen's University, Belfast.

Kirby, P. (1999) *Listening to Young Children: the Mosaic Approach*. London: Save the Children.

Lansdown, G. (2001) 'Children's participation in democratic decision making'. UNICEF. Available at: http://www.unicef-icad.org/publications/pdf/insight.pdf.

Lewis, A. (2010) 'Silence in the context of "child voice"', *Children & Society*, 24 (1): 14–23.

Lewis, A. and Lindsay, G. (2000) *Researching Children's Perspectives*. Philadelphia: Open University Press.

MacKay, F., Barret, W., Chrichton, R., (2007) 'Conclusions and implications for practice', in *Seeking and Taking Account of the Views of Children and Young People: A Psychological Perspective*. Available at: www.itscotland.com/pdp/. pp. 83–92.

MacNaughton, G., Hughes, P. and Smith, K. (2007) 'Young children's rights and public policy: practices and possiblities for citizenship in the early years' *Children & Society*, 21 (6): 458–69.

McKnorrie, K. (1995) *Children (Scotland) Act 1995*. Edinburgh: W. Green/Sweet & Maxwell.

Mill, M., Davis, J., Prout, A. and Tisdall, K. (2004) 'Moving the participation agenda forward; *Children of Society*, 18: 77–96.

Morrow, V. (2001) 'Using qualitative methods to elicit young people's perspectives on their environments: some ideas for community health initiatives', *Health Education Research*, 16 (3): 255–68.

National Archives (2012) Children Act 1989. Available at: www.legislation.gov.uk/ukpga/1989/41/contents (accessed 26 March 2012).

National Archives (2012) Children (Northern Ireland) Order (1995). Available at: www.legislation.gov.uk/nisi/1995/755/contents/made (accessed 27 March 2012).

National Youth Agency (2006) 'Involving children and young people – an introduction'. Available at: http://nya.org.uk/dynamic_files/hbr/sharedresources/Involving%20cyp%20-%20an%20introduction.pdf (accessed 12 March 2012).

NSPCC (2008) 'All about me: Child Line teachers' pack for children and young people with special educational needs (Keystage 2/Keystage 3). Available at: www.nspcc.org.uk/inform/resourcesforteachers/classroomresources/.

O'Kane, C. (2000) 'The development of participatory techniques: facilitating children's views about decisions which affect them', in P. Christensen and A. James (eds), *Research with Children: Perspectives and Practices*. London: Falmer Press. pp. 136–59.

Oliver, L. (2007) 'The contribution of participation in consultation online as a technique for seeking and taking into account the views of children and young people', in *Seeking and Taking Account of the Views of Children and Young People: a Psychological Perspective*. Available at: www.itscotland.com/pdp/. pp. 58–67.

Prout, A. (2001) 'Representing children: reflections on the 5–16 programme', *Children & Society*, 15 (3): 193–201.

Prout, A. (2002) 'Researching children as social actors: an introduction to the children 5–16 programme', *Children & Society*, 16 (2): 67–76.

Punch, S. (2002a) 'Interviewing strategies with young people: the "Secret Box", stimulus material and task-based activities', *Children & Society*, 16 (1): 45–56.
Punch, S. (2002b) 'Research with children: the same or different from research with adults?', *Childhood*, 9 (3): 321–41.
Rodenberg, P. (1993) *The Need for Words: Voice and the Text*. New York: Routledge.
Shier, H. (2001) 'Pathways to participation: openings, opportunities and obligations', *Children & Society*, 15 (2): 107–17.
Sinclair, R. (2004) 'Participation in practice: making it meaningful, effective and sustainable', *Children & Society*, 18 (2): 106–18.
Street, C. (2004) 'In-patient mental health services for young people – changing to meet new needs?', *Perspectives in Public Health*, 124 (3): 115–18.
Tisdall, E.K.M., Davis, J.M. and Gallogher, M. (2009) *Researching Children and Young People. Research Design, Method and Analysis*. London: Sage.
UNICEF (1989) Convention on the Rights of the Child. Available at: www.unicef.org/crc/ (accessed 12 March 2012).
UNICEF (2002) 'Children participating in research, monitoring and evaluation (M&E) – ethics and your responsibility as a manager'. Available at: www.unicef.org/evaluation/files/TechNote1_Ethics.pdf (accessed 12 March 2012).
Woolfson, R.C., Harker, M., Lowe, D., Shields, M., Banks, M., Campbell, L. and Fergusson, E. (2006) 'Consulting about consulting: Young people's views of consultation', *Educational Psychology in Practice*, 22 (4): 337–53.
Woolfson, R.C., Bryce, D., Mooney, L., Harker, M., Lowe, D. and Ferguson, E. (2008) 'Improving methods of consulting with young people: piloting a new model of consultation', *Educational Psychology in Practice*, 24 (1): 55–67.

Recommended reading for further study

Children's Society (2001) *Young People's Charter of Participation*. London: Children's Society.
Children's Rights Officers and Advocates (2002) *Up the Ladder of Participation*. London: CROA.
Fajerman, L., Treseder, P. and Connor, J. (2004) *Children are Service Users Too: a Guide to Consulting with Children and Young People*. London: Save the Children.
Greene, S. and Hogan, D. (eds) (2005) *Researching Children's Experience: Methods and Approaches*. London: Sage.
Kirby, P. (1999) *Involving Young Researchers – How to Enable Young People to Design and Conduct Research*. York: Joseph Rowntree Foundation.
MacBeath, J., Demetriou, H., Ruddick, J. and Myers, K (2003) *Consulting Pupils: a Toolkit for Teachers*. Cambridge: Pearson Publishing Company.
Madden, S. (2001) *Reaction Consultation Toolkit: a Practical Toolkit for Consulting with Children and Young People on Policy Issues*. Scotland Programme: Save the Children.
Shaw, C., Brady, L-M. and Davey, C. (2011) *Guidelines for Research with Children and Young People*. London: National Children's Bureau.
Shephard, C. (2002) *Participation – Spice It Up: Practical Tools for Engaging Children and You*. Save the Children.
Tolley, E., Girma, M., Stanton-Wharmby, A. Spate, A. and Milburn, J. (1998) *Young Opinions: great Ideas*. London: National Children's Bureau.
Treseder, P. and Crowley, A. (2001) *Taking the Initiative: Promoting Young People's Participation in Decision-Making in Wales*. London: Carnegie Young People Initiative.

Treseder, P. and Children's Rights Office and Save the Children Fund (1997) *Empowering Children & Young People: Training Manual*. London: Save the Children.

Youth Council for Northern Ireland (2001) *Seen and Heard? Consulting and Involving Young People Within the Public Sector*. Northern Ireland: Youth Council for Northern Ireland.

Weisner, T.S. (2005) *Discovering Successful Pathways in Children's Development: Mixed Methods in the Study of Childhood and Family Life*. Chicago, IL: University of Chicago Press.

White, P., Save the Children Fund and National Youth Agency (2001) *Local and Vocal: Promoting Young People's Involvement in Local Decision-Making – An Overview and Planning Guide*. London: Save the Children.

Willow, C. (1997) *Hear! Hear! Promoting Children and Young People's Democractic Participation in Local Government*. London: Local Government Information Unit and National Children's Bureau.

Websites

Having a Say at School. Research on Pupil Councils in Scotland. Available at: www.havingasayatschool.org.uk/ (accessed 26 March 2012).

In My Shoes. Available at: www.inmyshoes.org.uk/In_My_Shoes/Introduction.html (accessed 26 March 2012)

TEN

The ethics of doing research with children and young people

The aims of this chapter are:

- to explore the basis of contemporary ethical thinking in relation to research with children and young people;
- to examine the regulation of research activity with children and young people;
- to discuss levels of participation and ethics;
- to discuss the importance of informed consent in research with child and adolescent participants;
- to examine the process of gaining access to child and adolescent participants including tips for gaining research ethics committee approval;
- to provide a practical guide to assessing ethical versus non-ethical research.

Professionals who work with children learn many skills as part of their initial academic training, through working alongside more experienced practitioners, by reflecting on each new situation they encounter and in many other different and diverse ways. However, opportunities for observing experienced researchers in practice can be few and far between. Research in itself can be a time-consuming and lengthy process, making opportunities for observing end-to-end research studies in practice difficult to align with the modularity of academic study. Additionally, a great deal of the development of research design involves cognitive rather than overt behaviours, and the very nature of the researcher–participant relationship often makes it undesirable, if not impossible, to have an outsider present. Such intrusion can influence the research milieu, can be restrictive and can potentially have an effect on the internal validity of the research.

Ensuring that the process of undertaking research adheres to sound ethical principles is part of the general repertoire of researcher skills that the novice researcher will find difficult to observe or experience in practice. Inexperienced researchers can practise designing interview schedules or questionnaires, can rehearse their questioning techniques and enhance their powers of observation, but equipping themselves with a repertoire of skills that will prepare them for the ethical dilemmas they might meet when undertaking research with children and their families is much more challenging. That experienced researchers frequently do find themselves faced with ethical dilemmas is without doubt (Campbell, 2008; Powell and Smith, 2009; Schenk and Williamson, 2005) although paradoxically, according to Birbeck and Drummond (2007), it is not an area that is often discussed in the literature. We have then a situation where a fundamental part of the research process is difficult to experience in practice, is poorly described in the literature and yet we expect that the would-be researcher will have ensured that all potential ethical dilemmas have been considered prior to embarking on the research. Careful planning and knowledge of the potential pitfalls will help, but we cannot underestimate the unpredictability factor of working with children and the ethical dilemmas that may be faced, often at the most unexpected times.

This chapter explores how researchers, and in particular the novice researcher, can be prepared for at least some of those ethical challenges that might occur during the process of undertaking research in practice. As we have said previously, this is a practical text, and we will explore how the researcher can best be prepared for the unexpected, giving examples from our own experiences and the experiences of others. Before we do this, however, it is important that we examine the ethical principles that should underpin the preparation of our research. This examination inevitably includes looking at the foundation of contemporary ethical principles in research and at the differences that exist between professional groups, particularly in relation to the direct involvement of children and young people in research. This is a growing area of debate and the practical at the end of this chapter asks you to consider this point in relation to your own profession so that you can make up your own mind.

Basis of contemporary ethics in research with children and young people

The study of ethics in relation to research with children and young people involves an underlying knowledge of both general ethics theory and an exploration of the general principles of undertaking research on human participants and how these can be applied to children and young people. In many professions there remains a lack of specific ethical guidance about doing research with children and young people, which is probably partially attributed to the place that children and young people have held historically in society (see Chapter 1).

As we have discussed previously, it is only within the past few decades that societies have come to appreciate and recognize that children and young people have rights which are specific and which dictate that they should be consulted in matters that affect them. The current situation leaves the novice researcher to adapt a set of principles developed for research with adult subjects to children and adolescents. Some attempts have been made to do this with varying success and a helpful starting point is Schenk and Williamson's work (2005).

A useful place to start any discussion on the ethics of research involving children and young people is to focus on commonly held ethical principles that can act as an initial point of reference for novice researchers. Three ethical principles were established in the 1978 Belmont Report and a fourth (*non-maleficence* – meaning to avoid causing harm) was added by Beauchamp and Childress (2008), authors of a seminal book in this field called *Principles of Biomedical Ethics,* which was first published in 1979 and is now in its sixth edition (Beauchamp and Childress, 2008). The four widely held set of principles are as follows.

- *Autonomy*, which can be defined as self-rule that is free from both controlling interference by others and from limitations, such as inadequate understanding, that prevent meaningful choice (Beauchamp and Childress, 2008). Applying the principle of autonomy to children and adolescents means making sure that they are able to consent through free choice, without fear or worry that they will be disadvantaged if they refuse. It also requires that the researcher makes the information available in a form and at a level that is understandable to every child or adolescent so that they fully understand what they are required to do, should they agree to be part of the study, including what will happen to information gathered about them.
- *Non-maleficence*, which was originally combined with *beneficence* (doing good) as a single principle, asserts an obligation to do no harm. Beauchamp and Childress (2008) discuss how definitions of the word 'harm' can be very broad and that it is important that the term is understood. When working with children and adolescents the researcher must take reasonable, sufficient and appropriate steps to avoid causing pain, suffering, incapacitation, offense and death. A good example of forms of harm that can occur can be found in Keddie (2000) in a study of children and toys, where the researcher had to intervene to prevent physical harm on occasions but did not intervene to prevent non-physical harm in the form of stigmatization on another occasion.
- *Beneficence*, which requires that as professionals we act for the positive benefit of others and that we make judgments about the comparisons and relative weights of costs, risks and benefits, with probable overall benefits outweighing the risks to participants. This means in very basic terms that the researcher will need to be clear about what benefits there will be to the actual child or adolescent and to society, what risks are likely to occur to the child or adolescent and whether the benefits justify the risks.
- *Justice*, which is according the participant what is fair, equitable and appropriate treatment in light of what is due or owed (Beauchamp and Childress, 2008). This means that the researcher must make sure that all children and adolescents are treated fairly

and equally, and this includes consideration of who should be included in the study and who will be excluded. Information-gathering activities should not involve persons who are unlikely ever to benefit from the findings.

These are principles which, it could be argued, have relevance to our behaviour as moral human beings in all aspects of our personal and professional lives. In terms of undertaking research involving human participants, clearly we should act with morality and should not suppose that putting on a label that calls us *researchers* gives us licence to act in any way that is not moral. So why, then, did it become necessary to develop ethical codes that govern the way in which we undertake research? The simple answer is that abuse of the principles that guided research necessitated its regulation so that there should no longer be any room for subjective interpretation of what is or is not moral. Much of this abuse occurred in Nazi Germany during the Second World War and was brought to the attention of the world during the Nuremberg war trials (1945–1946). The messages that emerged were clear. In a book edited by Caplan (1992) titled *When Medicine Went Mad: Bioethics and the Holocaust,* Müller-Hill, when writing about the ethical implications of Nazi experimentation, states:

> The attempt of science to provide acceptable values and ethics has failed. Medicine and science should never again be trusted when they promise to deliver their own ethical values; these values have to come from other sources. (1992: 48)

The view that scientists should not self-regulate in relation to ethics and research involving human participants was deemed necessary not because of broken promises or because the so-called scientists involved in experimentation during the War were madmen. The view came about because not for the first time scientists committed crimes when they were part of a regime where obedience was paramount, in spite of existing codes of conduct and oaths of good practice. In the Nazi concentration camps, experimentation was aimed at advancing knowledge for the benefit of the Aryan community (a kind of warped and misguided beneficence) but at the expense of adults and children who were considered inferior. It is reported, for example, that Josef Mengele, one of the most infamous doctors of the era, who undertook experiments in Auschwitz-Birkenau, a Nazi concentration camp, on 1500 sets of twins (including many children), was interested in discovering the secrets of multiple births so that what was thought of as the superior race could be multiplied at twice the natural rate, and that he was also interested in discovering the hereditary basis of behaviour and physical characteristics. His methods were torturous, inhumane and frequently resulted in the deaths of the twins.

The value of such research must be questioned, and debate continues as to what should be done with data from these and other experiments. Kor (1992), a survivor of the twin experiments who was liberated from Auschwitz-Birkenau in January 1945, suggests that because the experiments were unethical the use of the data is also unethical. Kor also warns doctors and scientists in a way that is far more direct than any of the ethical codes in existence, by urging them to take the following pledge:

- to take a moral commitment never to violate anyone's human rights and human dignity;
- to promote a universal idea that says: 'Treat the subject of your experiments in a manner that you would want to be treated if you were in their place';
- to do your scientific work, but please, never stop being a human being. The moment you do, you are becoming a scientist for the sake of science alone, and you are becoming the Mengele of today. (1992: 7–8)

Regulation of research activity

Following the Second World War and the Nuremberg trials there was shock at what had happened under the guise of the term 'research' as well as determination that such atrocities should not occur in the future, resulting in various forms of governance and regulation that are briefly discussed below. While children and young people do not form a discrete group within this governance, they are clearly part of the overall concern. From the Nuremberg trials conducted following the War emerged the Nuremberg Code, which set out 10 moral, ethical and legal principles relating to research involving human participants. The Code, which was established in its final form in 1948, includes details relating to the necessity for voluntary consent of research participants, the need to ensure that the research is for the good of society, that research designs should have been previously tried out on animals and that unnecessary physical and mental suffering should be avoided. It also refers to the need to assess risk and the rights of research participants to withdraw from the experiment if they wish, as well as stating that the researcher should be scientifically qualified to undertake the experimentation.

The Geneva Conventions of 12 August 1949, and in particular the fourth Geneva Convention, formed an addition to international law in relation to civilians. The original convention of 1864 only applied to combatants, as did the Regulations Concerning the Laws and Customs of War on Land, annexed to the Fourth Hague Convention of 1907. The general provisions of the Geneva Convention Relating to the Protection of Civilian Persons in Time of War make important statements both about research and about children. Article 14 necessitates the setting up of safety zones, during hostilities, to protect children under the age of 15 and mothers of children under the age of seven years, and Article 82 states that during internment children and their families should be housed together to enable them to lead 'a proper family life' (Lossier, 1949: 184), whereas Article 147 prohibits 'wilful killing, torture or inhumane treatment, including biological experiments' (Lossier, 1949: 211, see also Boyden [2000] and the American Psychological Association [2010], for further discussion about conducting research with war-affected children).

The World Medical Association, conscious of violations of existing codes of conduct by physicians before and during the War, set up its own review to make sure doctors would be aware of their moral obligations to research subjects and adopted in 1954 a set of Principles for those in Research and Experimentation. After a number of revisions this was developed into the Declaration of Helsinki and was adopted by the World Medical Assembly in Helsinki in June 1964. It has been amended and clarified in a number of subsequent World Medical Assemblies. The most recent version, the sixth revision, was published by the World Medical Association in 2008 (World Medical Association, 2012). The Declaration of Helsinki provides a standard of international ethics in research involving human participants and, while it reinforces, elaborates and clarifies the details contained within the Nuremberg Code it also examines the issue of children as research participants in relation to informed consent. The Declaration discusses that not only should the informed consent of the child's legal guardian be sought but that where a minor child is able, the informed consent of the child should be sought *in addition* to that of the legal guardian. The issue of informed consent is discussed in more detail in the following section.

The United Nations was set up and had its charter adopted in 1945, following the collapse of its predecessor, the League of Nations, at the beginning of the War. It made provision for the establishment of a Commission on Human Rights, which set out to prepare an International Bill of Rights, later called the Universal Declaration, of Human Rights, following the General Assembly of the United Nations in 1948. Within the United Nations family are a number of specialized agencies that have relevance to research involving children, including the United Nations Educational, Scientific and Cultural Organization (UNESCO) and UNICEF. The Declaration of the Rights of the Child, first declared in 1959 and confirmed in the Convention on the Rights of the Child in 1989, sets out the fundamental human rights to which every child is entitled. Taking guidance from the Convention, UNICEF (2002) has provided useful recommendations for researchers undertaking studies with children and young people, and Schenk and Williamson (2005) have developed an excellent resource around ethical approaches to gathering data from children and young people in international settings.

In addition to the charters and conventions mentioned above, a number of professional groups have established their own codes which aim to regulate research within professions, for example, the British Psychological Society (2009), the

National Children's Bureau (Shaw et al., 2011), the British Sociological Association (2004) and the Medical Research Council (2004). Clearly, there are too many to mention within the confines of this chapter, but professionals and students hoping to enter the professions should be conversant with their own particular international codes as well as those that directly provide governance within their own countries. The ESRC (2010) has also produced a comprehensive *Framework for Research Ethics* which novice researchers from all professional groups may find helpful.

Clearly, the unethical experiments carried out during the Second World War are extreme examples and we could argue that they have little bearing on our behaviour today. However, in any research situation the *researcher* is potentially in a position of power and that power carries the potential for abuse. The relative power of adults on children and young people makes this a double-edged sword when involving children and adolescents as research participants. While there are varying extremes to which this abuse can exist, it is always important for researchers to consider the potential ethical implications of their work and to ensure that they are guided by the ethical principles we have referred to in this section.

Levels of participation and ethics

Any researcher should make sure that all possible ethical issues are considered when planning research and that steps are taken to manage risk. One key area that is fundamental to the level of risk relates to the level of participation of the child or adolescent in the research. Hart's (1992) eight-degree scale of participation provides a gradient of participation from 'manipulation' of the child in research to full participation with the research being child-initiated (see Figure 10.1). In medical research, participation is currently most likely to be at the least participative end of the range, whereas in social research the trend over the past decade or more has been towards much fuller participation so that the voices of children and young people are heard (see also Chapter 9; Balen et al., 2006; Campbell, 2008; Hill, 2005). However, we are likely to see a shift towards greater participation as we live in an age that is especially concerned that we should be involved in activities about us, e.g. The Big Society, the UK Government's 2010 flagship policy idea and Nothing About Us Without Us, which is the view that no policy should be decided without the full participation of those involved. Consequently, we expect that the current reluctance within some professional groups to involve children directly in research will become a thing of the past.

Whatever the level of participation, researchers have responsibilities to ensure that they protect children's and young people's best interests. The Freechild

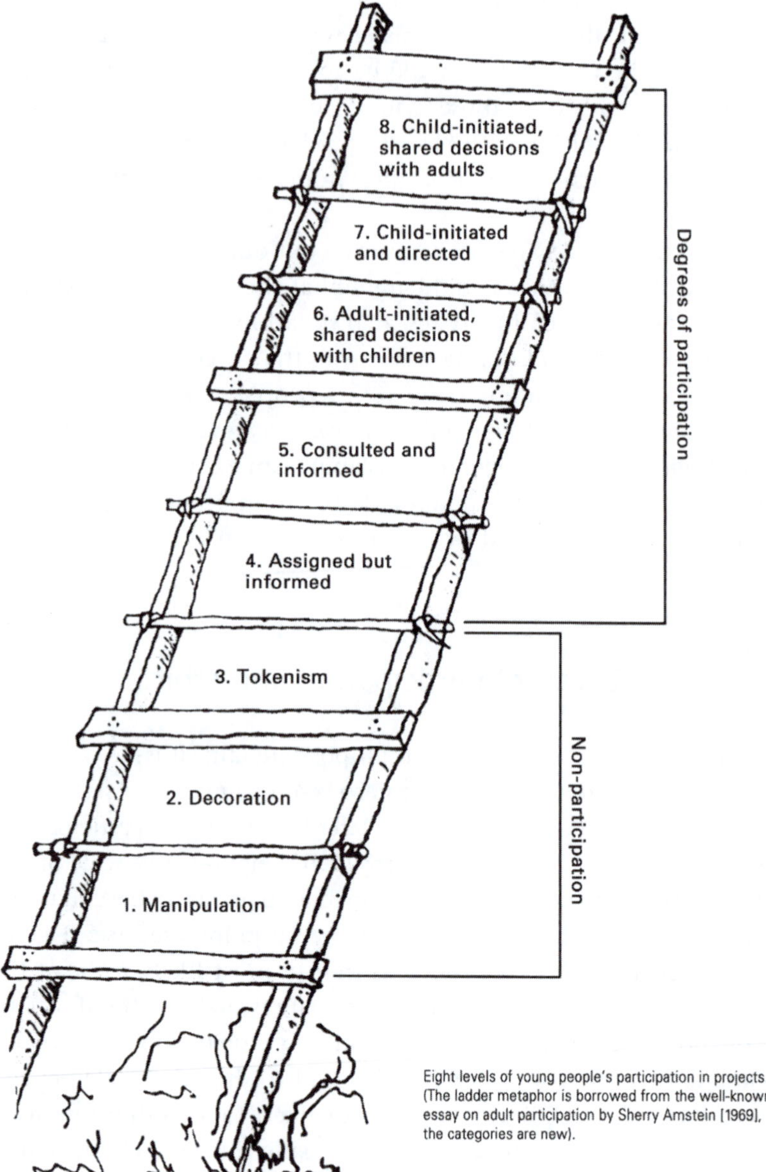

Figure 10.1 The ladder of participation.

Source: Reproduced with permission from the UNICEF Innocenti Research Centre.

Project (www.freechild.org/ladder.htm) has produced a useful adaptation of Hart's ladder and provides helpful detail in the form of a toolbox for researchers working with children and young people at each level of participation.

The debate about the extent to which children and young people should be directly involved in research is one we wish to highlight rather than continue. Suffice it to say that there has been a gradual change over the past two decades and the majority view in most circles is that children and adolescents have a right to participate and to have their voices heard, just as they also have a right to refuse to participate, and that research about children and young people should be *with* children and adolescents and not something that is done *to* them (Balen et al., 2006; Campbell, 2008; Coyne et al., 2009; Czymoniewicz et al., 2010; Dockett et al., 2009; Hill, 2006; Powell and Smith, 2009). Regardless of differences in professional stances, there are also commonalities between the professions in terms of the need to gain access to children and adolescents (either by *proxy* or directly), that informed assent and consent should be sought (from children and adolescents, as well as from significant adults) and that the ethical principles of autonomy, non-maleficence, beneficence and justice should be adhered to. A useful way of ensuring that novice researchers can ensure that they have considered all the ethical implications of an investigation is to identify *all* those who are involved in the study, including controls and those who are not directly being studied (e.g. the siblings of children or young people who are the actual research participants; or the babies of teenage mothers) and to go through each ethical principle with each person to ensure that all risk has been identified. It is useful during this process to collaborate with a more experienced researcher who is not involved in the particular study but who has some expertise in the area of investigation. This will facilitate reaching an objective viewpoint before

Table 10.1 Summary of good practice guidelines for research standards in general and in relation to children and young people

Standards for all participants	*Additional standards for consideration for children as participants*
Careful choice of participants related to the purpose of the research, and the likely costs and benefits	Which children stand to benefit from the research? How much of their time can we take up? How much intrusion is justified? What are the implications of failure?
Selection criteria	Is it ever justified to exclude children with learning or physical disabilities?
Engagement (respect, rapport, openness, listening)	Does it require extra time with children? Does it require the creation of innovative techniques?
Privacy, confidentiality, consent, choice of participation	Adults in the child's life usually need to be consulted regarding permissions as well as the child, and this includes resulting publications.

(Continued)

Table 10.1 (Continued)

Standards for all participants	*Additional standards for consideration for children as participants*
	Do young participants know and understand their right to decline or withdraw participation? Is there an element of coercion? What is too much responsibility for the child? Can older children still participate, if they wish, even if a parent declines?
Presentation of information on the purpose, processes and expectation of involvement for the child in the research	Is the information available and accessible to the child, parents, carers and professionals involved?
Control of research materials	How much responsibility is it reasonable to give the child? How much should adults intervene?
Review, revision and dissemination of research	Are the child and carers consulted on the research design, and can they contribute to the plan? Will they receive reports and do they have any control over the final reports? Can they reflect critically in terms of research evaluation?
Appropriate sources of funding	Should funding be accepted from an organization that does not always work in the interest of children?
Use of participatory methods	Are they sufficiently engaging and fun for children? Are they productive as well as fun? Are they well designed to address individual or group abilities or preferences? Is the language use appropriate? group abilities or preferences?
Appreciation and reward	Will children be thanked and rewarded for their efforts?
Careful choice of context	Is the setting comfortable, safe and predictable for the child? Is it managed in terms of power relations and impression management?
Participant's perspective	How possible is it to overcome the power relations in research with children and to avoid adult interpretation of child views?

Sources: Alderson, P. and Dr Barnardo's Organization (1995) *Listening to Children: Children, Ethics and Social Research*. Ilford: Barnardos; Shaw, C., Brady, L-M. and Davey, C. (2011) *Guidelines for Research with Children and Young People*. London: National Children's Bureau; The British Psychological Society (2009) *Code of Ethics and Conduct*. Leicester: BPS. Available at: www.bps.org.uk/sites/default/files/documents/code_of_ethics_and_conduct.pdf (accessed 7 March 2012).

the novice researcher attempts to gain access. We will discuss this further later on in the chapter. See Figure 10.1 and Table 10.1 for summaries on the levels of participation and research and good practice guidelines.

Informed consent

As we mentioned in the previous section, one of the common factors in all ethical considerations, including regulatory frameworks, is the need to gain informed consent from research participants. According to the Declaration of Helsinki, sixth revision (World Medical Association, 2012), even though a child or young person may not be legally competent to give consent, researchers should gain informed *assent*. UNICEF, in its guidance on child participation, also makes it clear that parental consent is 'not an adequate standard in light of the rights of the child' (2002: 5). The *child* as well as the parent must be aware of the implications of the research, and the child, if able, should give assent in addition to the consent of the adult with parental responsibility. This means ensuring that, if they are capable of doing so, they *know* they have a choice as to whether to participate in the research – in other words that they are true volunteers – that they *know* that they have the right to withdraw from the research at any time if they so wish without detriment to their care, that they *know* exactly what their role in the research is, i.e. what they must do if they choose to participate, and that they *know* what will happen to the data that are generated from the research. Where a child or young person does not reside with their parent, Shaw et al. (2011) suggest gaining permission from resident parents and informing non-resident parents who have substantial contact with their children.

Gaining informed consent should involve giving appropriate information and advice that is relevant to the individual's understanding of the consequences of their participation – this includes the individual child and parents. For example, if participation involves taking a new drug participants should be informed of the potential side effects. Participants should also be given information that leaves no uncertainty about what will happen to the results of the research. They need to be aware that results may be published and who will ultimately have access to the research. We have seen a few examples in student dissertations of where written consent has been obtained on a form which promises that participants' names will not be used and confidentiality and anonymity will be upheld, but because of our local knowledge and involvement in early years practice we have been able to easily identify participants, particularly in some of the qualitative studies that are popular among sociology and health-care students. In some cases it has been necessary, because of the potential harmful effects of placing certain information in the public domain (such as the library or through publication), to restrict access to the final product. This is not ideal and might have been avoided with more careful planning.

Researchers must be particularly aware that age alone is not a foolproof indicator of a child's ability to understand or to give either consent or assent. We have found in the course of our work, for example, that we have needed to produce information leaflets aimed at children and young people of different ages, versions for adults, versions in large font for a parent with sight problems, and in four languages! Providing information to gain consent or assent is a very serious and sometimes time-consuming activity, but time expended in getting things right from the start can save time later on. For example, the research ethics committee may well want to see your information 'offers' before they will approve a study.

There are different legislative frameworks governing the subject of understanding and consent both within the UK and in other countries. In relation to England and Wales, while the Family Law Reform Act 1969 gives the right to consent to *treatment* to young people aged 16–17, and to younger children if they are mature enough to understand what is proposed, the legal position is less clear in relation to consent to *research*. Young people aged 16 and 17 with sufficient understanding may consent to research that aims to be of direct benefit to them, and children under 16 are able to given their full consent for research that is of direct benefit to them provided they satisfy the Gillick criteria of competence (*Gillick* v *West Norfolk and Wisbech Area Health Authority*, 1985) namely, that they have been counselled and do not wish to involve their parents and that they have sufficient maturity to understand the nature, purposes and likely outcome of the proposed research (similar provision is made in Scotland by the Age of Legal Capacity [Scotland] Act 1991). The position in relation to research that does not aim to offer direct benefits to the child is less clear, and the Medical Research Council (2004) guidelines are that there would have to be minimal risk to the individual child participant. In clinical trials, children who are not able to give consent should not be included if the same results can be obtained from those capable of giving consent (European Union, 2001). In practical terms, the best advice to researchers is to seek at all times to have the full cooperation of both children/young people and parents in participating in the research.

Gaining access

It might perhaps seem strange to discuss gaining access after our discussion about informed consent, rather than before. However, our reasons for doing this are because issues of informed consent should be considered prior to gaining access, mainly because those people whom you will approach to gain access will wish to know how you intend to gain consent from either the child or young person, the parents (or those with parental responsibility) or both. They will also wish to see copies of letters, leaflets or forms that you intend to send or issue to participants to gain their written consent.

Gaining access to research participants or research sites normally requires approaching what are known colloquially as *gatekeepers*, meaning basically those people who attempt to safeguard the interests of others and who can give formal or informal permission for research to proceed. In different countries and for different departments the procedures vary, so it is important to find what procedures apply to your own particular context. Sometimes the arrangements will be quite informal and at the discretion of managers of local establishments, while at other times they will be governed by very formal frameworks. For example, in the UK, in relation to research in the fields of health and social care and under arrangements between the four UK health departments, the National Research Ethics Service (NRES; www.nres.nhs.uk), which sits within the Health Research Authority, is responsible for supporting NHS Research Ethics Committees in all four countries and, since 2009, the Social Care Research Ethics Committees (SCREC). This system of research ethics committees (RECs) is very important in setting standards and in enforcing policy and legislation, and no research within the fields of health and social care involving patients, their organs, tissues or data may proceed without their prior approval. It is worth mentioning that RECs are not able to approve clinical trials of investigational medicinal products unless the REC has been specifically approved for this function by the UK Ethics Committee Authority, and there are separate committees for the approval of gene therapy research (Gene Therapy Advisory Committee) and for the Ministry of Defence.

The process of gaining consent from a REC should not be underestimated, although fortunately there are now 60-day maximum turnaround times set from the time of application to the outcome of the review. The process of application has also been significantly streamlined in recent years with the online integrated research application system (IRAS) firmly in place. The NRES website also contains a vast amount of useful information ranging from application flow charts to template letters, sample leaflets and much more. It might appear quite daunting, but in our experience the local REC coordinators are very helpful (contact details are on the NRES website). We have included in Figure 10.2 a few 'top tips' for negotiating through the system. For anyone intending to gain ethical approval from any committee, it is also useful to remember that committees tend to be made up of a mix of professional and lay representatives so make sure that you write your applications carefully and do not use technical language without explanation.

- Consult the National Research Ethics Service (NRES) site and prepare leaflets and consent forms appropriate to your study.
- Go to the Integrated Research Application System (IRAS) part of the website and complete the short e-learning module.
- Write down any remaining questions and then consult the FAQ section of the site to see if the answers are contained there.
- Make contact with the NRES coordinator as a matter of courtesy and to clear up any remaining issues. You may like to find out when meetings are so that you can make sure you are free if you are called to attend in person (and, if you are a student, that your supervisor has maximum notice of the date).
- Complete the IRAS and if you have a supervisor make sure that they are happy with the form. Remember that if you are a student below doctorate level the chief investigator will normally be the academic supervisor who will need to sign forms and provide a curriculum vitae.
- Remember to be very clear in your application and, if you are called to a meeting, about:
    - what each participant will be expected to do, i.e. your methodology and conduct;
    - how you will take care of children during and after your study. Doing research with children means working with people capable of participating and of consenting to participation, but who are also in need of protection.
- Cover every possible aspect of informed consent/assent. Get your leaflets and forms prepared in advance.
- Work out how you intend to report the research, particularly if any of your subjects might be identifiable because of unusual traits/unique identifiers.

Figure 10.2 Top tips for gaining ethical approval

Researchers proposing to undertake studies in the NHS should also consult with the research and development departments of the NHS trust or trusts that they wish to study within as there may be additional requirements for them. Other researchers outside of the NHS should check if there are formal processes that they must follow. We have included a set of questions that researchers should be able to answer before thinking about submitting applications but we do advise novice researchers to navigate round the NRES website, which is helpful even if the research does not require REC approval.

Other important gatekeepers are those who manage the research site or access to those people who are your intended participants, such as teachers, managers, matrons. Again these people can be extremely helpful and good communication with them is a prerequisite to success. For example, one of our students wished to replicate a study relating to safer sex among older school children, and after making some minor alterations to the proposed questionnaire, the head teacher allowed the researcher to give consent forms to children to give to their parents and to the children themselves. In this way the researcher, in liaison with the school, was able to give out the information they wanted in the way they wanted, rather than yet another letter from the school arriving along with the consent form for the next school outing! In Boxes 10.1 and 10.2 we have included two examples of how researchers have to be prepared to negotiate with gatekeepers and be flexible to overcome the challenges that frequently occur when doing research.

BOX 10.1

For their own good: recruiting children for research

The research used a postmodern approach, focusing on the discourses that children used to describe themselves and their perceptions of their levels of participation in decision-making following parental separation. The study explored three research questions.

- How are children's views of themselves in relation to adults reflected in their comments about their ability to participate in decisions that directly affect them following their parents' separation?
- To what extent do children's interview texts reflect the dominant discourses about rights and children?
- How are the dominant discourses about children reflected in children's views of their level of involvement in decisions about them after parental separation?

Recruitment of children to participate in this study, however, proved to be extremely difficult. Reasons for this delay in recruiting children related to both the requirements for obtaining ethical approval from the Human Research Ethics Committee at the university to which Campbell was attached at the time of the study, and to issues embedded in the recruitment process. The presence of gatekeepers, including the university's ethics committee, family services providers and parents meant that Campbell had difficulty in gaining access to children to directly inform them of the research. This resulted in the abandonment of a number of recruitment approaches and the adoption of a simpler, more direct approach that relied on accessing personal networks.

In all, eight months went by before the first interview could be undertaken.

Source: Campbell, A. (2008) 'For their own good: recruiting children for research', *Childhood*, 15 (1): 30–49.

BOX 10.2

Research with hospitalized children: ethical, methodological and organizational challenges

This study, which was set in three hospitals, investigated sick children's experiences of participation in consultation and decision making. The study aimed to use a mixture of focus group and individual interviews. Ethical approval to conduct the study was obtained from the three individual hospital research ethics committees. The researchers devised specific protocols for any unexpected or serious adverse incidents arising during the interview processes with the children.

In spite of careful planning, there were several factors that hindered the collection of data through focus groups and that led to the researchers conducting only six of the planned 18 focus groups (comprising 17 children) and 38 individual interviews, which was many more than intended. The researchers encountered difficulties arranging focus group discussions because of the need to obtain three children or more within the specified age bands (7–9, 10–13 and 14–16 years). The study was conducted over the winter months and thus wards experienced increased admission of children/infants under seven with respiratory infections. During the study, infection control measures were also being implemented to prevent the spread of the winter vomiting bug in all three hospital sites. Consequently, bringing children together from different wards for focus groups was not always possible due to infection precautions. It was sometimes difficult to gather children together at a particular time because they experienced different daily routines (e.g. attending school, going to the playroom, physiotherapy treatments, X-rays, scans, meals, medication, doctors' rounds and family visits). Reduced length of stay meant that frequently children were discharged earlier than expected and acute illnesses meant that some children were too sick to participate in interviews.

In this study the researchers found solutions to challenges such as shifting to individual interviews rather than focus groups and moving the timings of interviews to Saturdays when there was less activity at the research sites.

Source: Coyne, I., Hayes, E. and Gallagher, P. (2009) 'Research with hospitalized children: ethical, methodological and organizational challenges', *Childhood*, 16 (3): 413–29.

Gatekeepers to the actual children, particularly when research is taking place with younger children or if it involves visiting the home environment or if it requires that children visit a special site, are the parents. If research involving children and young people is to be successful, then it is of prime importance that the relationship with parents is good. Fundamental to this process is gaining trust, which requires that you are honest and reliable and communicate well. Obvious features to maintaining a good relationship include such things as good manners – remembering to say a simple thank you may help to ensure that the parents turn up the next time.

Practical ethics involving children and young people

It is not our intention to provide a prescriptive or restrictive approach to ethics in research involving children and young people. Indeed it would be very difficult in any case because of the varied research approaches taken and the almost infinite research problems that could be studied. Ethics should be placed within the context of both the problem and the approach and should not be seen as an 'add-on'. It can appear sometimes in student dissertations that the same rather repetitive statements are made about informed consent, anonymity and confidentiality. The statements are without context and therefore fail to convince the reader that the researcher has thought through the ethical implications of *this* study as opposed to any other study. That is not to say that informed consent, anonymity and confidentiality are not important, because clearly they are. It is about ensuring that ethical principles are applied, which means examining the ethical implications of *your* study and ensuring that ethical principles are upheld in the context of *your* particular piece of research.

Practically, to this end, there are a number of questions that you can ask yourself as a researcher and which you can prepare answers to. There are many benefits of doing this, particularly, for example, if you are asked to attend an ethics committee meeting. The list of questions below, which we have divided into sections relating to the research process, is not finite but is designed to help you to focus on what can be a difficult task. It is also designed to reinforce the notion that ethics is not something the researcher should pay lip service to, but is of the utmost importance in any research study.

Problem

- Have any ethical difficulties been raised in any of the literature relating to the research problem? If so, what were these difficulties and how were they addressed?
- In your opinion, were they addressed in a satisfactory way? If so, why? If not, why not, and what could you do to provide a satisfactory solution?

Research questions

- Are your research questions necessary and of substance?
- Have the questions been answered before? If so, why are you doing the research?
- Do the questions require the involvement of child participants?
- Is the involvement direct or indirect (indirect might, for example, be when research is being undertaken with another family member, or in a school)?
- If you are involving children, have you considered issues such as informed assent?
- If you are not involving children are you certain that your research questions can be answered accurately by proxy?
- Could you answer your research aims without involving children? If yes, why are you involving them? Are there clear benefits to the children being involved?

Sampling

- How will children be recruited into your study?
- Why have you selected the particular sampling strategy?
- Will your participants understand the strategy (children can be hurt or consider it unfair that they are being excluded, as identified in a study by Hill [2006] – see Box 10.3)?
- When do you intend to approach your sample?
- What gatekeepers do you need to contact to gain permission?
- Have you got permission?
- Do you have relevant information about your study in an appropriate format to give to your sample (such as information appropriate to the first language of the child/young person or pictorial information)?
- How will you document their informed consent?
- Who do you need to gain informed consent from? Have you done so?
- If the research is being done with children, how will you demonstrate that their assent was based on understanding?
- How have you addressed confidentiality, including the issue of children and young people with unusual histories/backgrounds who might be identifiable because of their uniqueness?

BOX 10.3

Children's and young people's perspectives on methods used in research and consultation

The words 'fair' and 'unfair' are often used by children to express their judgements of approval and disapproval. Their notion of fairness encompasses ideas of both equity and equality. They tend to dislike situations where some (appear to) have more access to opportunities than others or receive more favourable treatment. With respect to research and consultation, this is linked to criteria for inclusion and differential attention. Children criticized consultation mechanisms that involved only a minority:

> … there are a lot of people besides us and they didn't get a chance to join in.

Young person 1: If it's in our school, it's always the same people that get picked for everything.
Young person 2: I've never been picked.
Young person 3: This is the first time I've been picked for anything.

They thought it was unfair for many to be left out and also thought the basis for selection was often biased (e.g. in favour of older pupils). Similarly, some children's views were thought to carry more weight either because they were more confident in group discussions or the adults were more inclined to take their views seriously. Underpinning these comments is a complaint about children's and young people's lack of entitlement to be engaged with participatory processes or to influence who is engaged. This reflects the views commonly held by children and adolescents that they lack rights and respect, especially in school contexts.

Children's concerns about fairness reflect both personal and collective considerations. While a few children appeared mainly concerned that their own views were ignored, many were eager (like statisticians) to see that research and consultation should be representative.

Source: Hill, M. (2006) 'Children's voices on ways of having a voice: children's and young people's perspectives on methods used in research and consultation', *Childhood*, 13 (1): 69–89.

Data collection instruments

- What do your participants need to do to provide you with your data?
- Are there any potential physical, psychological, social or emotional risks to the participants or those close to them? If so, are these negligible or more than negligible?
- How have you defined negligible? If they are more than negligible, how can they be justified?
- Have you explored every possible avenue to reduce risk? If not, why not?
- Have you checked this out with an objective third party?
- Have you assessed risks of harm to each child or young person?
- Will other children be affected directly or indirectly by your study (e.g. because they are in the environment where the study is taking place) and if so, have you assessed their risks?
- Have you considered risks to those collecting data or those who have been otherwise involved?
- What have you done to minimize any identified risk?

It is always useful when you have designed your data collection instruments to pilot or try out the instruments so that you can anticipate things that might go wrong. Involving children and/or young people in the process of design is a really good way of avoiding problems (Hill, 2006).

Data analysis and afterwards

- How have you ensured the ethical processing of data?
- Where will you store data?
- Would you be happy for such data about yourself to be stored in this way? If no, what will you do to address this?

- Are you breaking any data protection laws? If yes, how will you change things to ensure that you are not breaking the law?
- Do you break any promises or assurances made to your participants? If yes, why?
- What will happen to your data after your study has been completed?
- Do you have a plan for sharing results with those who participated?
- If your research involves children's drawings or diagrams, are there issues of ownership of the research 'data', and if so, have you considered how you will return these 'data' to the rightful owners?
- Finally, can you categorically state that, after answering all of these questions, you will do no harm to your participants?

Conclusion

We hope that by now you will have gained an understanding that ethics is not a part of the research process that can be dismissed without thought. The ethical implications of a particular study constitute an essential consideration that is of the utmost importance. Any researcher who does not give due consideration to ethics is not only doing potential harm to the research participants but is also potentially damaging their chosen profession and fellow professionals. We know of an example where one practitioner undertook research in a NHS primary care setting without adhering to ethical principles and without gaining consent from the appropriate gatekeepers. Not only were some of the research participants extremely distressed about the information given to them, but all research activity (including that which had been through the appropriate access processes) was stopped, leading to a great deal of distress for colleagues.

Giving appropriate thought to potential ethical dilemmas and approaching and gaining permission from relevant gatekeepers is essential before you start to collect data. Your responsibility as an ethical researcher does not, however, cease when all permissions have been granted and consent forms signed. It continues throughout the study and extends beyond. If you are party to information that is confidential at the time of its being given, then it must remain confidential, and if you have made promises to destroy data you must do so.

Ethics is a very serious business, and ignoring ethics can harm your participants, your colleagues and ultimately your own reputation as a professional and a researcher.

PUTTING RESEARCH INTO PRACTICE 10.1 – APPLYING ETHICAL CODES

1 Find out (e.g. from the library, the WWW or your professional association) what national and international codes exist that relate directly to your own actual or potential professional grouping.

2 Write down what the code or codes say about autonomy, non-maleficence, beneficence and justice. Does the code make specific reference to research involving children?

3 Next, find a piece of research undertaken by a professional from your field that involves children. Using the code or codes you have found, and the list of questions found in the section under 'Practical ethics involving children and young people', write down the strengths and weaknesses of the piece of research from an ethical perspective.

References

American Psychological Association (2010) *Ethical Principles of Psychologists and Code of Conduct (2010 Amendments)*. Available at: www.apa.org/ethics/code/index.aspx (accessed 7 March 2012).

Balen, R., Blyth, E., Calabretto, H., Fraser, C., Horrocks, C. and Manby, M. (2006) 'Involving children in health and social research: 'human becomings' or 'active beings'?', *Childhood*, 13 (1): 29–48.

Beauchamp, T.L. and Childress, J.F. (2008) *Principles of Biomedical Ethics*, 6th edn. New York: Oxford University Press.

Birbeck, D.J. and Drummond, M.J.N. (2007) 'Research with young children: contemplating methods and ethics', *Journal of Educational Enquiry*, 7 (2): 21–31.

Boyden, J. (2000) 'Conducting research with war-affected and displaced children: ethics & methods', *Cultural Survival Quarterly*, Issue 24.2 (Summer). Available at: www.culturalsurvival.org/publications/cultural-survival-quarterly/united-states/conducting-research-war-affected-and-displace (accessed 7 March 2012).

British Psychological Society (2009) *Code of Ethics and Conduct*. Leicester: BPS. Available at: www.bps.org.uk/sites/default/files/documents/code_of_ethics_and_conduct.pdf(accessed 7 March 2012).

British Sociological Association (2004) *Statement of Ethical Practice for the British Sociological Association 2002 (Appendix Updated 2004)*. Available at: www.britsoc.co.uk/NR/rdonlyres/801B9A62-5CD3-4BC2-93E1-FF470FF10256/0/StatementofEthicalPractice.pdf (accessed 7 March 2012).

Campbell, A. (2008) 'For their own good: recruiting children for research', *Childhood*, 15 (1): 30–49.

Caplan, A.L. (ed.) (1992) *When Medicine Went Mad: Bioethics and the Holocaust*. Totowa, NJ: Humana Press.

Coyne, I., Hayes, E. and Gallagher P. (2009) 'Research with hospitalized children: ethical, methodological and organizational challenges', *Childhood*, 16 (3): 413–29.

Czymoniewicz-Klippel, M.T., Brijnath, B. and Crockett, B. (2010) 'Ethics and the promotion of inclusiveness within qualitative research: case examples from Asia and the Pacific', *Qualitative Inquiry*, 16 (5): 332–41.

Dockett, S., Perry, B. and Einarsdottir, J. (2009) 'Researching with children: ethical tensions', *Journal of Early Childhood Research*', 7 (3): 283–98.

Economic and Social Research Council (2010) *Framework for Research Ethics*. Available at: www.esrc.ac.uk/about-esrc/information/research-ethics.aspx (accessed 7 March 2012).

European Union (2001) Directive 2001/20/EC of the European Parliament and the Council of 4 April 2001 on the approximation of the laws, regulations and administrative provisions of the Member States relating to the implementation of good clinical practice in the conduct of clinical trials on medicinal products for human use. Available at: http://eur-lex.europa.eu/smartapi/cgi/sga_doc?smartapi!celexapi!prod!CELEXnumdoc&lg=en&model=guicheti&numdoc=32001L0020 (accessed 7 March 2012).

Freechild Project. Ladder of Youth Voice. Available at: www.freechild.org/ladder.htm (accessed 26 March 2012).

Hart, R.A. (1992) *Children's Participation: from Tokenism To Citizenship.* Innocenti Essays No.4 Series. Florence, Italy: UNICEF International Children Development Centre.

Health Research Authority (2012) National Research Ethics Service. Available at: www.NRES.npsa.nhs.uk (accessed 7 March 2012).

Hill, M. (2005) 'Ethical considerations in researching children's experiences', in S. Greene and D. Hogan (eds), *Researching Children's Experience: Methods and Approaches.* London: Sage. pp. 61–86.

Hill, M. (2006) 'Children's voices on ways of having a voice: children's and young people's perspectives on methods used in research and consultation', *Childhood*, 13 (1): 69–89.

Keddie, A. (2000) 'Research with young children: some ethical considerations', *Journal of Educational Enquiry*, 1 (2): 72–81.

Kor, E.M. (1992) 'Nazi experiments as viewed by a survivor of Mengele's experiments', in A.L. Caplan (ed.), *When Medicine Went Mad: Bioethics and the Holocaust*. Totowa, NJ: Humana Press. pp. 3–8.

Lossier, J.G. (1949) 'The Red Cross and the International (sic) Declaration of Human Rights', *IRRC* , 5: 184–9.

Medical Research Council (2004) *Medical Research Involving Children.* London: MRC. Available at: www.mrc.ac.uk/Utilities/Documentrecord/index.htm?d=MRC002430 (accessed 7 March 2012).

Müller-Hill, B. (1992) 'Eugenics: the science and religion of the Nazis', in A.L. Caplan (ed.), *When Medicine Went Mad: Bioethics and The Holocaust*. Totowa, NJ: Humana Press. pp. 43–52.

Powell, M.A. and Smith, A.B. (2009) 'Children's participation rights in research', *Childhood,* 16 (1): 124–42.

Schenk, K. and Williamson, J. (2005) *Ethical Approaches to Gathering Information from Children and Adolescents in International Settings: Guidelines and Resources.* Washington, DC: Population Council.

Shaw, C., Brady, L-M. and Davey, C. (2011) *Guidelines for Research with Children and Young People.* London: National Children's Bureau.

UNICEF (1959) Declaration of the Rights of the Child. Available at: www.unicef.org/lac/spbarbados/Legal/global/General/declaration_child1959.pdf (accessed 7 March 2012).

UNICEF (1989) Convention on the Rights of the Child. Available at: www.unicef.org/crc/ (accessed 7 March 2012).

UNICEF (2002) Evaluation Technical Notes. Children Participating in Research, Monitoring and Evaluation (M&E) – Ethics and Your Responsibility as a Manager. Available at: www.unicef.org/evaluation/files/TechNote1_Ethics.pdf (accessed 7 March 2012).

World Medical Association (2012) Declaration of Helsinki – Ethical Principles for Medical Research Involving Human Subjects. Available at: www.wma.net/en/30publications/10policies/b3/ (accessed 7 March 2012).

Recommended reading for further study

Alderson, P. and Morrow, V. (2011) *The Ethics of Research with Children and Young People: a Practical Handbook*. London: Sage.

Beauchamp, T.L. and Childress, J.F. (2008) *Principles of Biomedical Ethics*, 6th edn. New York: Oxford University Press.

Mertens, D.M. and Ginsberg, P.E. (eds) (2009) *The Handbook of Social Research Ethics*. Thousand Oaks, CA: Sage.

ELEVEN
Communicating research

The aims of this chapter are:

- to introduce the need to communicate research widely;
- to discuss communicating with a variety of audiences;
- to share tips for publishing research.

Communicating the outcomes of research is an essential part of being a responsible researcher – even if the research did not go entirely to plan. There are various opportunities that researchers can use to share their research findings. In this chapter we look at some of the fundamental principles of communicating research, including writing up research reports, sharing your results with those that provided data for you, presenting results verbally at seminars and conferences and writing for publication. There is, after all, little point in spending time and effort undertaking research if you are not prepared to share your outcomes!

Writing up your research report

If you are a student enrolled at an academic institution undertaking a research dissertation you will be likely to have guidelines that you should follow for the presentation of your project report. Greasley (2011) provides an excellent text for students including a section about writing research projects and how the marking process works, so that you can make better judgements about what to include in your work and how to present it.

Likewise, if you are being funded to undertake research it is usual to negotiate with your sponsors what the final report will look like. Some sponsors will specify details such as font type and font size, the expected length of the report, referencing style and requirements, such as a glossary and use of appendices. It is always worth checking the details in advance so that you do not have to spend valuable time reformatting or, in some cases, rewriting your report. If you do not have any parameters to work with the following sections will give you some brief, helpful information about what you should include. This is by no means intended to be a definitive guide but discusses some of the issues you should consider.

To illustrate each section we have used a recently undertaken study looking at children's attendances at accident and emergency departments. A summary of the study is provided in Box 11.1.

BOX 11.1

An exploratory study of the reasons for frequent accident and emergency attendances in children aged 0–4 years in one locality in England

Children's accident and emergency (A&E) department visits have increased by 20% in each of the last two years across the seven general practices that make up the locality of Greenfields[1] – a small borough on the edge of London. This study aims to identify the reasons for the year-on-year increases with a view to making recommendations for possible interventions to try and reverse the increase in attendances.

There are two main reasons for wanting to explore A&E attendances. First, A&E is not a place that children should be exposed to unless it is absolutely necessary. Second, the evidence suggests that most of the symptoms that children are presenting with at A&E could be managed by general practitioners (GPs) or nurses. The Department of Health has identified that large numbers of patients visit A&E without an admission when GP practices are open (Department of Health, 2010). The cost to the NHS per year is £354 m. Nationally, 20% of attendances at A&E are children. Few attendances result in an admission. Those that end in an admission are likely to suffer from asthma and wheezing, feeding difficulties and tonsillitis.

The sample included in the study was all children aged 0–4 years from the seven practices who had attended A&E on four or more occasions in a rolling year at the census point of September 2010. The data management system was used to search for children with four or more attendances and there were 70 children identified in the group. Some children had many more than four attendances and one child had 13 attendances. Ethical approval for the study was given by the NHS ethics committee.

The methodology for the study was that health visitors contacted families (unless the GP advised against making contact). A leaflet explaining the study was developed and provided to participants and informed consent was obtained. Parents were interviewed by telephone and asked about the times they had attended A&E. Of the 70 children (from 69 families) four were not contacted on the advice of the GP, and nine did not respond or were not contactable. In all, 56 interviews took place.

Results showed that 42% of families had tried to contact their GP before attending A&E. The peak time for attendances was 18.00–20.00 h but 54% of A&E attendances were during GP surgery opening times. In line with national data, few attendances result in an admission and those that did end in an admission were children suffering from either asthma and wheezing, and feeding difficulties. Few families knew about the out-of-hours service and did not realize that if they called their GP practice out-of-hours they would be directed to other sources of support.

The results of this study found that, in line with national data, children were attending A&E with illnesses that did not result in admissions and that were amenable to treatment by the GP or the out-of-hours service. Recommendations from the study include introducing a self-management asthma programme and providing a 'fast-track' system in practices for children with asthma so that they can be seen urgently if required.

[1] The name of the borough is fictitious.

Writing for your audience

When you are writing your research report you should be clear about who your target audience is. This is something that should be agreed with sponsors if undertaking commercial research. It is important to make sure that the language that you use is appropriate for your intended audience. If you do not have an understanding of your audience you run the risk of producing a report that is too complex or, at worst, one that is patronizing. Greener discusses the use of language and jargon in particular. He writes:

> Nobody likes jargon. It's depressing ... to simply not understand what anyone is talking about because they seem intent in stringing together sentences that are based on obscure terms and acronyms that seem designed to obscure rather than provide understanding. (2011: 1)

It is also essential that you are consistent in your terminology. Two simple examples are the terms 'patient' and 'adolescent'. Some disciplines are happy to use the term patient whereas others might use 'service user' or 'client'; some disciplines will use adolescent whereas others use 'young person' or even 'teenager'. Check before you start to write your report that you use the correct words and terms.

Getting the balance right between simple language and technical language is often a challenge. For example, the audience for the full summarised report of the study in Box 11.1 were general practitioners and practice nurses. It was therefore acceptable to use a level of technical language as the audience in this case would all have an understanding of what *nebulizers* and *inhalers* are and so further explanation would not be required. Take another example, however, of the term *ventilation*. While a teacher was discussing the influenza epidemic with their class recently, a nine-year-old repeated that they had heard their mother, who was a nurse, saying that there were seven people in the intensive-care unit requiring ventilation. When the group were asked if they understood what this was, one boy said that it meant opening more windows so that people could get fresh air!

Title

The title of the project should reflect the content of what the report is about. The title should particularly include keywords. This is absolutely crucial if your report is going to be published and available on the WWW. A report with keywords in the title will be listed when keywords are searched for electronically (see Ford, 2011). When writing about research involving children it is helpful to include the appropriate keywords such as *children, neonates, school-aged children, adolescents*. It is also helpful to give an indication of the research approach such as *an ethnographic study, a randomized controlled trial, a case study, a systematic review.*

The title of the study in Box 11.1 identified that is was an *exploratory* study, and provided the age range of the children involved. It also included key words *accident* and *emergency*.

Contents page

The contents page should signpost your reader to the main sections and subsections of your report. You should also include a list of appendices and you can include a list of tables if you have included these in your report. Remember to do a final check when your report is complete as minor amendments to your text can alter the pagination.

Abstract or summary

The abstract of a report is a summary of the whole report – the aims, sample, methods, findings, conclusions and recommendations. It should be short (usually 250–300 words), factual and concise. Some journals will allow free access to abstracts but will require payment for the full text report so it is important that the abstract accurately reflects the report. The abstract is effectively the 'shop-front' or window of your report. It should entice readers to want to access the whole report.

A longer version of an abstract is an 'executive summary', which again should contain details of context, aims, sample, methods, the main results, and so on. Executive summaries are often developed so that they can be used as a 'stand-alone' summary of the main report.

The summary of the study in Box 11.1 provides some information about what the study is about and some context. It sets out the aims, the sample group, the methods (i.e. telephone interview), the main results, the conclusion and two key recommendations.

Introduction

Probably the most important section of the research report, the introduction should clearly set out the context of the study and the problem to be studied. It should include information about why the study is important, which might include referring to key policy drivers, the significance of the problem or issue being studied and what the research intends to do. Fetterman (2010) identifies the problem as being the 'driving force' of research, and as being instrumental in defining the selection of a research method.

Your introduction might include statements that relate your study to previous research, such as that you have taken a slightly different angle on a topic with a view to adding to the body of knowledge about a study topic. Your introduction should also make clear what the study is about, who was involved and where the study took place.

Our study in Box 11.1 only provides a brief introduction but does cover the key points of where the study took place, the significance of the problem and some of the national context.

Literature review/rationale

Research is done to increase or add to a body of knowledge and in this section you should set out concisely what the body of existing knowledge is. It is usual to review general literature and then move to specific literature that is absolutely pertinent to your research. All literature reviewed should be relevant. The reader should not be left wondering why you have included reference to a particular piece of literature – it should be clearly linked. If there is a large body of literature you might consider organizing the various articles under subheaded themes. When reviewing literature, it is helpful to the reader to specify the nature of the literature so the reader is clear as to whether the piece was original research, a systematic review, an opinion article, a piece of policy or legislation, and so on. It is helpful to include a brief description of your search strategy – how you came to include the literature that you have. All literature should be accurately referenced so that your reader can access the same literature you accessed. It is helpful at the end of the literature review to summarize how you have used the literature to inform the way you have approached your research.

Somekh and Lewin (2011) provide a very detailed section in their book on doing literature reviews and Jesson et al. (2011) provide a whole book on the subject – it is not a simple activity and takes time and effort to get it right!

It should be noted that in grounded theory research it is usual not to review the literature at the beginning of the report. Corbin and Strauss, seminal authors in this field write: 'there is no need to review all of the literature in the field beforehand, as is frequently done by researchers using quantitative research approaches' (2008: 35). The reasoning behind this is that while researchers need to be familiar with the area of study, they should not enter the fieldwork stage of their enquiry with preconceived ideas and should put their trust in their own abilities to generate knowledge and make their own discoveries (see also Birks and Mills, 2010 for a comprehensive introduction to grounded theory).

We do not provide the full literature review in our abstract in Box 11.1. The expectation would be that the literature review would expand on literature to include:

- the national policy drivers;
- national data around children's A&E attendance;
- data to show the psychological effects of frequent exposure to A&E;
- research undertaken in this field and the outcomes of that research.

Theoretical and conceptual frameworks

Research will, in simple terms, either generate theory through a process of inductive reasoning or test theory through a process of deductive reasoning. Fetterman (2010) identifies that these two traditional differences 'still hold' even with the introduction of new and innovative interdisciplinary research approaches (see, for example, Repko et al., 2012). Fetterman argues that the characteristics of the two traditional differences 'characterize the relationship between the problem, how it is articulated, researched and written about ...' (2010: 4).

Students will often mistakenly place a piece of research using induction or deductive reasoning on whether the piece includes qualitative or quantitative data (qualitative approaches will generally use inductive reasoning and quantitative approaches will generally use deductive reasoning). It is not, however, as simple as this. In our abstract in Box 11.1, for example, the study generates numerical information about how many times children attend A&E, what time of day they attended and other information that can be counted. However, the study does not use a quantitative approach – it is not testing theory. It is exploring reasons why children attend A&E with a view to generating theory that can be later tested.

A final point about theory is that theory does not need to be complex, grand or elaborate. Fetterman discusses that theory, particularly in research that sits at the purely inductive end of the spectrum can be 'personal theories about how the world or some small part of it works' (2010: 7). Greener (2011) argues that the important thing about a theory is that it is appropriate, easy to use and that it has 'explanatory power'. In other words, you should choose a theory that will help you make sense of the problem you are studying.

The purpose/aims, objectives and research questions

After the literature review, the purpose of the research should be clearly stated – and it should be consistent with what you have stated in your introduction. The idea of placing the purpose/aims/objectives/questions at this point is that it should logically flow from the review of the literature that shows what has gone before. As we have stated, research should add to the body of knowledge, so having set out what that body of knowledge is you then specify the purpose of your study and how it will add to the existing knowledge.

The purpose of your research can take a number of forms depending on your research approach. It might be a list of aims and objectives, research questions and a hypothesis. If you have more than one aim, objective, question or hypothesis, these should be placed in a logical order, which might be according to importance/priority or it might be the order in which you have studied the problem.

In our study in Box 11.1 the aim is stated in the abstract. In the full study you would expect to see an expanded set of objectives and research questions. It would not be appropriate to state a hypothesis in an exploratory study.

Methodology

Your methodology will generally comprise three parts: your sample, ethical considerations and how you collected your data. We briefly consider each of these parts in turn:

1 The first part of your methodology should outline the population(s) or sample(s) used. You should include information about why you have chosen that population or sample of the population, followed by the numbers used with any inclusion or exclusion criteria. You should provide a rationale for the numbers used and for the selection criteria. In this section of your report you need to outline the type of sample used and your sampling techniques, e.g. random sample, convenience sample, snowball sample. Fowler (2009) provides a very clear overview of sampling, including a debate on the challenging subject of how many subjects should be included in a sample. He also discusses other very current subjects such as sampling using the WWW and the challenges of sampling using the telephone, in the era of the mobile telephone!
2 The second part of your methodology should make clear what processes you followed to ensure that you protected your sample. This is particularly important when you are

doing research with children (see Hall and Coffey, 2011; see also Chapter 10). You should include information about the main ethical implications of your study, how you gained consent and assent, permissions that were sought from, for example, an ethics committee, and other related information. Part of protecting your sample is to make clear how you upheld confidentiality and anonymity.

3 The final part of your methodology should set out what your sample had to do to provide you with data. You should describe in detail your data collection tools and information about how you ensured that those tools were both reliable and valid. You should also include information about how you controlled variables (see also Chapters 5, 6, 7 and 8). If appropriate you should replicate the data collection tools that you used either in the text or in the appendices. There are a number of good detailed texts that can help you with developing data collection tools and techniques (Birks and Mills, 2010; Fowler, 2009; Greener, 2011; Liamputtong, 2011; Repko et al., 2012; Somekh et al., 2011).

In our study in Box 11.1 there is information provided about the children included in the study and the exclusion criteria (i.e. that the GP could request that a family is not contacted). You would expect in the full report to see more information about why the sample was selected in the way that it was. The study mentions that ethical approval was gained and informed consent was obtained from the parents. The methodology mentions only telephone interviews and in the full report more information would be provided about what questions, were asked and why, how information was recorded and who was undertaking the interviews, and what training the interviewers received.

Results

In quantitative research it is usual to have a separate section to report your results, followed by a discussion section. In qualitative research these two sections are often combined. Results, if reported separately, should be presented factually and in a value-free way – in other words you report what you found without discussion of the meaning of the results. If statistical tests are used you should explain which tests have been applied to which data and you should include both observed values and probability levels (see also Chapter 6). You should indicate if levels of statistical significance obtained are sufficient to reject any null hypotheses (see Argyrous, 2011; Vogt, 2011).

If you include tables and/or diagrams to highlight your results you should clearly explain what the tables/diagrams include in supportive text. In other words, introduce the table/diagram and then insert it within the text. Greasley (2011) has produced a section in his book on how **not** to present graphs and charts that is well worth reading.

In qualitative research you might use direct quotations or other information to bring alive your results and give a flavour of what was actually said in an interview or during a conversation. Fetterman (2010) identifies that verbatim quotations are extremely helpful in giving credibility to a research report and can help to bring to life characteristics of a situation or event. Again there should be supportive text so that a quote is set into context.

In our study in Box 11.1 there are some results provided but clearly the full report would include much more detail of how the data were sorted, coded and analysed. It would include tables to illustrate the times that children attended A&E and would further include some verbatim quotations about what parents said about not knowing about the out-of-hours service, for example.

Discussion

Your discussion section is where you interpret your data, linking your findings back to your aims/objectives, questions/hypotheses. In this section you should also interpret how your results add to the body of existing knowledge by comparing and contrasting your findings with previous research, with discussion about the possible reasons for similarities and differences. In this section you should refer to any limitations of your research such as that you used a weak form of sampling, or that you were unable to control for certain variables.

The discussion section is extremely important and it should be possible to read the discussion section and really understand what your research has achieved. The study in Box 11.1 mentions that the findings are in line with national data. The full report would then link back findings to other pieces of literature. It would mention the limitations of the sample, which was drawn from only seven practices.

Recommendations

Most research will have outcomes and implications, even if the outcome is to recommend that further research should be undertaken because the results were inconclusive. Research will often raise more questions than it answers, but this is all adding to the body of existing knowledge. By communicating even very minor or negative outcomes, you may at least help another researcher who was intending to do work similar to yours from wasting their time following a particular path. If you have recommendations, you should list these either in order of priority or in the order in which they were found through your research.

In our study in Box 11.1 there is reference to two main recommendations. Further, less important recommendations may be made in the full report, which would include tracking the future attendances of the cohort of children, producing information for families about alternatives to A & E attendance and information about the management in general practice of children attending with illnesses other than asthma.

Conclusion

Your conclusion should pull together the main points from your research and summarize in general terms what your research achieved. It is helpful here to revisit the aims of the study and highlight if those aims were met. If they were not met, it is helpful to reiterate why.

Providing feedback to research subjects

In this section of the chapter, we look at the importance of being able to communicate your research report to those who have contributed data to your study. We discussed the importance of involvement and participation in Chapter 9 and part of the work of the responsible researcher is to provide feedback. This applies to dissemination of your whole research report but may also apply to subsections of your research. For example, you may wish to validate that you have captured and interpreted information correctly through a process called 'member checking', which does exactly what it says – you check your findings with members of your sample.

When you are feeding information back to children or young people who have participated in your research you must ensure that the language and the medium used to provide feedback is appropriate to the understanding of the child or young person. Van Blerk and Ansell (2007) provide an interesting debate about this and use a system of posters, video and drama to provide feedback and disseminate their findings. They also discuss some of the challenges of locating children to provide feedback to when there is a time lapse between data collection and the completion of the report. If your participants are older children, it is worth considering using the communication media that children themselves use such as texts, email and even setting up a social network site with your participants so you can feedback electronically.

The NHS Evidence website also provides very clear guidance about producing documents that are in *Easy Read* versions primarily for people with learning disabilities. However, the guidance also gives some helpful information about how to provide information using pictures and symbols, video and audio technology, as well as how to lay out your documents and use appropriate language (NHS Evidence, 2008).

If you are providing information or a version of your research report for children, we have provided some helpful tips below:

- Define your audience.
- Decide what form of feedback is appropriate to the level of understanding of the group.
- Decide what you need to do to turn your work into an appropriate format.
- Decide if one format is sufficient or whether you should have more than one.
- Decide if you need help to do this – there are commercial websites that will do this for you or you could ask key members of the audience to help with this.
- Once you have your new format check it out with a couple of people in the audience.

Communicating through conferences and seminars

In this section we outline briefly some of the principles of communicating your research through the medium of conferences and seminars. It is another way of sharing your research with a wide audience of people. This section is not aimed at seasoned conference performers – we have all watched with awe at the skills of some presenters who appear to be able to go on stage with no notes and little preparation and enthral the audience. Most will actually have spent hours refining their presentation; so do not be fooled!

If you are to present to a large audience or to a small group you should familiarize yourself with your target audience, the venue of your presentation, the availability of audiovisual aids and other technology, the requirements for an abstract or summary and the form that this should be in, and anything else that the conference organizers have provided by way of information or equipment.

It is usual, nowadays, for presenters to present a set of slides and these can help you to prepare a pretty slick presentation of your report. The seasoned presenter may even use cartoons or pictures in the background that act as prompts and provide some humour on the way. If you are a novice presenter, it is safer to have a set of informative slides that you can talk about in your presentation. Experiment with the clever stuff when you, too, are a seasoned presenter!

In the rest of this section we provide a step-by-step guide to presenting using four main headings:

- Planning your time
- Preparing your presentation
- Being ready for questions
- Common pitfalls

Planning your time

Most of us will have sat in lectures or indeed conferences when the presenter goes over time. Even though the presentation might be interesting, it makes everyone in the audience uncomfortable including the organizers who will have fixed break points in the agenda, such as food breaks, and may have other presenters who are on a tight timescale and who need to present on time. If there are a number of concurrent sessions, as is common at large events, one presenter overrunning can cause chaos.

Therefore, if you are presenting you need to plan your time carefully. You need to allow time for introductions and for time at the end for questions – you need to factor in time for these activities.

If you are using slides, try not to have more than one slide per minute of your presentation (minus question time). This is a rough guide only and if you have a particularly complex slide allow longer for that slide.

It is helpful to do an outline of what you intend to cover and you can use this as your opening slide – simple headings are all that is required. For example, your outline slide might simply read:

Presentation outline

- Introduction to the study
- Aims and research questions
- Methodology
- Results
- Discussion
- Conclusions
- Recommendations
- Any questions?

Preparing your presentation

When preparing your presentation you should think about what is reasonable to achieve in your allocated time – do not try to cram too much in. You cannot possibly go through every part of your study (which might be anything up to 100,000 words) if you are presenting your PhD. Keep it simple and above all interesting. It is a really good tip to use some real (brief) examples from practice so that you bring your study to life.

For each slide define your heading. For each heading, with the exception of your results, have a few bullet points that succinctly walk people through your aims and methodology (including your sample, ethics and data collection). Briefly mention activities such as the validation of your data collection tools. People will not be particularly interested in things like your literature review even though you might have spent long and painstaking hours doing it.

As you are preparing your slides, make yourself a set of notes so that you can elaborate on your bullet points. In most software packages you can add notes to your slides and print out a copy of the slide with notes. Do not read from your slides and do not put too much information on slides – arrange the main items into bullet points and then talk about each item. Another rule of thumb is to have no more than eight bullet points on a slide.

What your audience is really interested in will be your results, so allow time within your presentation to walk people through what you found. If you are going to use tables and charts, then make sure that people will be able to read them. We have been in many conferences when a presenter puts up a wonderful table and then says 'you won't be able to read this but ...'. There is no point in having a slide if people cannot read it. If a table is absolutely crucial and you are not able to project it so that people can see it, ask the organizers to include the table in the conference pack and then you will be able to ask the audience to look in their packs to see what you want them to see. Font size and font type are also important issues to consider when preparing slides. With regard to the former, ideally you should not use a font size smaller than 30 points. As to the latter, sans serif fonts work best (though avoiding the ubiquitous Helvetica). Serif fonts tend to get lost on the screen due to the relatively low resolution of most data projectors. Use the same font set throughout your slide presentation and use no more than two complementary fonts (e.g. Arial and Arial Bold).

When you are actually presenting, a good tip is to speak to someone in the middle of the centre aisle but occasionally look to your left, right and to the back so that you appear to be including the whole audience. It is not unusual for presenters to ask a colleague to sit in a seat half-way back and in the centre of the auditorium and speak to that friendly face. Remember to smile at appropriate points and to vary the tone of your voice. Speak slowly and clearly. If you lose your place or train of thought, take a deep breath and collect your thoughts, then carry on.

The last point is to practice. No good actor would ever go on stage without rehearsing their lines and you should not either. Practice what you are going to say, build in pauses, time yourself and rehearse in front of a friend or at least in front of the mirror.

Being ready for questions

If you are going to allow time for questions you should prepare what these might be. You will notice that when good politicians are asked questions they buy themselves some thinking time by repeating back the question. Practice doing this. If a question is too difficult or contentious, agree with the person asking the question that you would be happy to discuss the question in private.

You will find that some members of the audience will use question time to air an individual point or to make a statement. Get round these as best you can while remaining calm and polite. You might say something like: 'Thank you. That is a very interesting point of view and one that I have not had time to consider.' Never be tempted to argue with a member of the audience in public.

Members of the audience sometimes ask very long questions or will ask two, three or more questions. It is helpful, if you can (particularly if you are behind a podium or seated at a table on stage), to have a pen and jot down the latter questions. Repeat back the questions and deal with each – not necessarily in the order they were asked.

Common pitfalls

The last part of this section provides a guide to avoiding common pitfalls. There are too many to cover every eventuality but we have listed a few below:

- Only use humour if you are confident you can carry it off.
- Only be creative if you think you can carry it off.
- Avoid irritating your audience by being controversial, sexist and so on.
- Make it easy for the audience to navigate through your session – do not lose them.
- Try to include your audience by looking at them from time to time.
- Do not send them to sleep – vary you voice and be lively.

Writing for publication

The last section of this chapter looks at writing for publication and specifically in journals. This is part of being a responsible researcher – sharing widely your research. There are some good books on this subject, notably Epstein et al. (2007) and Sigismund Huff (2009). However, we have included a few top tips for getting published below:

- Choose your publication. You should aim to publish your research in an appropriate journal and you should check by looking at a couple of recent editions to make sure it is the type of journal that carries reports similar to yours. There is a 'pecking order' of journals. Peer-reviewed journals by the big publishing houses are generally thought to be the best, though they are consequently also often the hardest to get published in.
- If you have undertaken a major piece of research and want to publish more than one paper you should write about different aspects of your report and may aim to publish in different journals. This is a useful thing to do if you have undertaken multidisciplinary

research and want to be able to share your findings with different audiences. You must not, however, submit the same article to more than one journal concurrently.

- Get the publishing guidelines for the journal. These will tell you what is required, e.g. length and/or structure of the abstract, word limit, referencing style. Big publishers get thousands of manuscripts sent to them and will usually not consider articles that do not conform to their requirements.
- Write your article in the style of the publishing guidelines. You might find it helpful to look at a couple of recent articles in the journal and check that you are roughly producing your articles in line with the published ones, e.g. how many words did they use for each section, did they use diagrams or tables, and so on.
- Get a colleague to read your finished article to make sure it makes sense and to iron out any errors or inconsistencies.
- Submit your articles in the format stated in the publishing guidelines.
- Be prepared to wait. It may take some weeks for your articles to go through the scrutiny process.
- Be prepared for rejection – do not take it personally. If you get feedback, act on it. If feedback suggests you rework the article and then it will be considered, submit it to the same journal. If not, try another journal – there are hundreds!
- If your article is accepted subject to making changes (this is not uncommon), make changes as quickly as you can and resubmit.
- Once accepted you will receive proofs for checking. Make sure you do this thoroughly and quickly.
- There are few better feelings than seeing your work in print so persevere!

PUTTING RESEARCH INTO PRACTICE 11.1 – GETTING PUBLISHED

This exercise aims to give you help if you are thinking about getting your work into print.

1 Select a piece of work you have done either as a student or as a professional. This might be an essay, a piece of research, an audit or anything you are proud of.
2 Spend an hour or so in the library looking through journals to see if you can identify a journal that has published similar material to yours.
3 Search on the WWW for the journal's guidelines for publication.
4 Try and rewrite your chosen piece following the correct style outline in the journal guidelines.
5 Submit it.

References

Argyrous, G. (2011) *Statistics for Research*, 3rd edn. London: Sage.
Birks, M. and Mills, J. (2010) *Grounded Theory: a Practical Guide*. London: Sage.
Corbin, J.M. and Strauss, A.L. (2008) *Basics of Qualitative Research: Techniques and Procedures for Developing Grounded Theory*, 3rd edn. Los Angeles, CA: Sage.

Epstein, D., Kenway, J. and Boden, R. (2007) *Writing for Publication*. London: Sage.
Fetterman, D.M. (2010) *Ethnography: Step-by-Step*. Los Angeles, CA: Sage.
Ford, N. (2011) *The Essential Student's Guide to Using the Web for Research*. London: Sage.
Fowler, F.J. (2009) *Survey Research Methods*, 4th edn. Los Angeles, CA: Sage.
Greasley, P. (2011) *Doing Essays & Assignments: Essential Tips for Students*. London: Sage.
Greener, I. (2011) *Designing Social Research: a Guide for the Bewildered*. London: Sage.
Hall, T. and Coffey, A. (eds) (2011) *Researching Young People*. London: Sage.
Jesson, J., Matheson, L. and Lacey, F.M. (2011) *Doing Your Literature Review: traditional and Systematic Techniques*. London: Sage.
Liamputtong, P. (2011) *Focus Group Methodology: Principle and Practice*. London: Sage.
NHS Evidence (n.d.) 'How to make information accessible: a guide to writing easy read documents'. Available at: http://www.changepeople.co.uk (accessed 14 May 2012).
Repko, A.F., Newell, W.H. and Szostak, R. (2012) *Case Studies in Interdisciplinary Research*. Los Angeles: Sage Publications.
Somekh, B. and Lewin, C. (eds) (2011) *Theory and Methods in Social Research*, 2nd edn. London: Sage.
Sigismund Huff. A. (2009) *Designing Research for Publication*. California: Sage Publications
van Blerk, L. and Ansell, N. (2007) 'Participatory feedback and dissemination with and for children: reflections from research with young migrants in southern Africa', Children's Geographies, 5 (3): 313–24.
Vogt, W.P (ed.) (2011) *Quantitative Research Methods for Professionals in Education and Other Fields*. Boston, MA: Pearson/Allyn and Bacon.

Recommended reading for further study

Epstein, D., Kenway, J. and Boden, R. (2007) *Writing for Publication*. London: Sage Publications.
Thomas, D. and Hodge, I.D. (2010) *Designing and Managing Your Research Project: core Skills for Social and Health Research*. London: Sage.
Welch-Ross, M.K. and Fasig, L.G. (2007) *Handbook on Communicating and Disseminating Behavioral Science*. Los Angeles: Sage Publications.

TWELVE

Themes and perspectives

The aim of this chapter is to draw together, and examine, the main common themes that emerge from doing research with children.

This book has brought together research knowledge intended to support the professional working with children and young people in using research intelligently, and to help prepare the would-be researcher by focusing on the special nature of children and on doing research with children and young people. We came to feel that this book was necessary, partly through our own observations when working with students preparing to work with children and adolescents, and partly through our own experiences of doing research. Research texts that are generic tend to pay very little attention to the differences between undertaking research involving children and young people and undertaking research with adults; there may perhaps be a couple of lines or a paragraph given over to the special nature of children and young people, but generally there is little or nothing at all. So the idea of this book was originally born. We are delighted that in preparing this third edition we have been able to refer to other research texts that are specifically about children and young people, which we were not able to do when the first edition was written. There has been a real impetus to make sure that doing research with children and young people is seen as a discipline in its own right and we are glad to have contributed to its emergence.

What we have attempted to do in our book is to draw out those aspects of undertaking research involving children and adolescents that are different, such as special techniques, participatory methods and ethical implications. In other chapters we have taken generic aspects and applied them to children's and young people's settings so that the reader can grasp that all research must be contextualized. We will consider this more fully later on.

What has become apparent, however, through the writing of the book, is that there are a number of common themes and perspectives that recur within each chapter and that are worthy of emphasis as we draw together what we hope you will find an exciting and meaningful text.

Children are different

At the very beginning of this book we discussed the special place children and young people hold in our society. They are not little adults but are developing and growing beings who have their own specific characteristics. The growing number of professional programmes focusing specifically on children and young people emphasizes the fact that working with them requires a different and distinct set of skills. This is also true of research involving them. The techniques required to gather data (see Chapters 7 and 8), the ethical considerations (see Chapter 10) and the underpinning theories (see Chapter 2) are different from those involved in researching with adult subjects. Children and young people perceive and understand the world in a different way from adults, and while the adult researcher cannot, for very obvious reasons, see the world from the child's or young person's perspective, acknowledging that children's worlds are different is a sound starting point.

It is important to realize, too, that children and young people do not represent a homogeneous group. Within the overarching phase of childhood and adolescence there exist a multitude of differences – differences which can be the result of age, gender, ethnicity and culture, education, social class, upbringing and so on. The list is indeed endless. We hope that after reading this book you will have an understanding of the importance of the differences that exist between child and adult and between child and child, and some of the factors that contribute to those differences.

Knowledge is the key to success

Our second theme, which clearly relates strongly to the first, is that the successful researcher undertaking research involving children and young people must not only be aware that they are different, but must also have an underlying knowledge of the child and young person from a number of perspectives. These include knowledge of theories of emotion and cognition, of learning and personality, of physical growth and development, and of children's relationships – in Chapter 2 we have discussed these theories in more detail. Apart from these basic skills, the would-be researcher will also need to develop special skills that relate to the particular problem being studied and be able to frame research questions in an appropriate way (see Chapter 5). These can be achieved through wide reading and through critical analysis of previous research undertaken in a particular field. This is important if the researcher is to develop research protocols that are sensitive and appropriate. Embracing theory is fundamental to the research process, and time taken to enhance your knowledge base is time well spent.

Knowledge is also something we can absorb through a variety of activities, not least through our everyday practice and through the observation of others who are more skilled than ourselves. The professions have traditionally relied in part on this type of apprenticeship system whereby the student professional will work alongside those who have more experience. The amount of knowledge and how meaningful that knowledge is to us is a very individual thing. We are certainly not sponges who will absorb knowledge purely by being in a certain environment – unfortunately. We have to observe what is going on around us, ask questions and seek clarification from the literature when we do not get satisfactory answers. We must learn to be reflective practitioners so that each new experience is thought about, compared with our past experiences and made sense of.

Special techniques

Imagine for a moment the ridiculous thought of a researcher entering a neonatal unit in a hospital and attempting to interview the babies (see Figure 12.1). We have discussed earlier that children and young people are different and that the researcher should hold a knowledge base that will enable greater understanding of the differences. Hand in hand with this knowledge is the repertoire of research skills that can capture the world of the child or young person. Interviewing babies is an extreme example of incompetence but there are many grey areas between total incompetence and total competence. In the second section of the book we have placed strong focus on the special skills and techniques that can be used when undertaking research involving children. In Chapters 6, 7 and 8 we have looked at both quantitative and qualitative methods and have given examples of some of the many techniques that can be used. As with all research techniques, these require practice and careful consideration. We hope that this book will help you to become both discerning and discriminating when designing research. It is not enough to 'pick off the shelf' a tool designed for adult subjects. Undertaking research with children and young people requires special tools just as it requires special skills. We do not pretend to have all the answers by any means, but the important point to make here is that you should use your knowledge of child and adolescence development, and your experiences of working with children and young

Figure 12.1 Interviewing the very young …

people, to inform your choices. Too often students compartmentalize their knowledge into rigid boxes which disallow the integration of their knowledge. Research involves you using all your skills and learning about children and young people, because it draws on so many theories either directly or indirectly (see Chapter 2).

Approaching research from different perspectives

Linked to the need to employ special techniques when undertaking research with children and young people is the fourth theme that has permeated our discussion. This is the consideration of the place of both qualitative and quantitative methods within research involving children and young people. There is room for both paradigms as we have discussed in Chapter 3. The researcher needs to identify the most appropriate approach based on previous work in the field and the research problem the researcher is seeking to address.

Throughout the book we have referred to both research approaches and have highlighted where one approach may be favoured over another. Both research approaches carry with them a set of discrete skills, methods and techniques as we have discussed in Chapters 7 and 8. We have pointed to the danger that the researcher might 'bend' the approach to match their own expertise rather than adopting the approach most appropriate to the research problem. Such decisions should logically flow from the problem rather than the research preferences of the researcher. It is worth acknowledging here that most professional disciplines involving children and young people now acknowledge that both qualitative and quantitative approaches have a place in generating and building our knowledge about children.

Training

Our fifth key theme, which again has clear links to those mentioned above, is training. We are aware of the difficulties of being able to observe researchers directly when they are gathering data, as this may sometimes interfere with the researcher–participant relationship. There are, however, other ways of learning: through simulation, role-play, in the laboratory, and so on. It is also useful when learning research skills to engage expert supervision, which is the usual arrangement for students learning research as part of an academic course. There is, we believe, also a role for supervision after you have qualified, when you are undertaking research. Your supervisor might well be a colleague or a peer, rather than someone with vast amounts of experience in undertaking research, but the advantage of this type of mentoring is that it brings a fresh and more objective perspective to what you are doing. In any case, two heads are always better than one, we are told.

There are also other informal ways of gaining training when you are undertaking research. We know from experience that even the most eminent researchers are usually more than willing to discuss their research in depth with novices and students. We have had several students who have engaged in protracted international email exchanges that have enabled them to gain great insight into why a researcher took a particular decision, or why they did not pursue a specific avenue of enquiry. We have also found that, on the whole, researchers are willing to share with you their ideas and even their data collection instruments so long as they have access to your results. Even if you cannot engage on such a scale, if you are undertaking a study around a particular topic which is of interest to an experienced researcher, that person is likely to be interested in what you are doing and why.

Inter-agency working

Another theme we wish to draw out in our conclusions is the professional working relationships of those involved with children. In Chapter 5 we provide, for example, a discussion about how academic disciplines each have preferred approaches to asking research questions. However, professionals rarely work in isolation and those involved in working with children and young people will most usually be part of a multidisciplinary team, working with professionals from different agencies. In terms of research this is an important consideration. Integrated children's services are becoming the norm and research has to acknowledge and work with this assumption in mind. This requires two considerations. First, when undertaking research that looks at service provision, the researcher will need to consider the perspectives of the different professionals involved in the particular care pathway. Second, researchers must consider when writing about their research that it will not only be people from a single professional group who will access the work (see Chapter 11). Other professionals (and indeed parents and children themselves) will access professional journals and the researcher should bear that in mind when writing. Most professional journals are much more willing than previously to consider publication of a broad range of research, rather than being restricted to a particular research 'type'.

The voice of children and young people

On a different note, there have appeared throughout the book a number of perspectives and thoughts on the actual involvement of children and young people in research, which is our penultimate theme. As we have said in the book, there is general agreement that children and young people must have a voice and be able to participate in research; the debate is about the extent to which this should occur. In Chapter 9 we have discussed the continued emphasis placed on participatory methods when undertaking research with children and provided many examples of participation by children and adolescents. We have referred to various models that can help the researcher to make decisions about participation, which range from a somewhat tokenistic involvement to children taking the role of researcher themselves. Those designing research need to make sure that they consider a whole range of factors when involving children and young people, from undertaking risk assessments of the 'field' in which research takes place, to considering the ethical implications, to giving children the right to be consulted about issues that affect them.

Part of our inability to resolve the debate may stem from our own different academic backgrounds and associated views that stem from our own professionalization. In all fields we have noted progress, but the progress has been slower in some academic fields than in others. We are, however, not alone in experiencing some disagreement, and we have referred in the book to the different professional points of view that exist. In practice we should perhaps embrace such differences as they make us question the origins of our colleagues' views rather than ignoring them. Certainly, in this era of inter-professional research and education we welcome the challenges these different perspectives bring. Our learning is certainly richer because these differences make us reflect on our own point of view as well as the views of others. What is important is that we should not allow our differences to halt our progress in research terms. A spirit of cooperation, respect and trust will enable healthy collaboration to take place and we must all make sure that, as a minimum, we uphold the rights of the child or young person to be consulted about matters that involve them as upheld by law (see Chapters 9 and 10).

Contextualization

Our final theme, which has been emphasized again and again, is that research involving children and young people, whether their involvement is direct or indirect, must be placed into a context. The three of us are experienced at supervising research, doing research and reading research, and with experience comes an almost intuitive understanding of what is 'good' research and what is not. We believe the answer is contextualization. That is, the ability of the researcher to really demonstrate that the research problem, the sampling, the choice of tools, the ethics and all other aspects of the research process exist in a meaningful rather than a stagnant way. Children and young people themselves lead complex lives, and we have already referred to the need to understand the developing child/young person. In Chapter 2 we have discussed the emergent theories that recognize that the child or young person is part of a social system and we have addressed the links between the child or young person's outer social world and inner psychological world. It is so important that the researcher gains an understanding of particularly the social ecological model of the child/young person in context. Children and young people are not mere recipients of their environment, but they influence what goes on within their worlds and are active in making the environment what it is. Therefore, as a researcher, whatever your professional background and research tradition, it is so important that you take a holistic approach to the study of children and young people. Only then can you understand children and young people and only then can you start to make sense of their worlds through that enigmatic process called research.

Author index

Subject index

188312